ZORA NEALE HURSTON was born c. 1891 in Eatonville, Florida, the first incorporated Black town in America. The nine secure years she spent there, and which she describes in *Dust Tracks on a Road*, ended when her mother died and her father, a Baptist preacher and thrice mayor of the town, remarried. She characterised her life from then on as 'a series of wanderings'— occasional work, intermittent schooling, time as a wardrobe assistant with a travelling theatre troupe—until she enrolled as a full-time student at Baltimore's Morgan Academy. Moving to Washington D.C. in 1918, she became a part-time student at Howard University and began to write, gaining the attention of some of the major figures of the Harlem Renaissance with her essays and short fiction. She moved to New York in 1925 and broadened her contact with both the Black and white literary communities. There she also earned a scholarship to Barnard College, where she studied Cultural Anthropology under Franz Boas. After graduating in 1928 she spent four years doing research on folklore in the South. Her collection of tales, songs, games and hoodoo practices from that time were published in *Mules and Men* (1935). Her first novel about Black life, *Jonah's Gourd Vine*, was published in 1934, followed by *Their Eyes Were Watching God* (1937; Virago, 1986), *Moses, Man of the Mountain* (1939), *Dust Tracks on a Road* (1942) and *Seraph on the Suwanee* (1948), as well as another collection of folklore, *Tell My Horse* (1938). Her standing as the most accomplished figure in Afro-American letters in the 1930s has endured as a new generation of Black women writers, Alice Walker and Toni Morrison among them, have acknowledged their debt to her work.

By the 1950s, however, Hurston had largely withdrawn from public life. Her increasingly conservative philosophy was expressed in essays written for the *American Legion Magazine* and *American Mercury* and in her controversial attack on the Supreme Court's 1954 ruling on school desegregation. Her argument, that the pressure for integration denied the value of existing Black institutions, alienated many of her contemporaries. She spent the last years of her life in ill-health and poverty and died in Port Pierce, Florida, in January 1960

•

DUST TRACKS ON A ROAD

•

AN AUTOBIOGRAPHY

• • • • •

ZORA NEALE HURSTON

With a New Introduction by
DELLITA L. MARTIN

Virago

Published by VIRAGO PRESS Limited 1986
41 William IV Street, London WC2N 4DB

First published by J. B. Lippincott Company
Copyright 1942 by Zora Neale Hurston
Copyright © renewed 1970 by John C. Hurston

This edition published by arrangement with Harper & Row Publishers,
Inc., New York

Introduction © Dellita L. Martin 1986

Appendix © 1984 by Harper & Row Publishers, Inc.

British Library Cataloguing in Publication Data

Hurston, Zora Neale
    Dust tracks on a road: an autobiography.—
    2nd ed.—(Virago non-fictional classics)
    1. Hurston, Zora Neale—Biography   2. Novelists,
    American—20th century—Biography
    I. Title   II. Hemenway, Robert E.
    813'.52   P53515.0789Z/

ISBN 0-86068-663-9

Printed in Finland by Werner Söderström
a member of Finnprint

CONTENTS

	Introduction	vii
I	My Birthplace	3
II	My Folks	12
III	I Get Born	27
IV	The Inside Search	33
V	Figure and Fancy	61
VI	Wandering	84
VII	Jacksonville and After	97
VIII	Backstage and the Railroad	116
IX	School Again	144
X	Research	174
XI	Books and Things	206
XII	My People! My People!	215
XIII	Two Women in Particular	238
XIV	Love	249
XV	Religion	266
XVI	Looking Things Over	280
	Appendix:	287
	My People, My People!	291
	The Inside Light—Being a Salute to Friendship	307
	Seeing the World as It Is	322

INTRODUCTION

Mary Burgher's essay, 'Images of Self and Race in the Autobiographies of Black Women', asserts that the essence of the Black female whom we see in various works consists of an outer shield of strength and tenacity and an inner core of tenderness and compassion.[1] Although Burgher primarily outlines the hardships and limitations under which Black women in general, and Black female writers in particular, have laboured, she contends that their genius, sensitivity, resourcefulness and enthusiasm have often counteracted the negative effects of harsh circumstances. Moreover, these qualities have inspired the writers to give artistic expression to the spirit of the group. Black female writers, then, heroically celebrate Black female experiences in auto-biographical literature, and Burgher comments, 'the life stories of Black women are poignant and sensitive definitions of self and compelling expressions of the unchanging needs and ideals of the Black race.'[2] Thus, Black female autobiography reflects the pattern of the communal self defined by Stephen Butterfield as characteristic of Black autobiography where 'the unity of the personal and the mass voice remains a dominant tradition'.[3]

The communal self is *not* a distinguishing trait of *Dust*

Tracks on a Road, hereafter referred to as *Dust Tracks*.[4] Instead I would like to focus on the contradictory, elusive and ambivalent self that unfolds in the autobiography of Zora Neale Hurston. It is an image that conflicts with the bold, self-confident posture one perceives in Hurston's fiction and essays, and one which propelled her to achieve success as a writer. Because of this incongruity, the reader comes away from *Dust Tracks* not only knowing very little of real value about the person, but also questioning the authenticity of her vision as a writer. In fact, Hurston's life story tends to neutralize her literary accomplishments if one does not carefully weigh it against the accounts given by others about her. Thus, one can only view *Dust Tracks* as the beginning of the decline of a great personality.

The early chapters (I-V) of the autobiography do recount the sense of shared life that Hurston knew in Eatonville, Florida, through the experiencing voice of the happy, energetic, curious and fiercely independent Black girl-child. However, in the latter part of the work we hear the narrating voice of the rugged-individualist, successful Black female author who has made it against the odds; in short, the old 'boot straps' theory. Robert Hemenway aptly points out that the two voices cannot be reconciled successfully into one autobiographical self and that the problem of voice largely accounts for the sense of confusion and inconsistency in *Dust Tracks*. Hemenway states: 'She was trapped in *Dust Tracks* by the personal identification she cultivated as one of the folk, for it limited her freedom to account for her experience as a part of the larger world.'[5] The literary dilemma that Hurston faced, then, was to find an appropriate voice for the post-Eatonville Zora.[6] I agree with Hemenway if the two voices and the worlds they imply are considered as mutually exclusive spheres; that is, if Hurston's achievement was *in spite of* her background. If, however, Hurston the writer 'made it' *because of* her environment, *because of* the training, self-assurance and self-reliance that she culled from her life in Eatonville—and I suggest that she in all likelihood held the latter view—then her success story is a natural, logical outcome of the moulding received during her early years, and the two voices can very definitely constitute one self. The problem is that Hurston is ambivalent about the two; therefore, the reader is left to reconcile them as best she can.

At first *Dust Tracks* is a delightfully humorous portrayal of Hurston's effervescent personality. One of the youngest siblings of eight, she is her mother's favourite child and the only one who is left to follow her own whims and desires. At the age of seven, however, Zora begins to see a series of frightening visions which give her '... a feeling of difference from others ... a feeling of terrible aloneness.' (*DT*, 58-9) Poignantly aware of her premature knowledge, Hurston is 'driven inward' into a world of vivid dreams and colourful fantasies that satisfy her craving for action. Until 'the coming of the pronouncements', Zora is essentially a happy child, secure in the knowledge of who she is. Her camelot vanishes definitively at the age of nine or ten when the first vision, her mother's death, materializes and the family is broken up. Hurston's reminiscence some thirty-three years later still conveys the immensity of her loss: 'That hour began my wanderings ... in spirit.' (*DT*, 89)

Throughout the early chapters of *Dust Tracks*, the reader is impressed with Hurston's continuous rebellion, even belligerence at times. For example, one Christmas Zora's father chides her for being too ambitious when she requests a black riding horse with white leather saddle and bridles:

'Lemme tell you something right now, my young lady; you ain't white. Riding horse! Always trying to wear de big hat! I don't know how you got in this family nohow. You ain't like none of de rest of my young'uns.' (*DT*, 38) Zora's grandmother prophesies dire things for her, fearing that the white folks 'gowine to lynch you, yet' because of her brazenness. (*DT*, 46) When Zora is sent with an older brother and sister to a school in Jacksonville after their mother's death, she is promptly shipped back home because she cannot and will not conform to the rules. But the hearth offers neither understanding nor comfort because of the proverbial wicked stepmother; and the circle of family and friends within which Zora drifts is not receptive to her desire for that 'book-reading business', which is a holdback and an unrelieved evil, if not downright sin, for a Black girl-child. In essence, Hurston's rejection of 'the pigeonhole way of life', her very presence as a 'crow in a pigeon's nest', contributed greatly to a deep sense of alienation from the people and culture she had known all her life. She states: 'I wanted what they could not conceive of. I could not reveal myself for lack of expression and then for lack of hope of understanding, even if I could have found the words. I was not comfortable to have around. Strange things must have looked out of my eyes like Lazarus after his resurrection.' (*DT*, 117) The vision of the *poète maudit*, the alienated rebel pitted against the world, looms clearly in Chapter VIII, which serves as backdrop to the rest of the autobiography. From the time Hurston declares her independence up until the final chapters, her story has the strong flavour of the Horatio Alger myth, of how through hard work, thrift, education and perseverance the protagonist rises from rags and anonymity to fame, if not to wealth.

At fourteen Zora seeks book knowledge, not as an end in itself, but as a vehicle for channelling and articulating the visions and dreams dammed up inside. Thus, her formal education at Morgan Academy, Howard University and Barnard College fully satisfies this need in that it introduces her to the world of literature, a meeting that finds an eager mate in 'the hemisphere of her imagination', according to Hemenway. It is at Barnard that Hurston declares her intent to pursue a writing career/vocation, although she becomes captivated with anthropology as a result of meeting Franz Boas. Hemenway comments:

When Hurston became fascinated with anthropology, she acquired the relatively rare opportunity to confront her culture both emotionally and analytically, both as subject and as object. She had lived Afro-American folklore before she knew that such a thing existed as a scientific concept or had special value as evidence of the adaptive creativity of a unique subculture. Hurston came to know that her parents and their neighbors perpetuated a rich oral literature without self-consciousness, a literature illustrating a creativity seldom recognized and almost universally misunderstood.[7]

Even though Hurston was to get sidetracked into anthropological research in the 1930s, during 1925 and 1926 she considered herself a writer and a contributor to the literary movement known as the Harlem Renaissance.

Hurston's first nationally published work was a story called 'Drenched in Light', which is important because it reveals the author's sense of self-acceptance and a healthy attitude toward her immediate culture, even the joy she felt at growing up in Eatonville. According to Hemenway, '. . . it was her manifesto of selfhood, an affirmation of her origins.'[8]

More significant was the fact that the story illustrates a philosophy of life that was refreshing considering the trend of the time: 'I am not tragically colored.' With such a vision motivating her, Hurston could proceed to make literature out of the Eatonville experience.[9]

Despite Hurston's declaration of pride in race and culture, the reader is puzzled by the ambivalence with which she approaches these at times, and there do seem to be two souls in conflict in the one dark body. Steeped in the culture of her birth, Zora Neale Hurston is unique among the Black writers of the 1920s in that she 'contributed an authentic folk experience to the esthetic mix of the Renaissance',[10] and she achieved in fact what others merely attempted. All of her stories, essays, novels and folklore collections are permeated with a sense of the wholeness of the Afro-American cultural tradition, at least the one she was familiar with in West Florida. Hurston's strong self-concept enabled her to take for granted what other writers tried too self-consciously to prove. Yet in spite of her reputation as an established writer, or at least a promising one, and despite her status as a very important figure of the Harlem Renaissance circle, Hurston only mentions in passing this significant period of Afro-American literature—and then begrudgingly, referring to it as the 'so-called Negro Renaissance'. Why? The reasons are probably as complex as Zora's personality, and it is a challenge even to speculate on them.

The peculiar disorientation of *Dust Tracks*, which critics like Alice Walker and Mary Helen Washington have noted, represents a gap in our understanding although it does not necessarily lessen our appreciation of her works. In her seminal essay 'In Search of Our Mothers' Gardens',[11]

Walker refers to the autobiography as 'oddly false-sounding'. And Washington observes: 'Zora used all sorts of manipulative and diversionary tactics in the autobiography to avoid any real self-disclosure. The sections on her adult life are a study in the art of subterfuge.'[12] One can certainly understand Hurston's reluctance to reveal certain aspects of her personal life, especially since they often involved embarrassing and painful episodes. Less comprehensible, however, is Hurston's apologetic, defensive and contradictory attitude toward the racial consciousness and cultural affirmation one sees clearly in the early chapters of *Dust Tracks* as well as in all her fictional works. States Hemenway: 'Zora seems to be both an advocate for the universal, demonstrating that this black woman does not look at the world in racial terms, and the celebrant of a unique upbringing in an all-black village.'[13]

We know now as Hurston knew then that race/ethnicity and universality are not necessarily mutually exclusive and that constant attempts to pit the one against the other serve no useful purpose. However, considering the strong case that Hurston makes for the beauty, health and viability of Afro-American culture, and considering Hurston's close encounters with the hard, cold reality of American racism, as well as her acute awareness of international colonialism, the two perspectives clash stridently, and the reader is sorely disappointed that she does not take a firm stance one way or the other. In light of Hurston's firm belief that Black writers often compromise their personal and artistic integrity by dwelling on the tragic aspects of the race question, one understands her decision to balance the picture by portraying in her works the positive, celebratory side of the Afro-American ethos. On the other hand, Chapter XII, 'My

People! My People!', and Chapter XVI, 'Looking Things Over', are, frankly, embarrassing, because they illustrate an ambivalent, servile, unconvincingly naive attitude which contradicts the previous dignified posture. For example, Hurston states that slavery is a thing of the past, so that it does not matter who raped her female ancestor. Or witness passages like the following:

For me to pretend that I am Old Black Joe and waste my time on his problems, would be just as ridiculous as for the government of Winston Churchill to bill the Duke of Normandy the first of every month, or for the Jews to hang around the pyramids trying to picket Old Pharaoh. While I have a handkerchief over my eyes crying over the landing of the first slaves in 1619, I might miss something swell that is going on in 1942. (*DT*, 284)

You, who play the zig-zag lightning of power over the world, with the grumbling thunder in your wake, think kindly of those who walk in the dust. And you who walk in humble places, think kindly too, of others. There has been no proof in the world so far that you would be less arrogant if you held the lever of power in your hands. Let us all be kissing-friends . . . (*DT*, 286)

I agree with Mary Helen Washington that the above excerpts represent a simplistic, dangerously naive viewpoint, and one that would lead to Hurston's right-wing politics of the 1950s, which many construed to be anti-Black.[14] Ann Rayson captures the paradox of the very last quote by referring to it as 'both naively ridiculous and camp in a finely ironic self-parody'.[15] However, Hemenway argues in Hurston's favour that her dilemma might well have come from '. . . a paradox of personal pride'. Hurston, he comments, may have been special, but she also believed that her hard-won success grew from the self-reliance, independence, and self-confidence inspired by familial and communal origins. These qualities helped her compete and brought her fame. To describe the discrimination she encountered might suggest that such self-reliance was a defensive reaction to white oppression; it might imply that racial discrimination worked, that it created compensatory black behavior. Absolutely obsessed with the fear that she might be found to engage in self-pity, Zora apparently believed that writing about the race problem might mean that Eatonville, an independent, self-governing black community, could be misinterpreted as a self-defensive civic refuge from the white world.[16]

Even Hurston's insistence on her uniqueness and her messianic role, which she fails to develop through the framework of the twelve visions, loses its flavour in the context of her ambivalence.[17] Moreover, while it helps to know that the manuscript version of *Dust Tracks* is much more outspoken on American Jim Crow and jingoism, the autobiography ultimately does more harm to Hurston's literary reputation than any of her subsequent works, which reject the Black experience altogether. Washington observes, 'the mask Hurston assumed in *Dust Tracks* was a sign of the growing evisceration of her work',[18] and Hemenway notes that the commercially successful autobiography ironically spells the end of Hurston's 'mission to celebrate black folkways' publicly.[19] The latter critic concludes:

Her total career, not her autobiography, is the proof of her achievement and the best index to her life and art. Only when considered in that total context can the book be properly assessed, for it is an autobiography at war with itself. Apparently written self-consciously with a white audience in mind, probably because of editorial suggestions, it illustrates the contradictions, ambivalence, and disappointment of Zora Hurston's personal and professional life in the early 1940s.[20]

What are we left with, then? On the one hand, there is the external perspective that Hemenway provides: '. . . the chief value of her autobiography . . . [is] its documentation of the Eatonville scene and what it meant to a woman who would rise by force of will and talent to become nationally known.'[21] On the other hand, I suggest that the portrait of the indomitable Black woman (the 'Amazon', if you will) that one sees in *Dust Tracks*, while real, is a foil to the inner self, the abandoned, alienated, vulnerable child-woman. It is compensatory to a large extent, but not for reasons that have anything to do with race or culture, and it is an image which, more often than not, fits the trail-blazer. One senses that Zora never got over the pain of rejection and misunderstanding from her father; never entirely discarded the guilt associated with her inability to see that her mother's death wishes were honoured; never quite forgave the family who did not or could not take care of her needs, even though she understood why; never completely reconciled herself to the people who let her down, the love affairs and marriages that failed, the fellow artists who ostracized her, and the society that would eventually vilify her. The title of the work itself may well reflect Hurston's desire for self-effacement, as far as her personal existence was concerned, and instead hints at the need to be judged solely on the basis of her priceless legacy to Afro-American and American literature and culture. Or it may intimate the author's final resignation of self to the fate of all humankind—for dust tracks are either blurred by time or are soon blown away like the chaff. Because Hurston adjusted well to whatever circumstances she found herself in, because she drank so lustily from the cup of life, savouring the honey and the gall, she was essentially the joker, the public face of a very agitated private self, the outer manifestation of a spirit in flux. And the twain did meet, only to stare across the gap at one another in that infinite posture of stalemate which we know of as *Dust Tracks on a Road*.

Dellita L. Martin, 1985

NOTES

1 Mary Burgher, 'Images of Self and Race in the Autobiographies of Black Women,' in Bell, Parker and Guy-Sheftall, eds, *Sturdy Black Bridges: Visions of Black Women in Literature*, New York: Anchor Books, 1979, p. 108.

2 *Ibid.*, p. 107.

3 Stephen Butterfield, *Black Autobiography in America*, Amherst: University of Massachusetts Press, 1974, p. 3.

4 Zora Neale Hurston, *Dust Tracks on a Road*, London: Virago Press, 1986. All citations are from this edition and they will carry the letters 'DT' to refer to pages in the text.

5 Robert Hemenway, *Zora Neale Hurston: A Literary Biography*, Urbana: University of Illinois Press, 1977, p. 279.

6 *Ibid.*, p. 283.

7 *Ibid.*, p. 22.

8 *Ibid.*, p. 11.

9 *Ibid.*

10 *Ibid.*, p. 51.

11 Alice Walker, 'In Search of Our Mothers' Gardens,' *In Search of Our Mothers' Gardens*, London: The Women's Press, 1984, p. 231.

12 Mary Helen Washington, Introduction to *I Love Myself When I Am Laughing*, New York: The Feminist Press, 1979, p. 20.

13 Hemenway, p. 276.

14 Washington, p. 22.

15 Ann Rayson, '*Dust Tracks on a Road*: Zora Neale Hurston and the Form of Black Autobiography', *Negro American Literature Forum*, 7 (Summer, 1973), p. 39.

16 Hemenway, p. 283.

17 *Ibid.*

18 Washington, p. 20.

19 Hemenway, p. 288.

20 *Ibid.*, p. 278.

21 *Ibid.*, p. 277.

I
My Birthplace

Like the dead-seeming, cold rocks, I have memories within that came out of the material that went to make me. Time and place have had their say.

So you will have to know something about the time and place where I came from, in order that you may interpret the incidents and directions of my life.

I was born in a Negro town. I do not mean by that the black back-side of an average town. Eatonville, Florida, is, and was at the time of my birth, a pure Negro town—charter, mayor, council, town marshal and all. It was not the first Negro community in America, but it was the first to be incorporated, the first attempt at organized self-government on the part of Negroes in America.

Eatonville is what you might call hitting a straight lick with a crooked stick. The town was not in the original plan. It is a by-product of something else.

It all started with three white men on a ship off the coast of Brazil. They had been officers in the Union Army. When the bitter war had ended in victory for their side, they had set out for South America. Perhaps the post-war distress made their native homes depressing. Perhaps it was just that they were young, and it was hard for them to return to the monotony of everyday being after the excitement of military life, and they, like numerous other young men, set out to find new frontiers.

But they never landed in Brazil. Talking together on the ship, these three decided to return to the United States and try their fortunes in the unsettled country of South Florida. No doubt the same thing which had moved them to go to Brazil caused them to choose South Florida.

This had been dark and bloody country since the mid-1700's. Spanish, French, English, Indian, and American blood had been bountifully shed.

The last great struggle was between the resentful Indians and the white planters of Georgia, Alabama, and South Carolina. The strong and powerful Cherokees, aided by the conglomerate Seminoles, raided the plantations and carried off Negro slaves into Spanish-held Florida. Ostensibly they were carried off to be slaves to the Indians, but in reality the Negro men were used to swell the ranks of the Indian fighters against the white plantation owners. During lulls in the long struggle, treaties were signed, but invariably broken. The sore point of returning escaped Negroes could not be settled satisfactorily to either side. Who was an Indian and who was a Negro? The whites contended all who had Negro blood. The Indians contended all who spoke their language belonged to the tribe. Since it was an easy matter to teach a slave to speak enough of the language to pass in a short time, the question could never be settled. So the wars went on.

The names of Oglethorpe, Clinch and Andrew Jackson are well known on the white side of the struggle. For the Indians, Miccanopy, Billy Bow-legs and Osceola. The noble Osceola was only a sub-chief, but he came to be recognized by both sides as the ablest of them all. Had he not been captured by treachery, the struggle would have lasted much longer than it did. With an offer of friendship, and a new rifle (some say a beautiful sword) he was lured to the fort seven miles outside of St. Augustine, and captured. He was confined in sombre Fort Marion that still stands in that city, escaped, was recaptured, and died miserably in the prison of a fort in Beaufort, South Carolina. Without his leadership, the Indian cause collapsed. The Cherokees and most of the Seminoles, with their Negro adherents, were moved west. The beaten Indians were moved to what is now Oklahoma. It was far from the then settlements of the whites. And then too, there seemed to be nothing there that white people wanted, so it was a good place for Indians. The wilds of Florida heard no more clash of battle among men.

The sensuous world whirled on in the arms of ether for a generation or so. Time made and marred some

men. So into this original hush came the three fron-
tier-seekers who had been so intrigued by its prospects
that they had turned back after actually arriving at
the coast of Brazil without landing. These young men
were no poor, refuge-seeking, wayfarers. They were
educated men of family and wealth.

The shores of Lake Maitland were beautiful, probably one reason they decided to settle there, on the
northern end where one of the old forts—built against
the Indians, had stood. It had been commanded by
Colonel Maitland, so the lake and the community
took their names in memory of him. It was Mosquito
County then and the name was just. It is Orange
County now for equally good reason. The men persuaded other friends in the north to join them, and
the town of Maitland began to be in a great rush.

Negroes were found to do the clearing. There was
the continuous roar of the crashing of ancient giants
of the lush woods, of axes, saws and hammers. And
there on the shores of Lake Maitland rose stately
houses, surrounded by beautiful grounds. Other settlers flocked in from upper New York State, Minnesota and Michigan, and Maitland became a center of
wealth and fashion. In less than ten years, the Plant
System, later absorbed into the Atlantic Coast Line
Railroad, had been persuaded to extend a line south
through Maitland, and the private coaches of millionaires and other dignitaries from North and South
became a common sight on the siding. Even a presi-

dent of the United States visited his friends at Maitland.

These wealthy homes, glittering carriages behind blooded horses and occupied by well-dressed folk, presented a curious spectacle in the swampy forests so dense that they are dark at high noon. The terrain swarmed with the deadly diamond-back rattlesnake, and huge, decades-old bull alligators bellowed their challenge from the uninhabited shores of lakes. It was necessary to carry a lantern when one walked out at night, to avoid stumbling over these immense reptiles in the streets of Maitland.

Roads were made by the simple expedient of driving buggies and wagons back and forth over the foot trail, which ran for seven miles between Maitland and Orlando. The terrain was as flat as a table and totally devoid of rocks. All the roadmakers had to do was to curve around the numerous big pine trees and oaks. It seems it was too much trouble to cut them down. Therefore, the road looked as if it had been laid out by a playful snake. Now and then somebody would chop down a troublesome tree. Way late, the number of tree stumps along the route began to be annoying. Buggy wheels bumped and jolted over them and took away the pleasure of driving. So a man was hired to improve the road. His instructions were to round off the tops of all stumps so that the wheels, if and when they struck stumps, would slide off gently instead of jolting the teeth out of riders as before.

This was done, and the spanking rigs of the bloods whisked along with more assurance.

Now, the Negro population of Maitland settled simultaneously with the white. They had been needed, and found profitable employment. The best of relations existed between employer and employee. While the white estates flourished on the three-mile length of Lake Maitland, the Negroes set up their hastily built shacks around St. John's Hole, a lake as round as a dollar, and less than a half-mile wide. It is now a beauty spot in the heart of Maitland, hard by United States Highway Number 17. They call it Lake Lily.

The Negro women could be seen every day but Sunday squatting around St. John's Hole on their haunches, primitive style, washing clothes and fishing, while their men went forth and made their support in cutting new ground, building, and planting orange groves. Things were moving so swiftly that there was plenty to do, with good pay. Other Negroes in Georgia and West Florida heard of the boom in South Florida from Crescent City to Cocoa and they came. No more back-bending over rows of cotton; no more fear of the fury of the Reconstruction. Good pay, sympathetic white folks and cheap land, soft to the touch of a plow. Relatives and friends were sent for.

Two years after the three adventurers entered the primeval forests of Mosquito County, Maitland had grown big enough, and simmered down enough, to consider a formal city government.

Now, these founders were, to a man, people who had risked their lives and fortunes that Negroes might be free. Those who had fought in the ranks had thrown their weight behind the cause of Emancipation. So when it was decided to hold an election, the Eatons, Lawrences, Vanderpools, Hurds, Halls, the Hills, Yateses and Galloways, and all the rest including Bishop Whipple, head of the Minnesota diocese, never for a moment considered excluding the Negroes from participation. The whites nominated a candidate, and the Negroes, under the aggressive lead of Joe Clarke, a muscular, dynamic Georgia Negro, put up Tony Taylor as their standard-bearer.

I do not know whether it was the numerical superiority of the Negroes, or whether some of the whites, out of deep feeling, threw their votes to the Negro side. At any rate, Tony Taylor became the first mayor of Maitland with Joe Clarke winning out as town marshal. This was a wholly unexpected turn, but nobody voiced any open objections. The Negro mayor and marshal and the white city council took office peacefully and served their year without incident.

But during that year, a yeast was working. Joe Clarke had asked himself, why not a Negro town? Few of the Negroes were interested. It was too vaulting for their comprehension. A pure Negro town! If nothing but their own kind was in it, who was going to run it?

With no white folks to command them, how would they know what to do? Joe Clarke had plenty of confidence in himself to do the job, but few others could conceive of it.

But one day by chance or purpose, Joe Clarke was telling of his ambitions to Captain Eaton, who thought it a workable plan. He talked it over with Captain Lawrence and others. By the end of the year, all arrangements had been made. Lawrence and Eaton bought a tract of land a mile west of Maitland for a town site. The backing of the whites helped Joe Clarke to convince the other Negroes, and things were settled.

Captain Lawrence at his own expense erected a well-built church on the new site, and Captain Eaton built a hall for general assembly and presented it to the new settlement. A little later, the wife of Bishop Whipple had the first church rolled across the street and built a larger church on the same spot, and the first building was to become a library, stocked with books donated by the white community.

So on August 18, 1886, the Negro town, called Eatonville, after Captain Eaton, received its charter of incorporation from the state capital, Tallahassee, and made history by becoming the first of its kind in America, and perhaps in the world. So, in a raw, bustling frontier, the experiment of self-government for Negroes was tried. White Maitland and Negro Eatonville have lived side by side for fifty-six years without a single instance of enmity. The spirit of the founders has reached beyond the grave.

The whole lake country of Florida sprouted with life—mostly Northerners, and prosperity was everywhere. It was in the late eighties that the stars fell, and many of the original settlers date their coming "just before, or just after the stars fell."

II
My Folks

Into this burly, boiling, hard-hitting, rugged-individualistic setting walked one day a tall, heavy-muscled mulatto who resolved to put down roots.

John Hurston, in his late twenties, had left Macon County, Alabama, because the ordeal of share-cropping on a southern Alabama cotton plantation was crushing to his ambition. There was no rise to the thing.

He had been born near Notasulga, Alabama, in an outlying district of landless Negroes, and whites not too much better off. It was "over the creek," which was just like saying on the wrong side of the railroad tracks. John Hurston had learned to read and write somehow between cotton-choppings and cotton-picking, and it might have satisfied him in a way. But somehow he took to going to Macedonia Baptist Church on the right side of the creek. He went one time, and met up with dark-brown Lucy Ann Potts, of the land-owning Richard Potts, which might have given him the going habit.

He was nearly twenty years old then, and she was fourteen. My mother used to claim with a smile that she saw him looking and looking at her up there in the choir and wondered what he was looking at her for. She wasn't studying about *him*. However, when the service was over and he kept standing around, never far from her, she asked somebody, "Who is dat bee-stung yaller nigger?"

"Oh, dat's one of dem niggers from over de creek, one of dem Hurstons—call him John I believe."

That was supposed to settle that. Over-the-creek niggers lived from one white man's plantation to the other. Regular hand-to-mouth folks. Didn't own pots to pee in, nor beds to push 'em under. Didn't have no more pride than to let themselves be hired by poor-white trash. No more to 'em than the stuffings out of a zero. The inference was that Lucy Ann Potts had asked about nothing and had been told.

Mama thought no more about him, she said. Of course, she couldn't help noticing that his gray-green eyes and light skin stood out sharply from the black-skinned, black-eyed crowd he was in. Then, too, he had a build on him that made you look. A stud-looking buck like that would have brought a big price in slavery time. Then, if he had not kept on hanging around where she couldn't help from seeing him, she would never have remembered that she had seen him two or three times before around the cotton-gin in Notasulga, and once in a store. She had wondered then who he was, handling bales of cotton like suit-cases.

After that Sunday, he got right worrisome. Slipping her notes between the leaves of hymn-books and things like that. It got so bad that a few months later she made up her mind to marry him just to get rid of him. So she did, in spite of the most violent opposition of her family. She put on the little silk dress which she had made with her own hands, out of goods bought from egg-money she had saved. Her ninety pounds of fortitude set out on her wedding night alone, since none of the family except her brother Jim could bear the sight of her great come-down in the world. She who was considered the prettiest and the smartest black girl was throwing herself away and disgracing the Pottses by marrying an over-the-creek nigger, and a bastard at that. Folks said he was a certain white man's son. But here she was, setting out to walk two miles at night by herself, to keep her pledge to him at the church. Her father, more tolerant than her mother, decided that his daughter was not going alone, nor was she going to walk to her wedding. So he hitched up the buggy and went with her. Nobody much was there. Her brother Jim slipped in just before she stood on the floor.

So she said her words and took her stand for life, and went off to a cabin on a plantation with him. She never forgot how the late moon shone that night as his two hundred pounds of bone and muscle shoved open the door and lifted her in his arms over the door-sill.

That cabin on a white man's plantation had to be all for the present. She had been pointedly made to know that the Potts plantation was nothing to her any more. Her father soon softened and was satisfied to an extent, but her mother, never. To her dying day her daughter's husband was never John Hurston to her. He was always "dat yaller bastard." Four years after my mother's marriage, and during her third pregnancy, she got to thinking of the five acres of cling-stone peaches on her father's place, and the yearning was so strong that she walked three miles to get a few. She was holding the corners of her apron with one hand and picking peaches with the other when her mother spied her, and ordered her off the place.

It was after his marriage that my father began to want things. Plantation life began to irk and bind him. His over-the-creek existence was finished. What else was there for a man like him? He left his wife and three children behind and went out to seek and see.

Months later he pitched into the hurly-burly of South Florida. So he heard about folks building a town all out of colored people. It seemed like a good place to go. Later on, he was to be elected Mayor of Eatonville for three terms, and to write the local laws. The village of Eatonville is still governed by the laws formulated by my father. The town clerk still consults a copy of the original printing which seems to be the only one in existence now. I have tried every way I know how to get this copy for my library, but so far it has not been possible. I had it once, but the town clerk came and took it back.

When my mother joined Papa a year after he had settled in Eatonville, she brought some quilts, her featherbed and bedstead. That was all they had in the house that night. Two burlap bags were stuffed with Spanish moss for the two older children to sleep on. The youngest child was taken into the bed with them.

So these two began their new life. Both of them swore that things were going to better, and it came to pass as they said. They bought land, built a roomy house, planted their acres and reaped. Children kept coming—more mouths to feed and more feet for shoes. But neither of them seemed to have minded that. In fact, my father not only boasted among other men about "his house full of young'uns" but he boasted that he had never allowed his wife to go out and hit a lick of work for anybody a day in her life. Of weaknesses, he had his share, and I know that my mother was very unhappy at times, but neither of them ever made any move to call the thing off. In fact, on two occasions, I heard my father threaten to kill my mother if she ever started towards the gate to leave him. He was outraged and angry one day when she said lightly that if he did not want to do for her and his children, there was another man over the fence waiting for his job. That expression is a folk-saying and Papa had heard it used hundreds of times by other women, but he was outraged at hearing it from Mama. She definitely understood, before he got through carrying on, that the saying was not for her lips.

On another occasion Papa got the idea of escorting the wife of one of his best friends, and having the friend escort Mama. But Mama seemed to enjoy it more than Papa thought she ought to—though she had opposed the idea when it was suggested—and it ended up with Papa leaving his friend's wife at the reception and following Mama and his friend home, and marching her into the house with the muzzle of his Winchester rifle in her back. The friend's wife, left alone at the hall, gave both her husband and Papa a good cussing out the next day. Mama dared not laugh, even at that, for fear of stirring Papa up more. It was a month or so before the two families thawed out again. Even after that, the subject could never be mentioned before Papa or the friend's wife, though both of them had been red-hot for the experiment.

My mother rode herd on one woman with a horse-whip about Papa, and "spoke out" another one. This, instead of making Papa angry, seemed to please him ever so much. The woman who got "spoken out" threatened to whip my mother. Mama was very small and the other woman was husky. But when Papa heard of the threats against Mama, he notified the outside woman that if she could not whip him too, she had better not bring the mess up. The woman left the county without ever breaking another breath with Papa. Nobody around there knew what became of her.

So, looking back, I take it that Papa and Mama, in spite of his meanderings, were really in love. Maybe he was just born before his time.

* * *

We lived on a big piece of ground with two big chinaberry trees shading the front gate and Cape jasmine bushes with hundreds of blooms on either side of the walks. I loved the fleshy, white, fragrant blooms as a child but did not make too much of them. They were too common in my neighborhood. When I got to New York and found out that the people called them gardenias, and that the flowers cost a dollar each, I was impressed. The home folks laughed when I went back down there and told them. Some of the folks did not want to believe me. A dollar for a Cape jasmine bloom! Folks up north there must be crazy.

There were plenty of orange, grapefruit, tangerine, guavas and other fruits in our yard. We had a five-acre garden with things to eat growing in it, and so we were never hungry. We had chicken on the table often; home-cured meat, and all the eggs we wanted.

It was a common thing for us smaller children to fill the iron tea-kettle full of eggs and boil them, and lay around in the yard and eat them until we were full. Any left-over boiled eggs could always be used for missiles. There was plenty of fish in the lakes around the town, and so we had all that we wanted. But beef stew was something rare. We were all very happy whenever Papa went to Orlando and brought back something delicious like stew-beef. Chicken and fish were too common with us. In the same way, we treasured an apple. We had oranges, tangerines and grapefruit to use as hand-grenades on the neighbors' children. But apples were something rare. They came from way up north.

Our house had eight rooms, and we called it a two-story house; but later on I learned it was really one story and a jump. The big boys all slept up there, and it was a good place to hide and shirk from sweeping off the front porch or raking up the back yard.

Downstairs in the dining-room there was an old "safe," a punched design in its tin doors. Glasses of guava jelly, quart jars of pear, peach and other kinds of preserves. The left-over cooked foods were on the lower shelves.

There were eight children in the family, and our house was noisy from the time school turned out until bedtime. After supper we gathered in Mama's room, and everybody had to get their lessons for the next day. Mama carried us all past long division in arithmetic, and parsing sentences in grammar, by diagrams on the blackboard. That was as far as she had gone. Then the younger ones were turned over to my oldest brother, Bob, and Mama sat and saw to it that we paid attention. You had to keep on going over things until you did know. How I hated the multiplication tables—especially the sevens!

We had a big barn, and a stretch of ground well covered with Bermuda grass. So on moonlight nights, two-thirds of the village children from seven to eighteen would be playing hide and whoop, chick-mah-chick, hide and seek, and other boisterous games in our yard. Once or twice a year we might get permission to go and play at some other house. But that was most unusual. Mama contended that we had plenty of space to play in; plenty of things to play with; and, furthermore, plenty of us to keep each other's company. If she had her way, she meant to raise her children to stay at home. She said that there was no need for us to live like no-count Negroes and poor-white trash—too poor to sit in the house—had to come outdoors for any pleasure, or hang around somebody else's house. Any of her children who had any tendencies like that must have got it from the Hurston side. It certainly did not come from the Pottses. Things like that gave me my first glimmering of the universal female gospel that all good traits and leanings come from the mother's side.

Mama exhorted her children at every opportunity

to "jump at de sun." We might not land on the sun, but at least we would get off the ground. Papa did not feel so hopeful. Let well enough alone. It did not do for Negroes to have too much spirit. He was always threatening to break mine or kill me in the attempt. My mother was always standing between us. She conceded that I was impudent and given to talking back, but she didn't want to "squinch my spirit" too much for fear that I would turn out to be a mealy-mouthed rag doll by the time I got grown. Papa always flew hot when Mama said that. I do not know whether he feared for my future, with the tendency I had to stand and give battle, or that he felt a personal reference in Mama's observation. He predicted dire things for me. The white folks were not going to stand for it. I was going to be hung before I got grown. Somebody was going to blow me down for my sassy tongue. Mama was going to suck sorrow for not beating my temper out of me before it was too late. Posses with ropes and guns were going to drag me out sooner or later on account of that stiff neck I toted. I was going to tote a hungry belly by reason of my forward ways. My older sister was meek and mild. She would always get along. Why couldn't I be like her? Mama would keep right on with whatever she was doing and remark, "Zora is my young'un, and Sarah is yours. I'll be bound mine will come out more than conquer. You leave her alone. I'll tend to her when I figger she needs it." She meant by that that Sarah had a disposition like Papa's, while mine was like hers.

Behind Mama's rocking-chair was a good place to be in times like that. Papa was not going to hit Mama. He was two hundred pounds of bone and muscle and Mama weighed somewhere in the nineties. When people teased him about Mama being the boss, he would say he could break her of her headstrong ways if he wanted to, but she was so little that he couldn't find any place to hit her. My Uncle Jim, Mama's brother, used to always take exception to that. He maintained that if a woman had anything big enough to sit on, she had something big enough to hit on. That was his firm conviction, and he meant to hold on to it as long as the bottom end of his backbone pointed towards the ground—don't care who the woman was or what she looked like, or where she came from. Men like Papa who held to any other notion were just beating around the bush, dodging the issue, and otherwise looking like a fool at a funeral.

Papa used to shake his head at this and say, "What's de use of me taking my fist to a poor weakly thing like a woman? Anyhow, you got to submit yourself to 'em, so there ain't no use in beating on 'em and then have to go back and beg 'em pardon."

But perhaps the real reason that Papa did not take Uncle Jim's advice too seriously was because he saw how it worked out in Uncle Jim's own house. He could tackle Aunt Caroline, all right, but he had his hands full to really beat her. A knockdown didn't convince her that the fight was over at all. She would get up and come right on in, and she was nobody's weakling. It was generally conceded that he might get the edge on her in physical combat if he took a hammer or a trace-chain to her, but in other ways she always won. She would watch his various philandering episodes just so long, and then she would go into action. One time she saw all, and said nothing. But one Saturday afternoon, she watched him rush in with a new shoe-box which he thought that she did not see him take out to the barn and hide until he was ready to go out. Just as the sun went down, he went out, got his box, cut across the orange grove and went on down to the store.

He stopped long enough there to buy a quart of peanuts, two stalks of sugarcane, and then tripped on off to the little house in the woods where lived a certain transient light of love. Aunt Caroline kept right on ironing until he had gotten as far as the store. Then she slipped on her shoes, went out in the yard and got the axe, slung it across her shoulder and went walking very slowly behind him.

The men on the store porch had given Uncle Jim a laughing sendoff. They all knew where he was going and why. The shoes had been bought right there at the store. Now here came "dat Cal'line" with her axe on her shoulder. No chance to warn Uncle Jim at all. Nobody expected murder, but they knew that plenty of trouble was on the way. So they just sat and waited. Cal'line had done so many side-splitting things to Jim's lights of love—all without a single comment from her—that they were on pins to see what happened next.

About an hour later, when it was almost black dark, they saw a furtive figure in white dodging from tree to tree until it hopped over Clark's strawberry-patch fence and headed towards Uncle Jim's house until it disappeared.

"Looked mightily like a man in long drawers and nothing else," Walter Thomas observed. Everybody agreed that it did, but who and what could it be?

By the time the town lamp which stood in front of the store was lighted, Aunt Caroline emerged from the blackness that hid the woods and passed the store. The axe was still over her shoulder, but now it was draped with Uncle Jim's pants, shirt and coat. A new pair of women's oxfords were dangling from the handle by their strings. Two stalks of sugarcane were over her other shoulder. All she said was, "Good-evening, gentlemen," and kept right on walking towards home.

The porch rocked with laughter They had the answer to everything. Later on when they asked Uncle Jim how Cal'line managed to get into the lady's house, he smiled sourly and said, "Dat axe was her key." When they kept on teasing him, he said, "Oh, dat old stubborn woman I married, you can't teach her nothing. I can't teach her no city ways at all."

On another occasion, she caused another lady who couldn't give the community anything but love, baby, to fall off of the high, steep church steps on her head. Aunt Cal'line might have done that just to satisfy her curiosity, since it was said that the lady felt that anything more than a petticoat under her dresses would be an encumbrance. Maybe Aunt Caroline just wanted to verify the rumor. The way the lady tumbled, it left no doubt in the matter. She was really a free soul. Evidently Aunt Caroline was put out about it, because she had to expectorate at that very moment, and it just happened to land where the lady was bare. Aunt Caroline evidently tried to correct her error in spitting on her rival, for she took her foot and tried to grind it in. She never said a word as usual, so the lady must have misunderstood Aunt Caroline's curiosity. She left town in a hurry—a speedy hurry—and never was seen in those parts again.

So Papa did not take Uncle Jim's philosophy about handling the lady people too seriously. Every time Mama cornered him about some of his doings, he used to threaten to wring a chair over her head. She never even took enough notice of the threat to answer. She just went right on asking questions about his doings and then answering them herself until Papa slammed out of the house looking like he had been whipped all over with peach hickories. But I had better not let out a giggle at such times, or it would be just too bad.

Our house was a place where people came. Visiting preachers, Sunday school and B.Y.P.U. workers, and just friends. There was fried chicken for visitors, and other such hospitality as the house afforded.

Papa's bedroom was the guest-room. Store-bought towels would be taken out of the old round-topped trunk in Mama's room and draped on the washstand. The pitcher and bowl were scrubbed out before fresh water from the pump was put in for the use of the guest. Sweet soap was company soap. We knew that. Otherwise, Octagon laundry soap was used to keep us clean. Bleached-out meal sacks served the family for bath towels ordinarily, so that the store-bought towels could be nice and clean for visitors.

Company got the preference in toilet paper, too. Old newspapers were put out in the privy house for family use. But when company came, something better was offered them. Fair to middling guests got sheets out of the old Sears, Roebuck catalogue. But Mama would sort over her old dress patterns when really fine company came, and the privy house was well scrubbed, lime thrown in, and the soft tissue paper pattern stuck on a nail inside the place for the comfort and pleasure of our guests.

III
I Get Born

This is all hear-say. Maybe some of the details of my birth as told me might be a little inaccurate, but it is pretty well established that I really did get born.

The saying goes like this. My mother's time had come and my father was not there. Being a carpenter, successful enough to have other helpers on some jobs, he was away often on building business, as well as preaching. It seems that my father was away from home for months this time. I have never been told why. But I did hear that he threatened to cut his throat when he got the news. It seems that one daughter was all that he figured he could stand. My sister, Sarah, was his favorite child, but that one girl was enough. Plenty more sons, but no more girl babies to wear out shoes and bring in nothing. I don't think he ever got over the trick he felt that I played on him by getting born a girl, and while he was off from home at that. A little of my sugar used to sweeten his coffee right now. That is a Negro way of saying his patience was short with me. Let me change a few words with him—and I am of the word-changing kind—and he was ready to change ends. Still and all, I looked more like him than any child in the house. Of course, by the time I got born, it was too late to make any suggestions, so the old man had to put up with me. He was nice about it in a way. He didn't tie me in a sack and drop me in the lake, as he probably felt like doing.

People were digging sweet potatoes, and then it was hog-killing time. Not at our house, but it was going on in general over the country like, being January and a bit cool. Most people were either butchering for themselves, or off helping other folks do their butchering, which was almost just as good. It is a gay time. A big pot of hasslits cooking with plenty of seasoning, lean slabs of fresh-killed pork frying for the helpers to refresh themselves after the work is done. Over and above being neighborly and giving aid, there is the food, the drinks and the fun of getting together.

So there was no grown folks close around when Mama's water broke. She sent one of the smaller children to fetch Aunt Judy, the mid-wife, but she was gone to Woodbridge, a mile and a half away, to eat at a hog-killing. The child was told to go over there and tell Aunt Judy to come. But nature, being indifferent to human arrangements, was impatient. My mother had to make it alone. She was too weak after I rushed out to do anything for herself, so she just was lying there, sick in the body, and worried in mind, wondering what would become of her, as well as me.

She was so weak, she couldn't even reach down to where I was. She had one consolation. She knew I wasn't dead, because I was crying strong.

Help came from where she never would have thought to look for it. A white man of many acres and things, who knew the family well, had butchered the day before. Knowing that Papa was not at home, and that consequently there would be no fresh meat in our house, he decided to drive the five miles and bring a half of a shoat, sweet potatoes, and other garden stuff along. He was there a few minutes after I was born. Seeing the front door standing open, he came on in, and hollered, "Hello, there! Call your dogs!" That is the regular way to call in the country because nearly everybody who has anything to watch has biting dogs.

Nobody answered, but he claimed later that he heard me spreading my lungs all over Orange County, so he shoved the door open and bolted on into the house.

He followed the noise and then he saw how things were, and, being the kind of a man he was, he took out his Barlow Knife and cut the navel cord, then he did the best he could about other things. When the mid-wife, locally known as a granny, arrived about an hour later, there was a fire in the stove and plenty of hot water on. I had been sponged off in some sort of a way, and Mama was holding me in her arms.

As soon as the old woman got there, the white man

unloaded what he had brought, and drove off cussing about some blankety-blank people never being where you could put your hands on them when they were needed.

He got no thanks from Aunt Judy. She grumbled for years about it. She complained that the cord had not been cut just right, and the belly-band had not been put on tight enough. She was mighty scared I was going to have a weak back, and that I would have trouble holding my water until I reached puberty. I did.

The next day or so a Mrs. Neale, a friend of Mama's, came in and reminded her that she had promised to let her name the baby in case it was a girl. She had picked up a name somewhere which she thought was very pretty. Perhaps she had read it somewhere, or somebody back in those woods was smoking Turkish cigarettes. So I became Zora Neale Hurston.

There is nothing to make you like other human beings so much as doing things for them. Therefore, the man who grannied me was back next day to see how I was coming along. Maybe it was pride in his own handiwork, and his resourcefulness in a pinch, that made him want to see it through. He remarked that I was a God-damned fine baby, fat and plenty of lung-power. As time went on, he came infrequently, but somehow kept a pinch of interest in my welfare. It seemed that I was spying noble, growing like a gourd vine, and yelling bass like a gator. He was the kind of a man that had no use for puny things, so I was all to the good with him. He thought my mother was justified in keeping me.

But nine months rolled around, and I just would not get on with the walking business. I was strong, crawling well, but showed no inclination to use my feet. I might remark in passing, that I still don't like to walk. Then I was over a year old, but still I would not walk. They made allowances for my weight, but yet, that was no real reason for my not trying.

They tell me that an old sow-hog taught me how to walk. That is, she didn't instruct me in detail, but she convinced me that I really ought to try.

It was like this. My mother was going to have collard greens for dinner, so she took the dishpan and went down to the spring to wash the greens. She left me sitting on the floor, and gave me a hunk of cornbread to keep me quiet. Everything was going along all right, until the sow with her litter of pigs in convoy came abreast of the door. She must have smelled the cornbread I was messing with and scattering crumbs about the floor. So, she came right on in, and began to nuzzle around.

My mother heard my screams and came running. Her heart must have stood still when she saw the sow in there, because hogs have been known to eat human flesh.

But I was not taking this thing sitting down. I had been placed by a chair, and when my mother got inside the door, I had pulled myself up by that chair and was getting around it right smart.

As for the sow, poor misunderstood lady, she had no interest in me except my bread. I lost that in scrambling to my feet and she was eating it. She had much less intention of eating Mama's baby, than Mama had of eating hers.

With no more suggestions from the sow or anybody else, it seems that I just took to walking and kept the thing a-going. The strangest thing about it was that once I found the use of my feet, they took to wandering. I always wanted to go. I would wander off in the woods all alone, following some inside urge to go places. This alarmed my mother a great deal. She used to say that she believed a woman who was an enemy of hers had sprinkled "travel dust" around the doorstep the day I was born. That was the only explanation she could find. I don't know why it never occurred to her to connect my tendency with my father, who didn't have a thing on his mind but this town and the next one. That should have given her a sort of hint. Some children are just bound to take after their fathers in spite of women's prayers.

IV
The Inside Search

Grown people know that they do not always know the why of things, and even if they think they know, they do not know where and how they got the proof. Hence the irritation they show when children keep on demanding to know if a thing is so and how the grown folks got the proof of it. It is so troublesome because it is disturbing to the pigeonhole way of life. It is upsetting because until the elders are pushed for an answer, they have never looked to see if it was so, nor how they came by what passes for proof to their acceptances of certain things as true. So, if telling their questioning young to run off and play does not suffice for an answer, a good slapping of the child's bottom is held to be proof positive for anything from spelling Constantinople to why the sea is salt. It was told to the old folks and that had been enough for them, or to put it in Negro idiom, nobody didn't tell 'em, but they heard. So there must be something wrong with a child that questions the gods of the pigeonholes.

I was always asking and making myself a crow in

a pigeon's nest. It was hard on my family and sur-roundings, and they in turn were hard on me. I did not know then, as I know now, that people are prone to build a statue of the kind of person that it pleases them to be. And few people want to be forced to ask themselves, "What if there is no me like my statue?" The thing to do is to grab the broom of anger and drive off the beast of fear.

I was full of curiosity like many other children, and like them I was as unconscious of the sanctity of statu-ary as a flock of pigeons around a palace. I got few answers from other people, but I kept right on ask-ing, because I couldn't do anything else with my feel-ings.

Naturally, I felt like other children in that death, destruction and other agonies were never meant to touch me. Things like that happened to other people, and no wonder. They were not like me and mine. Nat-urally, the world and the firmaments careened to one side a little so as not to inconvenience me. In fact, the universe went further than that—it was happy to break a few rules just to show me preferences.

For instance, for a long time I gloated over the happy secret that when I played outdoors in the moonlight the moon followed me, whichever way I ran. The moon was so happy when I came out to play, that it ran shining and shouting after me like a pretty puppy dog. The other children didn't count.

But, I was rudely shaken out of this when I confided my happy secret to Carrie Roberts, my chum. It was cruel. She not only scorned my claim, she said that the moon was paying me no mind at all. The moon, my own happy private-playing moon, was out in its play yard to race and play with her.

We disputed the matter with hot jealousy, and nothing would do but we must run a race to prove which one the moon was loving. First, we both ran a race side by side, but that proved nothing because we both contended that the moon was going that way on account of us. I just knew that the moon was there to be with me, but Carrie kept on saying that it was herself that the moon preferred. So then it came to me that we ought to run in opposite directions so that Carrie could come to her senses and realize the moon was mine. So we both stood with our backs to our gate, counted three and tore out in opposite directions.

"Look! Look, Carrie!" I cried exultantly. "You see the moon is following me!"

"Aw, youse a tale-teller! You know it's chasing me."

So Carrie and I parted company, mad as we could be with each other. When the other children found out what the quarrel was about, they laughed it off. They told me the moon always followed them. The unfaithfulness of the moon hurt me deeply. My moon followed Carrie Roberts. My moon followed Matilda Clarke and Julia Moseley, and Oscar and Teedy Miller. But after a while, I ceased to ache over the moon's many loves. I found comfort in the fact that though I was not the moon's exclusive friend, I was still among those who showed the moon which way to go. That was my earliest conscious hint that the world didn't tilt under my footfalls, nor careen over one-sided just to make me glad.

But no matter whether my probings made me happier or sadder, I kept on probing to know. For instance, I had a stifled longing. I used to climb to the top of one of the huge chinaberry trees which guarded our front gate, and look out over the world. The most interesting thing that I saw was the horizon. Every way I turned, it was there, and the same distance away. Our house then, was in the center of the world. It grew upon me that I ought to walk out to the horizon and see what the end of the world was like. The daring of the thing held me back for a while, but the thing became so urgent that I showed it to my friend, Carrie Roberts, and asked her to go with me. She agreed. We sat up in the trees and disputed about what the end of the world would be like when we got there—whether it was sort of tucked under like the hem of a dress, or just was a sharp drop off into nothingness. So we planned to slip off from our folks bright and soon next morning and go see.

I could hardly sleep that night from the excitement of the thing. I had been yearning for so many months to find out about the end of things. I had no doubts about the beginnings. They were somewhere in the five acres that was home to me. Most likely in Mama's room. Now, I was going to see the end, and then I would be satisfied.

As soon as breakfast was over, I sneaked off to the meeting place in the scrub palmettoes, a short way from our house and waited. Carrie didn't come right away. I was on my way to her house by a round-about way when I met her. She was coming to tell me that she couldn't go. It looked so far that maybe we wouldn't get back by sundown, and then we would both get a whipping. When we got big enough to wear long dresses, we could go and stay as long as we wanted to. Nobody couldn't whip us then. No matter how hard I begged, she wouldn't go. The thing was too bold and brazen to her thinking. We had a fight, then. I had to hit Carrie to keep my heart from stifling me. Then I was sorry I had struck my friend, and went on home and hid under the house with my heartbreak. But I did not give up the idea of my journey. I was merely lonesome for someone brave enough to undertake it with me. I wanted it to be Carrie. She was a lot of fun, and always did what I told her. Well, most of the time, she did. This time it was too much for even her loyalty to surmount. She even tried to talk me out of my trip. I couldn't give up. It meant too much to me. I decided to put it off until I had something to ride on, then I could go by myself.

So for weeks I saw myself sitting astride of a fine horse. My shoes had sky-blue bottoms to them, and I was riding off to look at the belly-band of the world.

It was summer time, and the mockingbirds sang all night long in the orange trees. Alligators trumpeted from their stronghold in Lake Belle. So fall passed and then it was Christmas time.

Papa did something different a few days before Christmas. He sort of shoved back from the table after dinner and asked us all what we wanted Santa Claus to bring us. My big brothers wanted a baseball outfit. Ben and Joel wanted air rifles. My sister wanted patent leather pumps and a belt. Then it was my turn. Suddenly a beautiful vision came before me. Two things could work together. My Christmas present could take me to the end of the world.

"I want a fine black riding horse with white leather saddle and bridles," I told Papa happily.

"You, what?" Papa gasped. "What was dat you said?"

"I said, I want a black saddle horse with . . ."

"A saddle horse!" Papa exploded. "It's a sin and a shame! Lemme tell you something right now, my young lady; you ain't white.* Riding horse! Always trying to wear de big hat! I don't know how you got in this family nohow. You ain't like none of de rest of my young 'uns."

"If I can't have no riding horse, I don't want nothing at all," I said stubbornly with my mouth, but

---

* That is a Negro saying that means "Don't be too ambitious. You are a Negro and they are not meant to have but so much."

inside I was sucking sorrow. My longed-for journey looked impossible.

"I'll riding-horse you, Madam!" Papa shouted and jumped to his feet. But being down at the end of the table big enough for all ten members of the family together, I was near the kitchen door, and I beat Papa to it by a safe margin. He chased me as far as the side gate and turned back. So I did not get my horse to ride off to the edge of the world. I got a doll for Christmas.

Since Papa would not buy me a saddle horse, I made me one up. No one around me knew how often I rode my prancing horse, nor the things I saw in far places. Jake, my puppy, always went along and we made great admiration together over the things we saw and ate. We both agreed that it was nice to be always eating things.

I discovered that I was extra strong by playing with other girls near my age. I had no way of judging the force of my playful blows, and so I was always hurting somebody. Then they would say I meant to hurt, and go home and leave me. Everything was all right, however, when I played with boys. It was a shameful thing to admit being hurt among them. Furthermore, they could dish it out themselves, and I was acceptable to them because I was the one girl who could take a good pummeling without running home to tell. The fly in the ointment there, was that in my family it was not ladylike for girls to play with boys. No matter how young you were, no good could come of the thing. I used to wonder what was wrong with playing with boys. Nobody told me. I just mustn't, that was all. What was wrong with my doll-babies? Why couldn't I sit still and make my dolls some clothes?

I never did. Dolls caught the devil around me. They got into fights and leaked sawdust before New Year's. They jumped off the barn and tried to drown themselves in the lake. Perhaps, the dolls bought for me looked too different from the ones I made up myself. The dolls I made up in my mind, did everything. Those store-bought things had to be toted and helped around. Without knowing it, I wanted action.

So I was driven inward. I lived an exciting life unseen. But I had one person who pleased me always. That was the robust, gray-haired white man who had helped me get into the world. When I was quite small, he would come by and tease me and then praise me for not crying. When I got old enough to do things, he used to come along some afternoons and ask to take me with him fishing. He said he hated to bait his own hook and dig worms. It always turned out when we got to some lake back in the woods that he had a full can of bait. He baited his own hooks. In between fishing business, he would talk to me in a way I liked—as if I were as grown as he. He would tell funny stories and swear at every other word. He was always making me tell him things about my doings, and then he would tell me what to do about things. He called me Snidlits, explaining that Zora was a hell of a name to give a child.

"Snidlits, don't be a nigger," he would say to me over and over. "Niggers * lie and lie! Any time you catch folks lying, they are skeered of something. Lying is dodging. People with guts don't lie. They tell the truth and then if they have to, they fight it out. You lay yourself open by lying. The other fellow knows right off that you are skeered of him and he's more'n apt to tackle you. If he don't do nothing, he starts to looking down on you from then on. Truth is a letter from courage. I want you to grow guts as you go along. So don't you let me hear of you lying. You'll get 'long all right if you do like I tell you. Nothing can't lick you if you never get skeered."

My face was all scratched up from fighting one time, so he asked me if I had been letting some kid lick me. I told him how Mary Ann and I had started to fighting and I was doing fine until her older sister Janie and her brother Ed, who was about my size, had all doubleteened me.

"Now, Snidlits, this calls for talking. Don't you try to fight three kids at one time unlessen you just can't get around it. Do the best you can, if you have to. But learn right now, not to let your head start more than your behind can stand. Measure out the amount of

---

* The word Nigger used in this sense does not mean race. It means a weak, contemptible person of any race.

fighting you can do, and then do it. When you take on too much and get licked, folks will pity you first and scorn you after a while, and that's bad. Use your head!"

"Do de best I can," I assured him, proud for him to think I could.

"That's de ticket, Snidlits. The way I want to hear you talk. And while I'm on the subject, don't you never let nobody spit on you or kick you. Anybody who takes a thing like that ain't worth de powder and shot it takes to kill 'em, hear?"

"Yessir."

"Can't nothing wash that off, but blood. If anybody ever do one of those things to you, kill dead and go to jail. Hear me?"

I promised him I would try and he took out a peanut bar and gave it to me.

"Now, Snidlits, another thing. Don't you never threaten nobody you don't aim to fight. Some folks will back off of you if you put out plenty threats, but you going to meet some that don't care how big you talk, they'll try you. Then, if you can't back your crap with nothing but talk, you'll catch hell. Some folks puts dependence in bluffing, but I ain't never seen one that didn't get his bluff called sooner or later. Give 'em what you promise 'em and they'll look up to you even if they hate your guts. Don't worry over that part. Somebody is going to hate you anyhow, don't care what you do. My idea is to give 'em a good cause if it's got to be. And don't change too many words if you aim to fight. Lam hell out of 'em with the first lick and keep on lamming. I've seen many a fight finished with the first lick. Most folks can't stand to be hurt. But you must realize that getting hurt is part of fighting. Keep right on. The one that hurts the other one the worst wins the fight. Don't try to win no fights by calling 'em low-down names. You can call 'em all the names you want to, after the fight. That's the best time to do it, anyhow."

I knew without being told that he was not talking about my race when he advised me not to be a nigger. He was talking about class rather than race. He frequently gave money to Negro schools.

These talks went on until I was about ten. Then the hard-riding, hard-drinking, hard-cussing, but very successful man, was thrown from his horse and died. Nobody ever expected him to die in bed, so that part was all right. Everybody said that he had been a useful citizen, just powerful hot under the collar.

He was an accumulating man, a good provider, paid his debts and told the truth. Those were all the virtues the community expected. Any more than that would not have been appreciated. He could ride like a centaur, swim long distances, shoot straight with either pistol or guns, and he allowed no man to give him the lie to his face. He was supposed to be so tough, it was said that once he was struck by lightning and was not even knocked off his feet, but that lightning went off through the woods limping. Nobody found any fault with a man like that in a country where personal strength and courage were the highest virtues. People were supposed to take care of themselves without whining.

For example, two men came before the justice of the peace over in Maitland. The defendant had hit the plaintiff three times with his fist and kicked him four times. The justice of the peace fined him seven dollars—a dollar a lick. The defendant hauled out his pocketbook and paid his fine with a smile. The justice of the peace then fined the plaintiff ten dollars.

"What for?" he wanted to know. "Why, Mr. Justice, that man knocked me down and kicked me, and I never raised my hand."

"That is just what I'm fining you for, you yellow-bellied coudar! * Nobody with any guts would have come into court to settle a fist fight."

The community felt that the justice had told him what was right. In a neighborhood where bears and alligators raided hog-pens, wildcats fought with dogs in people's yards, rattlesnakes as long as a man and as thick as a man's forearm were found around back doors, a fist fight was a small skimption. As in all frontiers, there was the feeling for direct action. Decency was plumb outraged at a man taking a beating and then swearing out a warrant about it. Most of the settlers considered a courthouse a place to "law" over

* A coudar is a fresh-water terrapin.

property lines and things like that. That is, you went to law over it if neither party got too abusive and personal. If it came to that, most likely the heirs of one or the other could take it to court after the funeral was over.

So the old man died in high favor with everybody. He had done his cussing and fighting and drinking as became a man, taken care of his family and accumulated property. Nobody thought anything about his going to the county seat frequently, getting drunk, getting his riding-mule drunk along with him, and coming down the pike yelling and singing while his mule brayed in drunken hilarity. There went a man!

I used to take a seat on top of the gate-post and watch the world go by. One way to Orlando ran past my house, so the carriages and cars would pass before me. The movement made me glad to see it. Often the white travelers would hail me, but more often I hailed them, and asked, "Don't you want me to go a piece of the way with you?"

They always did. I know now that I must have caused a great deal of amusement among them, but my self-assurance must have carried the point, for I was always invited to come along. I'd ride up the road for perhaps a half-mile, then walk back. I did not do this with the permission of my parents, nor with their foreknowledge. When they found out about it later,

I usually got a whipping. My grandmother worried about my forward ways a great deal. She had known slavery and to her my brazenness was unthinkable.

"Git down offa dat gate-post! You li'l sow, you! Git down! Setting up dere looking dem white folks right in de face! They's gowine to lynch you, yet. And don't stand in dat doorway gazing out at 'em neither. Youse too brazen to live long."

Nevertheless, I kept right on gazing at them, and "going a piece of the way" whenever I could make it. The village seemed dull to me most of the time. If the village was singing a chorus, I must have missed the tune.

Perhaps a year before the old man died, I came to know two other white people for myself. They were women.

It came about this way. The whites who came down from the North were often brought by their friends to visit the village school. A Negro school was something strange to them, and while they were always sympathetic and kind, curiosity must have been present, also. They came and went, came and went. Always, the room was hurriedly put in order, and we were threatened with a prompt and bloody death if we cut one caper while the visitors were present. We always sang a spiritual, led by Mr. Calhoun himself. Mrs. Calhoun always stood in the back, with a palmetto switch in her hand as a squelcher. We were all little angels for the duration, because we'd better be.

She would cut her eyes and give us a glare that meant trouble, then turn her face towards the visitors and beam as much as to say it was a great privilege and pleasure to teach lovely children like us. They couldn't see that palmetto hickory in her hand behind all those benches, but we knew where our angelic behavior was coming from.

Usually, the visitors gave warning a day ahead and we would be cautioned to put on shoes, comb our heads, and see to ears and fingernails. There was a close inspection of every one of us before we marched in that morning. Knotty heads, dirty ears and fingernails got hauled out of line, strapped and sent home to lick the calf over again.

This particular afternoon, the two young ladies just popped in. Mr. Calhoun was flustered, but he put on the best show he could. He dismissed the class that he was teaching up at the front of the room, then called the fifth grade in reading. That was my class.

So we took our readers and went up front. We stood up in the usual line, and opened to the lesson. It was the story of Pluto and Persephone. It was new and hard to the class in general, and Mr. Calhoun was very uncomfortable as the readers stumbled along, spelling out words with their lips, and in mumbling undertones before they exposed them experimentally to the teacher's ears.

Then it came to me. I was fifth or sixth down the line. The story was not new to me, because I had read my reader through from lid to lid, the first week that Papa had bought it for me.

That is how it was that my eyes were not in the book, working out the paragraph which I knew would be mine by counting the children ahead of me. I was observing our visitors, who held a book between them, following the lesson. They had shiny hair, mostly brownish. One had a looping gold chain around her neck. The other one was dressed all over in black and white with a pretty finger ring on her left hand. But the thing that held my eyes were their fingers. They were long and thin, and very white, except up near the tips. There they were baby pink. I had never seen such hands. It was a fascinating discovery for me. I wondered how they felt. I would have given those hands more attention, but the child before me was almost through. My turn next, so I got on my mark, bringing my eyes back to the book and made sure of my place. Some of the stories I had re-read several times, and this Greco-Roman myth was one of my favorites. I was exalted by it, and that is the way I read my paragraph.

"Yes, Jupiter had seen her (Persephone). He had seen the maiden picking flowers in the field. He had seen the chariot of the dark monarch pause by the maiden's side. He had seen him when he seized Persephone. He had seen the black horses leap down Mount Aetna's fiery throat. Persephone was now in Pluto's dark realm and he had made her his wife."

The two women looked at each other and then back to me. Mr. Calhoun broke out with a proud smile beneath his bristly moustache, and instead of the next child taking up where I had ended, he nodded to me to go on. So I read the story to the end, where flying Mercury, the messenger of the Gods, brought Persephone back to the sunlit earth and restored her to the arms of Dame Ceres, her mother, that the world might have springtime and summer flowers, autumn and harvest. But because she had bitten the pomegranate while in Pluto's kingdom, she must return to him for three months of each year, and be his queen. Then the world had winter, until she returned to earth.

The class was dismissed and the visitors smiled us away and went into a low-voiced conversation with Mr. Calhoun for a few minutes. They glanced my way once or twice and I began to worry. Not only was I barefooted, but my feet and legs were dusty. My hair was more uncombed than usual, and my nails were not shiny clean. Oh, I'm going to catch it now. Those ladies saw me, too. Mr. Calhoun is promising to 'tend to me. So I thought.

Then Mr. Calhoun called me. I went up thinking how awful it was to get a whipping before company. Furthermore, I heard a snicker run over the room. Hennie Clark and Stell Brazzle did it out loud, so I would be sure to hear them. The smart-aleck was going to get it. I slipped one hand behind me and switched my dress tail at them, indicating scorn.

"Come here, Zora Neale," Mr. Calhoun cooed as I reached the desk. He put his hand on my shoulder and gave me little pats. The ladies smiled and held out those flower-looking fingers towards me. I seized the opportunity for a good look.

"Shake hands with the ladies, Zora Neale," Mr. Calhoun prompted and they took my hand one after the other and smiled. They asked me if I loved school, and I lied that I did. There was *some* truth in it, because I liked geography and reading, and I liked to play at recess time. Whoever it was invented writing and arithmetic got no thanks from me. Neither did I like the arrangement where the teacher could sit up there with a palmetto stem and lick me whenever he saw fit. I hated things I couldn't do anything about. But I knew better than to bring that up right there, so I said yes, I *loved* school.

"I can tell you do," Brown Taffeta gleamed. She patted my head, and was lucky enough not to get sandspurs in her hand. Children who roll and tumble in the grass in Florida, are apt to get sandspurs in their hair. They shook hands with me again and I went back to my seat.

When school let out at three o'clock, Mr. Calhoun told me to wait. When everybody had gone, he told me I was to go to the Park House, that was the hotel in Maitland, the next afternoon to call upon Mrs. Johnstone and Miss Hurd. I must tell Mama to see that I was clean and brushed from head to feet, and I must wear shoes and stockings. The ladies liked me, he said, and I must be on my best behavior.

The next day I was let out of school an hour early, and went home to be stood up in a tub of suds and be scrubbed and have my ears dug into. My sandy hair sported a red ribbon to match my red and white checked gingham dress, starched until it could stand alone. Mama saw to it that my shoes were on the right feet, since I was careless about left and right. Last thing, I was given a handkerchief to carry, warned again about my behavior, and sent off, with my big brother John to go as far as the hotel gate with me.

First thing, the ladies gave me strange things, like stuffed dates and preserved ginger, and encouraged me to eat all that I wanted. Then they showed me their Japanese dolls and just talked. I was then handed a copy of *Scribner's Magazine,* and asked to read a place that was pointed out to me. After a paragraph or two, I was told with smiles, that that would do.

I was led out on the grounds and they took my picture under a palm tree. They handed me what was to me then a heavy cylinder done up in fancy paper, tied with a ribbon, and they told me goodbye, asking me not to open it until I got home.

My brother was waiting for me down by the lake, and we hurried home, eager to see what was in the thing. It was too heavy to be candy or anything like that. John insisted on toting it for me.

My mother made John give it back to me and let me open it. Perhaps, I shall never experience such joy again. The nearest thing to that moment was the telegram accepting my first book. One hundred goldy-new pennies rolled out of the cylinder. Their gleam lit up the world. It was not avarice that moved me. It was the beauty of the thing. I stood on the mountain. Mama let me play with my pennies for a while, then put them away for me to keep.

That was only the beginning. The next day I received an Episcopal hymn-book bound in white leather with a golden cross stamped into the front cover, a copy of The Swiss Family Robinson, and a book of fairy tales.

I set about to commit the song words to memory. There was no music written there, just the words. But there was to my consciousness music in between them just the same. "When I survey the Wondrous Cross" seemed the most beautiful to me, so I committed that to memory first of all. Some of them seemed dull and without life, and I pretended they were not there. If white people liked trashy singing like that, there must be something funny about them that I had not noticed before. I stuck to the pretty ones where the words marched to a throb I could feel.

A month or so after the two young ladies returned to Minnesota, they sent me a huge box packed with clothes and books. The red coat with a wide circular collar and the red tam pleased me more than any of the other things. My chums pretended not to like anything that I had, but even then I knew that they were jealous. Old Smarty had gotten by them again. The clothes were not new, but they were very good. I shone like the morning sun.

But the books gave me more pleasure than the clothes. I had never been too keen on dressing up. It called for hard scrubbings with Octagon soap suds getting in my eyes, and none too gentle fingers scrubbing my neck and gouging in my ears.

In that box were Gulliver's Travels, Grimm's Fairy Tales, Dick Whittington, Greek and Roman Myths, and best of all, Norse Tales. Why did the Norse tales strike so deeply into my soul? I do not know, but they did. I seemed to remember seeing Thor swing his mighty short-handled hammer as he sped across the sky in rumbling thunder, lightning flashing from the tread of his steeds and the wheels of his chariot. The great and good Odin, who went down to the well of knowledge to drink, and was told that the price of a drink from that fountain was an eye. Odin drank deeply, then plucked out one eye without a murmur and handed it to the grizzly keeper, and walked away. That held majesty for me.

Of the Greeks, Hercules moved me most. I followed him eagerly on his tasks. The story of the choice of Hercules as a boy when he met Pleasure and Duty, and put his hand in that of Duty and followed her steep way to the blue hills of fame and glory, which she pointed out at the end, moved me profoundly. I resolved to be like him. The tricks and turns of the other Gods and Goddesses left me cold. There were other thin books about this and that sweet and gentle little girl who gave up her heart to Christ and good works. Almost always they died from it, preaching as they passed. I was utterly indifferent to their deaths. In the first place I could not conceive of death, and in the next place they never had any funerals that amounted to a hill of beans, so I didn't care how soon they rolled up their big, soulful, blue eyes and kicked the bucket. They had no meat on their bones.

But I also met Hans Andersen and Robert Louis Stevenson. They seemed to know what I wanted to hear and said it in a way that tingled me. Just a little below these friends was Rudyard Kipling in his Jungle Books. I loved his talking snakes as much as I did the hero.

I came to start reading the Bible through my mother. She gave me a licking one afternoon for repeating something I had overheard a neighbor telling her. She locked me in her room after the whipping, and the Bible was the only thing in there for me to read. I happened to open to the place where David was doing some mighty smiting, and I got interested. David went here and he went there, and no matter where he went, he smote 'em hip and thigh. Then he sung songs to his harp awhile, and went out and smote some more. Not one time did David stop and preach about sins and things. All David wanted to know from God was who to kill and when. He took care of the other details himself. Never a quiet moment. I liked him a lot. So I read a great deal more in the Bible, hunting for some more active people like David. Except for the beautiful language of Luke and Paul, the New Testament still plays a poor second to the Old Testament for me. The Jews had a God who laid about Him when they needed Him. I could see no use waiting till Judgment Day to see a man who was just crying for a good killing, to be told to go and roast. My idea was to give him a good killing first, and then if he got roasted later on, so much the better.

In searching for more Davids, I came upon Leviticus. There were exciting things in there to a child eager to know the facts of life. I told Carrie Roberts about it, and we spent long afternoons reading what Moses told the Hebrews not to do in Leviticus. In that way I found out a number of things the old folks would not have told me. Not knowing what we were actually reading, we got a lot of praise from our elders for our devotion to the Bible.

Having finished that and scanned the Doctor Book, which my mother thought she had hidden securely from my eyes, I read all the things which children write on privy-house walls. Therefore, I lost my taste for pornographic literature. I think that the people who love it got cheated in the matter of privy houses when they were children.

In a way this early reading gave me great anguish through all my childhood and adolescence. My soul was with the gods and my body in the village. People just would not act like gods. Stew beef, fried fat-back and morning grits were no ambrosia from Valhalla. Raking back yards and carrying out chamber-pots, were not the tasks of Thor. I wanted to be away from drabness and to stretch my limbs in some mighty struggle. I was only happy in the woods, and when the ecstatic Florida springtime came strolling from the sea, trance-glorifying the world with its aura. Then I hid out in the tall wild oats that waved like a glinty veil. I nibbled sweet oat stalks and listened to the wind soughing and sighing through the crowns of the lofty pines. I made particular friendship with one huge tree and always played about its roots. I named it "the loving pine," and my chums came to know it by that name.

In contrast to everybody about me, I was not afraid of snakes. They fascinated me in a way which I still cannot explain. I got no pleasure from their death.

I do not know when the visions began. Certainly I was not more than seven years old, but I remember the first coming very distinctly. My brother Joel and I had made a hen take an egg back and been caught as we turned the hen loose. We knew we were in for it and decided to scatter until things cooled off a bit. He hid out in the barn, but I combined discretion with pleasure, and ran clear off the place. Mr. Linsay's house was vacant for a spell. He was a neighbor who was off working somewhere at the time. I had not thought of stopping there when I set out, but I saw a big raisin lying on the porch and stopped to eat it. There was some cool shade on the porch, so I sat down, and soon I was asleep in a strange way. Like clearcut stereopticon slides, I saw twelve scenes flash before me, each one held until I had seen it well in every detail, and then be replaced by another. There was no continuity as in an average dream. Just disconnected scene after scene with blank spaces in between. I knew that they were all true, a preview of things to come, and my soul writhed in agony and shrunk away. But I knew that there was no shrinking. These things had to be. I did not wake up when the last one flickered and vanished, I merely sat up and saw the Methodist Church, the line of moss-draped oaks, and our strawberry patch stretching off to the left.

So when I left the porch, I left a great deal behind me. I was weighed down with a power I did not want. I had knowledge before its time. I knew my fate. I knew that I would be an orphan and homeless. I knew that while I was still helpless, that the comforting circle of my family would be broken, and that I would have to wander cold and friendless until I had served my time. I would stand beside a dark pool of water and see a huge fish move slowly away at a time when I would be somehow in the depth of despair. I would hurry to catch a train, with doubts and fears driving me and seek solace in a place and fail to find it when I arrived, then cross many tracks to board the train again. I knew that a house, a shotgun-built house that needed a new coat of white paint, held torture for me, but I must go. I saw deep love betrayed, but I must feel and know it. There was no turning back. And last of all, I would come to a big house. Two women waited there for me. I could not see their faces, but I knew one to be young and one to be old. One of them was arranging some queer-shaped flowers such as I had never seen. When I had come to these women, then I would be at the end of my pilgrimage, but not the end of my life. Then I would know peace and love and what goes with those things, and not before.

These visions would return at irregular intervals. Sometimes two or three nights running. Sometimes weeks and months apart. I had no warning. I went to bed and they came. The details were always the same, except in the last picture. Once or twice I saw the old faceless woman standing outdoors beside a tall plant with that same off-shape white flower. She turned suddenly from it to welcome me. I knew what was going on in the house without going in, it was all so familiar to me.

I never told anyone around me about these strange things. It was too different. They would laugh me off as a story-teller. Besides, I had a feeling of difference from my fellow men, and I did not want it to be found out. Oh, how I cried out to be just as everybody else! But the voice said No. I must go where I was sent. The weight of the commandment laid heavy and made me moody at times. When I was an ordinary child, with no knowledge of things but the life about me, I was reasonably happy. I would hope that the call would never come again. But even as I hoped I knew that the cup meant for my lips would not pass. I must drink the bitter drink. I studied people all around me, searching for someone to fend it off. But I was told inside myself that there was no one. It gave me a feeling of terrible aloneness. I stood in a world of vanished communion with my kind, which is worse than if it had never been. Nothing is so desolate as a place where life has been and gone. I stood on a soundless island in a tideless sea.

Time was to prove the truth of my visions, for one by one they came to pass. As soon as one was fulfilled, it ceased to come. As this happened, I counted them off one by one and took consolation in the fact that one more station was past, thus bringing me nearer the end of my trials, and nearer to the big house, with the kind women and the strange white flowers.

Years later, after the last one had come and gone, I read a sentence or a paragraph now and then in the columns of O. O. McIntyre which perhaps held no special meaning for the millions who read him, but in which I could see through those slight revelations that he had had similar experiences. Kipling knew the feeling for himself, for he wrote of it very definitely in his Plain Tales From the Hills. So I took comfort in knowing that they were fellow pilgrims on my strange road.

I consider that my real childhood ended with the coming of the pronouncements. True, I played, fought and studied with other children, but always I stood apart within. Often I was in some lonesome wilderness, suffering strange things and agonies while other children in the same yard played without a care. I asked myself why me? Why? Why? A cosmic loneliness was my shadow. Nothing and nobody around me really touched me. It is one of the blessings of this world that few people see visions and dream dreams.

V
Figure and Fancy

Nothing that God ever made is the same thing to more than one person. That is natural. There is no single face in nature, because every eye that looks upon it, sees it from its own angle. So every man's spice-box seasons his own food.

Naturally, I picked up the reflections of life around me with my own instruments, and absorbed what I gathered according to my inside juices.

There were the two churches, Methodist and Baptist, and the school. Most people would say that such institutions are always the great influences in any town. They would say that because it sounds like the thing that ought to be said. But I know that Joe Clarke's store was the heart and spring of the town.

Men sat around the store on boxes and benches and passed this world and the next one through their mouths. The right and the wrong, the who, when and why was passed on, and nobody doubted the conclusions. Women stood around there on Saturday nights and had it proven to the community that their husbands were good providers, put all of their money in their wives' hands and generally glorified them. Or right there before everybody it was revealed that one man was keeping some other woman by the things the other woman was allowed to buy on his account. No doubt a few men found that their wives had a brand new pair of shoes oftener than he could afford it, and wondered what she did with her time while he was off at work. Sometimes he didn't have to wonder. There were no discreet nuances of life on Joe Clarke's porch. There was open kindnesses, anger, hate, love, envy and its kinfolks, but all emotions were naked, and nakedly arrived at. It was a case of "make it and take it." You got what your strengths would bring you. This was not just true of Eatonville. This was the spirit of that whole new part of the state at the time, as it always is where men settle new lands.

For me, the store porch was the most interesting place that I could think of. I was not allowed to sit around there, naturally. But, I could and did drag my feet going in and out, whenever I was sent there for something, to allow whatever was being said to hang in my ear. I would hear an occasional scrap of gossip in what to me was adult double talk, but which I understood at times. There would be, for instance, sly references to the physical condition of women, irregular love affairs, brags on male potency by the parties of the first part, and the like. It did not take me long to know what was meant when a girl was spoken of as "ruint" or "bigged."

For instance, somebody would remark, "Ada Dell is ruint, you know." "Yep, somebody was telling me. A pitcher can go to the well a long time, but its bound to get broke sooner or later." Or some woman or girl would come switching past the store porch and some man would call to her, "Hey, Sugar! What's on de rail for de lizard?" Then again I would hear some man say, "I got to have my ground-rations. If one woman can't take care of it, I gits me another one." One man told a woman to hold her ear close, because he had a bug to put in her ear. He was sitting on a box. She stooped over to hear whatever it was he had to whisper to her. Then she straightened up sharply and pulled away from him. "Why, you!" she exclaimed. "The idea of such a thing! Talking like dat to me, when you know I'm a good church-worker, and you a deacon!" He didn't seem to be ashamed at all. "Dat's just de point I'm coming out on, sister. Two clean sheets can't dirty one 'nother, you know." There was general laughter, as the deacon moved his foot so that I could get in the store door. I happened to hear a man talking to another in a chiding manner and say, "To save my soul, I can't see what you fooled with her for. I'd just as soon pick up a old tin can out of the trash pile."

But what I really loved to hear was the menfolks holding a "lying" session. That is, straining against each other in telling folks tales. God, Devil, Brer Rabbit, Brer Fox, Sis Cat, Brer Bear, Lion, Tiger, Buzzard, and all the wood folk walked and talked like natural men. The wives of the story-tellers might yell from backyards for them to come and tote some water, or chop wood for the cook-stove and never get a move out of the men. The usual rejoinder was, "Oh, she's got enough to go on. No matter how much wood you chop, a woman will burn it all up to get a meal. If she got a couple of pieces, she will make it do. If you chop up a whole boxful, she will burn every stick of it. Pay her no mind." So the story-telling would go right on.

I often hung around and listened while Mama waited on me for the sugar or coffee to finish off dinner, until she lifted her voice over the tree tops in a way to let me know that her patience was gone: "You Zora-a-a! If you don't come here, you better!" That had a promise of peach hickories in it, and I would have to leave. But I would have found out from such story-tellers as Elijah Moseley, better known as "Lige," how and why Sis Snail quit her husband, for instance. You may or may not excuse my lagging feet, if you know the circumstances of the case:

One morning soon, Lige met Sis Snail on the far side of the road. He had passed there several times in the last few years and seen Sis Snail headed towards the road. For the last three years he had stepped over her several times as she crossed the road, always forging straight ahead. But this morning he found her clean across, and she seemed mighty pleased with herself, so he stopped and asked her where she was headed for.

"Going off to travel over the world," she told him. "I done left my husband for good."

"How come, Sis Snail? He didn't ill-treat you in no ways, did he?"

"Can't exactly say he did, Brother Lige, but you take and take just so much and then you can't take no more. Your craw gits full up to de neck. De man gits around too slow to suit me, and look like I just can't break him of it. So I done left him for good. I'm out and gone. I gits around right fast, my ownself, and I just can't put up with nobody dat gits around as slow as he do."

"Oh, don't leave de man too sudden, Sis Snail. Maybe he might come to move round fast like you do. Why don't you sort of reason wid de poor soul and let him know how you feel?"

"I done tried dat until my patience is all wore out. And this last thing he done run my cup over. You know I took sick in de bed—had de misery in my side so bad till I couldn't rest in de bed. He heard me groaning and asked me what was de matter. I told him how sick I was. Told him, 'Lawd, I'm so sick!' So he said 'If you's sick like dat, I'll go git de doctor for you.' I says, 'I sho would be mighty much obliged if you would.' So he took and told me, 'I don't want you laying there and suffering like dat. I'll go git de doctor right away. Just lemme go git my hat.'

"So I laid there in de bed and waited for him to go git de doctor. Lawd! I was so sick! I rolled from pillar to post. After seven I heard a noise at de door, and I said, 'Lawd, I'm so glad! I knows dats my husband done come back wid de doctor.' So I hollered out and asked, 'Honey, is dat you done come back wid de doctor?' And he come growling at me and giving me a short answer wid, 'Don't try to rush me. I ain't gone yet.' It had done took him seven years to git his hat and git to de door. So I just up and left him."

Then one late afternoon, a woman called Gold, who had come to town from somewhere else, told the why and how of races that pleased me more than what I learned about race derivations later on in Ethnology. This was her explanation:

God did not make folks all at once. He made folks sort of in His spare time. For instance one day He had a little time on his hands, so He got the clay, seasoned it the way He wanted it, then He laid it by and went on to doing something more important. Another day He had some spare moments, so He rolled it all out, and cut out the human shapes, and stood them all up against His long gold fence to dry while He did some important creating. The human shapes all got dry, and when He found time, He blowed the breath of life in them. After that, from time to time, He would call everybody up, and give them spare parts. For instance, one day He called everybody and gave out

feet and eyes. Another time He give out toe-nails that
Old Maker figured they could use. Anyhow, they had
all that they got up to now. So then one day He said,
"Tomorrow morning, at seven o'clock *sharp,* I aim
to give out color. Everybody be here on time. I got
plenty of creating to do tomorrow, and I want to give
out this color and get it over wid. *Everybody* be
'round de throne at seven o'clock tomorrow morning!"

So next morning at seven o'clock, God was sitting
on His throne with His big crown on His head and
seven suns circling around His head. Great multitudes was standing around the throne waiting to get
their color. God sat up there and looked, east, and He
looked west, and He looked north and He looked
Australia, and blazing worlds were falling off His
teeth. So He looked over to His left and moved His
hands over a crowd and said, "You's yellow people!"
They all bowed low and said, "Thank you, God," and
they went on off. He looked at another crowd, moved
His hands over them and said, "You's red folks!"
They made their manners and said, "Thank you, Old
Maker," and they went on off. He looked towards the
center and moved His hand over another crowd and
said, "You's white folks!" They bowed low and said,
"Much obliged, Jesus," and they went on off. Then
God looked way over to the right and said, "Look
here, Gabriel, I miss a lot of multitudes from around
the throne this morning." Gabriel looked too, and

said, "Yessir, there's a heap of multitudes missing from round de throne this morning." So God sat there an hour and a half and waited. Then He called Gabriel and said, "Looka here, Gabriel, I'm sick and tired of this waiting. I got plenty of creating to do this morning. You go find them folks and tell 'em they better hurry on up here and they expect to get any color. Fool with me, and I won't give out no more."

So Gabriel run on off and started to hunting around. Way after while, he found the missing multitudes lying around on the grass by the Sea of Life, fast asleep. So Gabriel woke them up and told them, "You better get up from there and come on up to the throne and get your color. Old Maker is might wore out from waiting. Fool with Him and He won't give out no more color."

So as the multitudes heard that, they all jumped up and went running towards the throne hollering, "Give us our color! We want our color! We got just as much right to color as anybody else." So when the first ones got to the throne, they tried to stop and be polite. But the ones coming on behind got to pushing and shoving so till the first ones got shoved all up against the throne so till the throne was careening all over to one side. So God said, "Here! Here! Git back! Git back!" But they was keeping up such a racket that they misunderstood Him, and thought He said, "Git black!" So they just got black, and kept the thing a-going.

In one way or another, I heard dozens more of these tales. My father and his preacher associates told the best stories on the church. Papa, being moderator of the South Florida Baptist Association, had numerous preacher visitors just before the Association met, to get the politics of the thing all cut and dried before the meetings came off. After it was decided who would put such and such a motion before the house, who would second it, and whom my father would recognize first and things like that, a big story-telling session would get under way on our front porch, and very funny stories at the expense of preachers and congregations would be told.

No doubt, these tales of God, the Devil, animals and natural elements seemed ordinary enough to most people in the village. But many of them stirred up fancies in me. It did not surprise me at all to hear that the animals talked. I had suspected it all along. Or let us say, that I wanted to suspect it. Life took on a bigger perimeter by expanding on these things. I picked up glints and gleams out of what I heard and stored it away to turn it to my own uses. The wind would sough through the tops of the tall, long-leaf pines and say things to me. I put in the words that the sounds put into me. Like "Woo woo, you wooo!" The tree was talking to me, even when I did not catch the words. It was talking and telling me things. I have mentioned the tree near our house that got so friendly I named it "the loving pine." Finally all of my play-mates called it that too. I used to take a seat at the foot of that tree and play for hours without any toys. We talked about everything in my world. Sometimes we just took it out in singing songs. That tree had a mighty fine bass voice when it really took a notion to let it out.

There was another tree that used to creep up close to the house around sundown and threaten me. It used to put on a skull-head with a crown on it every day at sundown and make motions at me when I had to go out on the back porch to wash my feet after supper before going to bed. It never bothered around during the day. It was just another pine tree about a hundred feet tall then, standing head and shoulders above a grove. But let the dusk begin to fall, and it would put that crown on its skull and creep in close. Nobody else ever seemed to notice what it was up to but me. I used to wish it would go off somewhere and get lost. But every evening I would have to look to see, and every time, it would be right there, sort of shaking and shivering and bowing its head at me. I used to wonder if sometime it was not going to come in the house.

When I began to make up stories I cannot say. Just from one fancy to another, adding more and more detail until they seemed real. People seldom see themselves changing.

So I was making little stories to myself, and have no memory of how I began. But I do remember some of the earliest ones.

I came in from play one day and told my mother how a bird had talked to me with a tail so long that while he sat up in the top of the pine tree his tail was dragging the ground. It was a soft beautiful bird tail, all blue and pink and red and green. In fact I climbed up the bird's tail and sat up the tree and had a long talk with the bird. He knew my name, but I didn't know how he knew it. In fact, the bird had come a long way just to sit and talk with me.

Another time, I dashed into the kitchen and told Mama how the lake had talked with me, and invited me to walk all over it. I told the lake I was afraid of getting drowned, but the lake assured me it wouldn't think of doing *me* like that. No, indeed! Come right on and have a walk. Well, I stepped out on the lake and walked all over it. It didn't even wet my feet. I could see all the fish and things swimming around under me, and they all said hello, but none of them bothered me. Wasn't that nice?

My mother said that it was. My grandmother glared at me like open-faced hell and snorted.

"Luthee!" (She lisped.) "You hear dat young 'un stand up here and lie like dat? And you ain't doing nothing to break her of it? Grab her! Wring her coat tails over her head and wear out a handful of peach hickories on her back-side! Stomp her guts out! Ruin her!"

"Oh, she's just playing," Mama said indulgently.

"Playing! Why dat lil' heifer is lying just as fast as a horse can trot. Stop her! Wear her back-side out. I bet if I lay my hands on her she'll stop it. I vominates a lying tongue."

Mama never tried to break me. She'd listen some-times, and sometimes she wouldn't. But she never seemed displeased. But her mother used to foam at the mouth. I was just as sure to be hung before I got grown as gun was iron! The least thing Mama could do to straighten me out was to smack my jaws for me. She outraged my grandmother scandalously by not doing it. Mama was going to be responsible for my downfall when she stood up in judgment. It was a sin before the living justice, that's what it was. God knows, grandmother would break me or kill me, if she had her way. Killing me looked like the best one, anyway. All I was good for was to lay up and wet the bed half of the time and tell lies, besides being the spitting image of dat good-for-nothing yaller bastard. I was the punishment God put on Mama for marrying Papa. I ought to be thrown in the hogslops, that's what. She could beat me as long as I last.

I knew that I did not have to pay too much atten-tion to the old lady and so I didn't. Furthermore, how was she going to tell what I was doing inside? I could keep my inventions to myself, which was what I did most of the time.

One day, we were going to have roasting-ears for dinner and I was around while Mama was shucking the corn. I picked up an inside chunk and carried it off to look at. It was such a delicate, blushy green. I crawled under the side of the house to love it all by myself.

In a few minutes, it had become Miss Corn-Shuck, and of course needed some hair. So I went back and picked up some cornsilk and tied it to the pointed end. We had a lovely time together for a day or two, and then Miss Corn-Shuck got lonesome for some company.

I do not think that her lonesomeness would have come down on her as it did, if I had not found a cake of sweet soap in Mama's dresser drawer. It was a cake of Pears' scented soap. It was clear like amber glass. I could see straight through it. It delighted my senses just as much as the tender green corn-shuck. So Miss Corn-Shuck fell in love with Mr. Sweet Smell then and there. But she said she could not have a thing to do with him unless he went and put on some clothes. I found a piece of red and white string that had come around some groceries and made him a suit of clothes. Being bigger in the middle than he was on either end, his pants kept falling off—sometimes over his head and sometimes the other way. So I cut little notches in his sides around the middle and tied his suit on. To other people it might have looked like a cake of soap with a bit of twine tied around it, but Miss Corn-Shuck and I knew he had on the finest clothes in the world. Every day it would be different, because Mr. Sweet Smell was very particular about what he wore. Besides he wanted Miss Corn-Shuck to admire him.

There was a great mystery about where Mr. Sweet Smell came from. I suppose if Mama had been asked, she would have said that it was the company soap, since the family used nothing but plain, yellow Octagon laundry soap for bathing. But I had not known it was there until I happened to find it. It might have been there for years. Whenever Miss Corn-Shuck asked him where his home was, he always said it was a secret which he would tell her about when they were married. It was not very important anyway. We knew he was some very high-class man from way off—the farther off the better.

But sad to say, Miss Corn-Shuck and Mr. Sweet Smell never got married. They always meant to, but before very long, Miss Corn-Cob began to make trouble. We found her around the kitchen door one day, and she followed us back under the house and right away started her meanness. She was jealous of Miss Corn-Shuck because she was so pretty and green, with long silky hair, and so Miss Corn-Cob would make up all kinds of mean stories about her. One day there was going to be a big party and that was the first time that the Spool People came to visit. They used to hop off of Mama's sewing machine one by one until they were a great congregation—at least fifteen or so. They didn't do anything much besides second the motion on what somebody else did and said, so they must have been the common people.

Reverend Door-Knob was there, too. He used to live on the inside of the kitchen door, but one day he rolled off and came under the house to be with us. Unconsciously he behaved a lot like Mayor Joe Clarke. He was roundish and reddish brown, and used to laugh louder than anything when something funny happened. The spool people always laughed whenever he laughed. They used to cry too, whenever Mr. Sweet Smell or Miss Corn-Shuck cried. They were always doing whatever they saw other people do. That was the way the Spool People were.

When Mr. Sweet Smell left his fine house in the dresser drawer that day, he came through the kitchen and brought a half can of condensed milk for the refreshments. Everybody liked condensed milk for refreshment. Well, Miss Corn-Cob sneaked around and ate up all the refreshments and then she told everybody that Miss Corn-Shuck ate it. That hurt Mr. Sweet Smell's feelings so bad till he went home and so he didn't marry Miss Corn-Shuck that day. Reverend Door-Knob was so mad with Miss Corn-Cob that he threw her clear over the house and she landed in the horse trough, which everybody said, served her just right.

But not getting married that day sort of threw Mr.

Sweet Smell in a kind of fever. He was sick in the bed for several days. Miss Corn-Shuck went to see him every day, and that was very nice. He rubbed off some of his smell on her because she was so nice to come to see him.

Some people might have thought that Miss Corn-Shuck's green dress had faded and her silky hair all dried up. But that was because they didn't know any better. She just put on a brownish cloak over it, so it wouldn't get dirty. She would let me see it any time I wanted to. That was because she liked me better than anyone else except Mr. Sweet Smell. She lay under the mattress of my bed every night. Mr. Sweet Smell always went home to the dresser drawer. The Spool People slept on the sill under the house because Reverend Door-Knob used to sleep there. They couldn't do a thing unless they saw somebody else doing it. They wore a string around their waist, trying to dress up like Mr. Sweet Smell.

Miss Corn-Cob played a very mean trick once. Miss Corn-Shuck and Mr. Sweet Smell were going to get married down by the lake. The lake had kindly moved into the washbasin for the occasion. A piece of cold cornbread had turned into a magnificent cake. Plenty of egg-nogg had come out of a cake of shaving soap. The bride and groom were standing side by side and ready. When what did Miss Corn-Cob do? She shoved Reverend Door-Knob into the lake, because she knew he couldn't swim. Here everybody was waiting and nobody would have known where the preacher was if one of the Spool People had not seen him kicking down at the bottom of the lake and rescued him.

While he was getting dry and putting on a fresh suit of clothes, Miss Corn-Cob sent our old domi-necker rooster to steal the wedding cake. So the wedding had to be put off until Christmas because then there would be plenty of cake for everybody. The Spool People said they were glad of it, because there ought to be enough cake to go around if you wanted a really nice wedding. The lake told everybody good-bye, jumped out in the yard and went on home. It could not stay off too long, because it would be missed and people would not know what to think.

Miss Corn-Cob went and hid down a gopher hole for a whole week. Every night she used to cry so loud that we could hear her at the house. You see she was scared of the dark. Her mama gave her a good whipping when she got back home and everybody stood around and said, "Goody! Goody! Goody! Goody! Goody!" Because that makes everybody feel bad. That is, no child likes to hear another one gloating "Goody!" when he is in trouble.

They all stayed around the house for years, holding funerals and almost weddings and taking trips with me to where the sky met the ground. I do not know exactly when they left me. They kept me company for so long. Then one day they were gone. Where? I do not know. But there is an age when children are fit company for spirits. Before they have absorbed too much of earthy things to be able to fly with the unseen things that soar. There came a time when I could look back on the fields where we had picked flowers together but they, my friends, were nowhere to be seen. The sunlight where I had lost them was still of Midas gold, but that which touched me where I stood had somehow turned to gilt. Nor could I return to the shining meadow where they had vanished. I could not ask of others if they had seen which way my company went. My friends had been too shy to show themselves to others. Now and then when the sky is the right shade of blue, the air soft, and the clouds are sculptured into heroic shapes, I glimpse them for a moment, and believe again that the halcyon days have been.

When inanimate things ceased to commune with me like natural men, other dreams came to live with me. Animals took on lives and characteristics which nobody knew anything about except myself. Little things that people did or said grew into fantastic stories.

There was a man who turned into an alligator for my amusement. All he did was live in a one-room house by himself down near Lake Belle. I did the rest myself. He came into the village one evening near dusk and stopped at the store. Somebody teased him about living out there by himself, and said that if he did not hurry up and get married, he was liable to go wild.

I saw him tending his little garden all day, and otherwise just being a natural man. But I made an image of him for after dark that was different. In my imagination, his work-a-day hands and feet became the reptilian claws of an alligator. A tough, knotty hide crept over him, and his mouth became a huge snout with prong-toothed, powerful jaws. In the dark of the night, when the alligators began their nightly mysteries behind the cloaking curtain of cypress trees that all but hid Lake Belle, I could see him crawling from his door, turning his ugly head from left to right to see who was looking, then gliding down into the dark waters to become a 'gator among 'gators. He would mingle his bellow with other bull 'gator bellows and be strong and terrible. He was the king of 'gators and the others minded him. When I heard the thunder of bull 'gator voices from the lake on dark nights, I used to whisper to myself, "That's Mr. Pendir! Just listen at him!"

I kept adding detail. For instance, late one afternoon, my mother had taken me for a walk down around Lake Belle. On our way home, the sun had set. It was good and dark when we came to the turning-off place that would take us straight home. At that spot, the trees stood apart, and the surface of the lake was plain. I saw the early moon laying a shiny track across the water. After that, I could picture the full moon laying a flaming red sword of light across the water. It was a road of yellow-red light made for Mr. Pendir to tread. I could see him crossing the lake down this flaming road wrapped in his awful majesty, with thousands on thousands of his subject-'gators moving silently along beside him and behind him in an awesome and mighty convoy.

I added another chapter to the Pendir story when a curious accident happened in the village. One old woman, Mrs. Bronson, went fishing in Blue Sink late one afternoon and did not return. The family, who had opposed the idea of a woman of Mrs. Bronson's age going off to Blue Sink to fish so late in the day, finally became worried and went out to hunt for her. They went around the edge of the lake with lanterns and torches and called and called, but they could not see her, and neither did she answer. Finally, they found her, though people were beginning to be doubtful about it. Blue Sink drops down abruptly from its shores, and is supposed to be bottomless. She was in the lake, at the very edge, still alive, but unable to crawl out. She did not even cry out when she heard herself being called and could discern the moving lanterns. When she was safely home in bed, she said that she had sat there till sundown because she knew the fish would begin to bite. She did catch a few. But just as black dark came on, a terrible fear came on her somehow, and something like a great wind struck her and hurled her into the water. She had fallen on the narrow inside rim of the lake, otherwise she would have sunk into the hidden deeps. She said that she screamed a few times for help, but something rushed across Blue Sink like a body-fied wind and commanded her to hush-up. If she so much as made another sound, she would never get out of that lake alive. That was why she had not answered when she was called, but she was praying inside to be found.

The doctor came and said that she had suffered a stroke. One whole side of her body was paralyzed, so when she tumbled over into the lake, she could not get out. Her terror and fear had done the rest. She must have had two or three horrible hours lying there in the edge of the water, hard put to it to keep her face above water, and expecting the attack of an alligator, water moccasin, gar fish, and numerous other creatures which existed only in her terrified mind. It is a wonder that she did not die of fright.

Right away, I could see the mighty tail of Mr. Pendir slapping Old Lady Bronson into the lake. Then he had stalked away across the lake like the Devil walking up and down in the earth. But when she had screamed, I pictured him re-crossing to her, treading the red-gold of his moon-carpet, with his mighty minions swimming along beside him, his feet walking the surface like a pavement. The soles of his feet never even being damp, he drew up his hosts around her and commanded her to hush.

The old woman was said to dabble in hoodoo, and some said that Pendir did too. I had heard often enough that it was the pride of one hoodoo doctor to "throw it back on the one that done it." What could be more natural then than for my 'gator-man to get peeved because the old lady had tried to throw something he did back on him? Naturally, he slapped her in to the lake. No matter what the doctor said, I knew the real truth of the matter.

I told my playmates about it and they believed it right away. I got bold and told them how I had seen Mr. Pendir turning into a 'gator at night and going down into the lake and walking the water. My chums even believed part of it in a way. That is, they liked the idea and joined in the game. They became timid in the presence of the harmless little man and on the sly would be looking for 'gator signs on him. We pretended a great fear of him. Lest we meet him in 'gator form some night and get carried off into the lake, and die on that terrible road of light.

I told them how he couldn't die anyway. That is, he couldn't die anymore. He was not a living man. He had died a long time ago, and his soul had gone to the 'gators. He had told me that he had no fear of death because he had come back from where other folks were going.

The truth of the matter was, that poor Mr. Pendir was the one man in the village who could not swim a lick. He died a very ordinary death. He worked too long in the hot sun one day, and some said on an empty stomach, and took down sick. Two days later he just died and was buried and stayed where he was put. His life had not agreed with my phantasy at any point. He had no female relatives around to mourn loud and make his funeral entertaining, even, and his name soon ceased to be called. The grown folks of the village never dreamed what an exciting man he had been to me. Even after he was dead and buried, I would go down to the edge of Lake Belle to see if I could run across some of his 'gator hides that he had sloughed off at daybreak when he became a man again. My phantasies were still fighting against the facts.

VI
Wandering

I knew that Mama was sick. She kept getting thinner and thinner and her chest cold never got any better. Finally, she took to bed.

She had come home from Alabama that way. She had gone back to her old home to be with her sister during her sister's last illness. Aunt Dinky had lasted on for two months after Mama got there, and so Mama had stayed on till the last.

It seems that there had been other things there that worried her. Down underneath, it appeared that Grandma had never quite forgiven her for the move she had made twenty-one years before in marrying Papa. So that when Mama suggested that the old Potts place be sold so that she could bring her share back with her to Florida, her mother, urged on by Uncle Bud, Mama's oldest brother, refused. Not until Grandma's head was cold, was an acre of the place to be sold. She had long since quit living on it, and it was pretty well run down, but she wouldn't, that was all. Mama could just go on back to that yaller rascal she had married like she came. I do not think that the money part worried Mama as much as the injustice and spitefulness of the thing.

Then Cousin Jimmie's death seemed to come back on Mama during her visit. How he came to his death is an unsolved mystery. He went to a party and started home. The next morning his headless body was found beside the railroad track. There was no blood, so the train couldn't have killed him. This had happened before I was born. He was said to have been a very handsome young man, and very popular with the girls. He was my mother's favorite nephew and she took it hard. She had probably numbed over her misery, but going back there seemed to freshen up her grief. Some said that he had been waylaid by three other young fellows and killed in a jealous rage. But nothing could be proved. It was whispered that he had been shot in the head by a white man unintentionally, and then beheaded to hide the wound. He had been shot from ambush, because his assailant mistook him for a certain white man. It was night. The attacker expected the white man to pass that way, but not Jimmie. When he found out his mistake, he had forced a certain Negro to help him move the body to the railroad track without the head, so that it would look as if he had been run over by the train. Anyway, that is what the Negro wrote back after he had moved to Texas years later. There was never any move to prove the charge, for obvious reasons. Mama took the whole thing very hard.

It was not long after Mama came home that she began to be less active. Then she took to bed. I knew she was ailing, but she was always frail, so I did not take it too much to heart. I was nine years old, and even though she had talked to me very earnestly one night, I could not conceive of Mama actually dying. She had talked of it many times.

That day, September 18th, she had called me and given me certain instructions. I was not to let them take the pillow from under her head until she was dead. The clock was not to be covered, nor the looking-glass. She trusted me to see to it that these things were not done. I promised her as solemnly as nine years could do, that I would see to it.

What years of agony that promise gave me! In the first place, I had no idea that it would be soon. But that same day near sundown I was called upon to set my will against my father, the village dames and village custom. I know now that I could not have succeeded.

I had left Mama and was playing outside for a little while when I noted a number of women going inside Mama's room and staying. It looked strange. So I went on in. Papa was standing at the foot of the bed looking down on my mother, who was breathing hard. As I crowded in, they lifted up the bed and turned it around so that Mama's eyes would face the east. I thought that she looked to me as the head of the bed was reversed. Her mouth was slightly open, but her

breathing took up so much of her strength that she could not talk. But she looked at me, or so I felt, to speak for her. She depended on me for a voice.

The Master-Maker in His making had made Old Death. Made him with big, soft feet and square toes. Made him with a face that reflects the face of all things, but neither changes itself, nor is mirrored anywhere. Made the body of Death out of infinite hunger. Made a weapon for his hand to satisfy his needs. This was the morning of the day of the beginning of things.

But Death had no home and he knew it at once.

"And where shall I dwell in my dwelling?" Old Death asked, for he was already old when he was made.

"You shall build you a place close to the living, yet far out of the sight of eyes. Wherever there is a building, there you have your platform that comprehends the four roads of the winds. For your hunger, I give you the first and last taste of all things."

We had been born, so Death had had his first taste of us. We had built things, so he had his platform in our yard.

And now, Death stirred from his platform in his secret place in our yard, and came inside the house.

Somebody reached for the clock, while Mrs. Mattie Clarke put her hand to the pillow to take it away.

"Don't!" I cried out. "Don't take the pillow from under Mama's head! She said she didn't want it moved!"

I made to stop Mrs. Mattie, but Papa pulled me away. Others were trying to silence me. I could see the huge drop of sweat collected in the hollow at Mama's elbow and it hurt me so. They were covering the clock and the mirror.

"Don't cover up that clock! Leave that looking-glass like it is! Lemme put Mama's pillow back where it was!"

But Papa held me tight and the others frowned me down. Mama was still rasping out the last morsel of her life. I think she was trying to say something, and I think she was trying to speak to me. What was she trying to tell me? What wouldn't I give to know! Perhaps she was telling me that it was better for the pillow to be moved so that she could die easy, as they said. Perhaps she was accusing me of weakness and failure in carrying out her last wish. I do not know. I shall never know.

Just then, Death finished his prowling through the house on his padded feet and entered the room. He bowed to Mama in his way, and she made her manners and left us to act out our ceremonies over unimportant things.

I was to agonize over that moment for years to come. In the midst of play, in wakeful moments after midnight, on the way home from parties, and even in the classroom during lectures. My thoughts would escape occasionally from their confines and stare me down.

Now, I know that I could not have had my way against the world. The world we lived in required those acts. Anything else would have been sacrilege, and no nine-year-old voice was going to thwart them. My father was with the mores. He had restrained me physically from outraging the ceremonies established for the dying. If there is any consciousness after death, I hope that Mama knows that I did my best. She must know how I have suffered for my failure.

But life picked me up from the foot of Mama's bed, grief, self-despisement and all, and set my feet in strange ways. That moment was the end of a phase in my life. I was old before my time with grief of loss, of failure, and of remorse. No matter what the others did, my mother had put her trust in me. She had felt that I could and would carry out her wishes, and I had not. And then in that sunset time, I failed her. It seemed as she died that the sun went down on purpose to flee away from me.

That hour began my wanderings. Not so much in geography, but in time. Then not so much in time as in spirit.

Mama died at sundown and changed a world. That is, the world which had been built out of her body and her heart. Even the physical aspects fell apart with a suddenness that was startling.

My oldest brother was up in Jacksonville in school, and he arrived home after Mama had passed. By then, she had been washed and dressed and laid out on the ironing-board in the parlor.

Practically all of the village was in the front yard and on the porch, talking in low tones and waiting. They were not especially waiting for my brother Bob. They were doing that kind of waiting that people do around death. It is a kind of sipping up the drama of the thing. However, if they were asked, they would say it was the sadness of the occasion which drew them. In reality it is a kind of feast of the Passover.

Bob's grief was awful when he realized that he was too late. He could not conceive at first that nothing could be done to straighten things out. There was no ear for his excuse nor explanation—no way to ease what was in him. Finally it must have come to him that what he had inside, he must take with him wherever he went. Mama was there on the cooling board with the sheet draped over her blowing gently in the wind. Nothing there seemed to hear him at all.

There was my sister Sarah in the kitchen crying and trying to quiet Everett, who was just past two years old. She was crying and trying to make him hush at the same time. He was crying because he sensed the grief around him. And then, Sarah, who was fifteen, had been his nurse and he would respond to her mood, whatever it was. We were all grubby bales of misery, huddled about lamps.

I have often wished I had been old enough at the time to look into Papa's heart that night. If I could know what that moment meant to him, I could have

set my compass towards him and been sure. I know that I did love him in a way, and that I admired many things about him. He had a poetry about him that I loved. That had made him a successful preacher. He could hit ninety-seven out of a hundred with a gun. He could swim Lake Maitland from Maitland to Winter Park, and no man in the village could put my father's shoulders to the ground. We were so certain of Papa's invincibility in combat that when a village woman scolded Everett for some misdemeanor, and told him that God would punish him, Everett, just two years old, reared back and told her, "He better not bother me. Papa will shoot Him down." He found out better later on, but that goes to show you how big our Papa looked to us. We had seen him bring down bears and panthers with his gun, and chin the bar more times than any man in competing distance. He had to our knowledge licked two men who Mama told him had to be licked. All that part was just fine with me. But I was Mama's child. I knew that she had not always been happy, and I wanted to know just how sad he was that night.

I have repeatedly called up that picture and questioned it. Papa cried some too, as he moved in his awkward way about the place. From the kitchen to the front porch and back again. He kept saying, "Poor thing! She suffered so much." I do not know what he meant by that. It could have been love and pity for her suffering ending at last. It could have been remorse mixed with relief. The hard-driving force was no longer opposed to his easy-going pace. He could put his potentialities to sleep and be happy in the laugh of the day. He could do next year or never, what Mama would have insisted must be done today. Rome, the eternal city, meant two different things to my parents. To Mama, it meant, you must build it today so it could last through eternity. To Papa, it meant that you could plan to lay some bricks today and you have the rest of eternity to finish it. With all time, why hurry? God had made more time than anything else, anyway. Why act so stingy about it?

Then too, I used to notice how Mama used to snatch Papa. That is, he would start to put up an argument that would have been terrific on the store porch, but Mama would pitch in with a single word or a sentence and mess it all up. You could tell he was mad as fire with no words to blow it out with. He would sit over in the corner and cut his eyes at her real hard. He was used to being a hero on the store porch and in church affairs, and I can see how he must have felt to be always outdone around home. I know now that that is a griping thing to a man—not to be able to whip his woman mentally. Some women know how to give their man that conquesting feeling. My mother took her over-the-creek man and bare-knuckled him from brogans to broadcloth, and I am certain that he was proud of the change, in public. But in the house, he might have always felt over-the-

creek, and because that was not the statue he had made for himself to look at, he resented it. But then, you cannot blame my mother too much if she did not see him as his entranced congregations did. The one who makes the idols never worships them, however tenderly he might have molded the clay. You cannot have knowledge and worship at the same time. Mystery is the essence of divinity. Gods must keep their distances from men.

Anyway, the next day, Sam Moseley's span of fine horses, hitched to our wagon, carried my mother to Macedonia Baptist Church for the last time. The finality of the thing came to me fully when the earth began to thud on the coffin.

That night, all of Mama's children were assembled together for the last time on earth. The next day, Bob and Sarah went back to Jacksonville to school. Papa was away from home a great deal, so two weeks later I was on my way to Jacksonville, too. I was under age, but the school had agreed to take me in under the circumstances. My sister was to look after me, in a way.

The midnight train had to be waved down at Maitland for me. That would put me into Jacksonville in the daytime.

As my brother Dick drove the mile with me that night, we approached the curve in the road that skirts Lake Catherine, and suddenly I saw the first picture of my visions. I had seen myself upon that curve at night leaving the village home, bowed down with grief that was more than common. As it all flashed back to me, I started violently for a minute, then I moved closer beside Dick as if he could shield me from those others that were to come. He asked me what was the matter, and I said I thought I heard something moving down by the lake. He laughed at that, and we rode on, the lantern showing the roadway, and me keeping as close to Dick as I could. A little, humped-up, shabby-backed trunk was behind us in the buckboard. I was on my way from the village, never to return to it as a real part of the town.

Jacksonville made me know that I was a little colored girl. Things were all about the town to point this out to me. Streetcars and stores and then talk I heard around the school. I was no longer among the white people whose homes I could barge into with a sure sense of welcome. These white people had funny ways. I could tell that even from a distance. I didn't get a piece of candy or a bag of crackers just for going into a store in Jacksonville as I did when I went into Galloway's or Hill's at Maitland, or Joe Clarke's in Eatonville.

Around the school I was an awful bother. The girls complained that they couldn't get a chance to talk without me turning up somewhere to be in the way. I broke up many good "He said" conferences just by showing up. It was not my intention to do so. What I wanted was for it to go full steam ahead and let me listen. But that didn't seem to please. I was not in the "he said" class, and they wished I would kindly please stay out of the way. My underskirt was hanging, for instance. Why didn't I go some place and fix it? My head looked like a hoo-raw's nest. Why didn't I go comb it? If I took time enough to match my stockings, I wouldn't have time to be trying to listen in on grown folk's business. These venerable old ladies were anywhere from fifteen to eighteen.

In the classroom I got along splendidly. The only difficulty was that I was rated as sassy. I just had to talk back at established authority and that established authority hated backtalk worse than barbed-wire pie. My brother was asked to speak to me in addition to a licking or two. But on the whole, things went along all right. My immediate teachers were enthusiastic about me. It was the guardians of study-hour and prayer meetings who felt that their burden was extra hard to bear.

School in Jacksonville was one of those twilight things. It was not dark, but it lacked the bold sunlight that I craved. I worshipped two of my teachers and loved gingersnaps with cheese, and sour pickles. But I was deprived of the loving pine, the lakes, the wild violets in the woods and the animals I used to know. No more holding down first base on the team with my brothers and their friends. Just a jagged hole where my home used to be.

At times, the girls of the school were lined up two

and two and taken for a walk. On one of these occasions, I had an experience that set my heart to fluttering. I saw a woman sitting on a porch who looked at a distance like Mama. Maybe it *was* Mama! Maybe she was not dead at all. They had made some mistake. Mama had gone off to Jacksonville and they thought that she was dead. The woman was sitting in a rocking-chair just like Mama always did. It must be Mama! But before I came abreast of the porch in my rigid place in line, the woman got up and went inside. I wanted to stop and go in. But I didn't even breathe my hope to anyone. I made up my mind to run away someday and find the house and let Mama know where I was. But before I did, the hope that the woman really was my mother passed. I accepted my bereavement.

VII
Jacksonville and After

My sister moped a great deal. She was Papa's favorite child, and I am certain that she loved him more than anything on earth, my baby brother Everett being next in her love. So two months after I came to school, Sarah said that she was sick and wanted to go home. Papa arranged for her to leave school.

That had very tragic results for Sarah. In a week or two after she left me in Jacksonville, she wrote back that Papa had married again. That hurt us all, somehow. But it was worse for Sarah, for my stepmother must have resented Papa's tender indulgence for his older daughter. It was not long before the news came back that she had insisted that Papa put Sarah out of the house. That was terrible enough, but it was not satisfactory to Papa's new wife. Papa must go over and beat Sarah with a buggy whip for commenting on the marriage happening so soon after Mama's death. Sarah must be driven out of town. So Sarah just married and went down on the Manater River to live. She took Everett with her. She probably left more behind her than she took away.

What Papa and Sarah felt during these times, I have never heard from either of them. I know that it must have plowed very deep with both of them.

God, how I longed to lay my hands upon my stepmother's short, pudgy hulk! No gun, no blade, no club would do. Just flesh against flesh and leave the end of the struggle to the hidden Old Women who sit and spin.

Papa had honored his first-born daughter from the day of her birth. If she was not foretold, she was certainly forewished. Three sons had come, and he was glad of their robust health, but after the first one he wanted a little girl child around the house. For several years then, it had been a wish deferred. So that when she did arrive, small, undersized, but a girl, his joy was boundless. He changed and washed her diapers. She was not allowed to cry as an infant, and when she grew old enough to let on, her wishes did not go unregarded. What was it Papa's girl-baby wanted to eat? She wanted two dolls instead of one? Bless her little heart! A cheeky little rascal! Papa would bring it when he came. The two oldest boys had to get out of their beds late one night and stay outdoors for an hour or more because little three-year-old Sarah woke up and looked out of the window and decided that she wanted to see the stars outdoors. It was no use for the boys to point out that she could see stars aplenty through the window. Papa thundered, "Get up and take dat young'un outdoors! Let her look at de stars just as long as she wants to. And don't let me hear a mutter out of you. If I hear one *grumble,* I'll drop your britches below your hocks and bust de hide on you!"

Sarah was diminutive. Even when she was small, you could tell that she never would grow much. She would be short like Papa's mother, and her own mother. She had something of both of them in her face. Papa delighted in putting the finest and the softest shoes on her dainty feet; the fluffiest white organdy dresses with the stiffest ribbon sashes. "Dat's a switching little gal!" He used to gloat.

She had music lessons on the piano. It did not matter that she was not interested in music, it was part of his pride. The parlor organ was bought in Jacksonville and shipped down as a surprise for Sarah on her tenth birthday. She had a gold ring for her finger, and gold earrings. When I begged for music lessons, I was told to dry up before he bust the hide on my back.

If the rest of us wanted to sneak jelly or preserves and get off without a licking, the thing to do was to get Sarah in on it. Papa might ignore the whipping-purge that Mama was organizing until he found that Sarah was mixed up in it. Then he would lay aside the county newspaper which he was given to reading, and shout at Mama, "Dat'll do! Dat'll do, Lulu! I can't stand all dat racket around de place." Of course, if Mama was really in the mood, Papa's protest would change no plans, but at times it would, and we would all escape because of Sarah. I have seen Papa actually snatch the switch out of Mama's hand when she got to Sarah. But if Mama thought that the chastisement was really in order, she would send out to the peach tree for another one and the whipping would go right on. Papa knew better than to stick his bill in when Mama was really determined. Under such circumstances, Sarah was certain to get some sort of a present on Monday when Papa came back from Sanford.

He had never struck her in his life. She never got but one from him, and that was this cruel thing at the instigation of our stepmother. Neither Papa nor Sarah ever looked at each other in the same way again, nor at the world. Nor did they look like the same people to the world who knew them. Their heads hung down and they studied the ground under their feet too much.

As for me, looking on, it made a tiger out of me. It did not matter so much to me that Sarah was Papa's favorite. I got my joys in other ways, and so, did not miss his petting. I do not think that I ever really wanted it. It made me miserable to see Sarah look like that. And six years later I paid the score off in a small way. It was on a Monday morning, six years after Sarah's heartbreak, that my stepmother threatened to beat me for my impudence, after vainly trying to get Papa to undertake the job. I guess that the memory of the time that he had struck Sarah at his wife's demand, influenced Papa and saved me. I do not think that she considered that a changed man might be in front of her. I do not think that she thought that I would resist in the presence of my father after all that had happened and had shown his lack of will. I do not think that she even thought that she could whip me if I resisted. She did think, if she thought at all, that all she had to do was to start on me, and Papa would be forced to jump in and finish up the job to her satisfaction in order to stay in her good graces. Old memories of her power over him told her to assert herself, and she pitched in. She called me a sassy, impudent heifer, announced that she was going to take me down a buttonhole lower, and threw a bottle at my head. The bottle came sailing slowly through the air and missed me easily. She never should have missed.

The primeval in me leaped to life. Ha! This was the very corn I wanted to grind. Fight! Not having to put up with what she did to us through Papa! Direct action and everything up to me. I looked at her hard. And like everybody else's enemy, her looks, her smells, her sounds were all mixed up with her doings, and she deserved punishment for them as well as her acts. The feelings of all those six years were pressing inside me like steam under a valve. I didn't have any thoughts to speak of. Just the fierce instinct of flesh on flesh—me kicking and beating on her pudgy self—those two ugly false teeth in front—her dead on the floor—grinning like a dead dog in the sun. Consequences be damned! If I died, let me die with my hands soaked in her blood. I wanted her blood, and plenty of it. That is the way I went into the fight, and that is the way I fought it.

She had the advantage of me in weight, that was all. It did not seem to do her a bit of good. Maybe she did not have the guts, and certainly she underestimated mine. She gave way before my first rush and found herself pinned against the wall, with my fists pounding at her face without pity. She scratched and clawed at me, but I felt nothing at all. In a few seconds, she gave up. I could see her face when she realized that I meant to kill her. She spat on my dress, then, and did what she could to cover up from my renewed fury. She had given up fighting except for trying to spit in my face, and I did not intend for her to get away.

She yelled for Papa, but that was no good. Papa was disturbed, no doubt of it, but he wept and fiddled in the door and asked me to stop, while her head was traveling between my fist and the wall, and I wished that my fist had weighed a ton. She tried to do something. She pulled my hair and scratched at me. But I had come up fighting with boys. Hair-pulling didn't worry me.

She screamed that she was going to get Papa's pistol and kill me. She tried to get across the room to the dresser drawer, but I knew I couldn't let that happen. So the fight got hotter. A friend of hers who weighed over two hundred pounds lived across the street. She heard the rumpus and came running. I visualized that she would try to grab me, and I realized that my stepmother would get her chance. So I grabbed my stepmother by the collar and dragged her to a hatchet against the wall and managed to get hold of it. As Mrs. G. waddled through the living-room door, I hollered to her to get back, and let fly with that hatchet with all that my right arm would do. It struck the wall too close to her head to make her happy. She reeled around and rolled down those front steps yelling that I had gone crazy. But she never came back and the fight went on. I was so mad when I saw my adversary sagging to the floor I didn't know what to do. I began to scream with rage. I had not beaten more than two years out of her yet. I made up my mind to stomp her, but at last Papa came to, and pulled me away.

I had a scratch on my neck and two or three on my arms, but that was all. I was not at all pacified. She owed me four more years. Besides there was her spit on the front of her dress. I promised myself to pay her for the old and the new too, the first chance I got. Years later, after I had graduated from Barnard and I was doing research, I found out where she was. I drove twenty miles to finish the job, only to find out that she was a chronic invalid. She had an incurable sore on her neck. I couldn't tackle her under such circumstances, so I turned back, all frustrated inside. All I could do was to wish that she had a lot more neck to rot.

The fight brought things to a head between Papa and his wife. She said Papa had to have me arrested, but Papa said he didn't have to do but two things— die and stay black. And then, he would never let me sleep in jail a night. She took the matter to the church and the people laughed. Most of them had been praying for something like that to happen. They were annoyed because she didn't get her head stomped. The thing rocked on for a few months. She demanded that Papa "handle" some of the sisters of the church who kept cracking her about it, but he explained that there was nothing he could do. They were old friends of my mother's and it was natural for them to feel as they did. There were two or three hot word-battles on the church grounds, and then she left Papa with the understanding that he could get her back when he had made "them good-for-nothing nigger wimmens know dat she was Mrs. Reverend." So she went on off with her lip hung down lower than a mason's apron.

Papa went to see a lawyer and he said to send her clothes to her if she had not come back after three weeks. And that is just what Papa did. She "lawed" for a divorce and he let it slide. The black Anne Boleyn had come at last to the morning and the axe. The simile ends there. The King really had an axe. It has always seemed to me under the provocation a sad lack that preachers could not go armed like that. Perhaps it is just as well that it has been arranged so that the state has taken over the business of execution.

Not every skunk in the world rates a first-class killing. Hanging is too good for some folks. They just need their behinds kicked. And that is all that woman rated. But, you understand, this was six years after I went up to Jacksonville. I put it in right here because I was thinking so hard.

But back to Jacksonville and the school. I had gotten used to the grits and gravy for breakfast, had found out how not to be bored at prayer-meeting—you could always write notes if you didn't go to sleep—and how to poke fun at acidulated disciplinarians, and how to slip through a crack in the fence and cross the street to the grocery store for gingersnaps and pickles which were forbidden between meals. I had generally made a sort of adjustment. Lessons had never worried me, though arithmetic still seemed an unnecessary evil.

Then, one day, the Second in Command sent for me to tell me that my room and board had not been paid. What was I going to do about it? I certainly didn't know. Then she gave me a free-hand opinion of the Reverend John Hurston that Chief Justice Taney could not have surpassed. Every few days after that I was called in and asked what was I going to do. After a while she did not call me in, she would just yell out of the window to where I might be playing in the yard. That used to keep me shrunk up inside. I got so I wouldn't play too hard. The call might come at any time. My spirits would not have quite so far to fall.

But I stayed out the year, but not because my bills were paid. I was put to scrubbing down the stair steps every Saturday, and sent to help clean up the pantry and do what I could in the kitchen after school. Then too, the city of Jacksonville had a spelling bee in all the Negro schools and I won it for my school. I received an atlas of the world and a Bible as prizes, besides so much lemonade and cake that I told President Collier that I could feel it coming through my skin. He had such a big laugh that I made up my mind to to hurry up and get grown and marry him. For his part, he didn't seem to know that he had been picked out. In fact, he seemed to be quite patient about it. Never tried to hurry my growth at all, and never mentioned the matter. He acted like he was satisfied with some stale, old, decrepit woman of twenty-five or so. It used to drive me mad. I comforted myself with the thought that he would cry his eyes out when I would suddenly appear before him, tall and beautiful and disdainful and make him beg me for a whole week before I would give in and marry him, and of course fire all of those old half-dead teachers who were hanging around him. Maybe they would drown themselves in the St. John's River. Oh, I might stop them just before they jumped in. I never did decide what to do with all my disgruntled rivals after I dragged them away from the river. They could rake up the yard, but a yard somewhere a long way from where *he* was. That would be better for everybody. A yard in Africa would be just dandy. They would naturally die of old age in a week or so.

I wrote some letters from him to me and read his tender words with tears in my eyes. I made us a secret post office behind the laundry. One day his letters to me would get written and buried, and the next day I would dig them up and read them. Then I would answer them and assure him he did not have to worry. I meant to marry him as soon as they let me put on long dresses, which I hoped would not be too far off. A month or two more ought to age me quite a bit.

This torrid love affair was conducted from a hole in the ground behind the laundry and came to an abrupt end. One of those same hateful teachers who was mean enough to get grown before I did, reported to my husband-in-reserve that it was I who put a wet brick in her bed while she was presiding over study hour in the chapel. So much fuss over nothing! Just a brick that had been soaked overnight in a rain-barrel placed between the sheets near the foot of the bed, and they made as much fuss about it as if ice cream had been abolished.

It was true that it was a coldish spell of weather in February and all that. But what fun would a cold brick be in June? I ask you!

Oh, the perfidy, the deceit of the man to whom I had given my love and all my lovely letters in the hole behind the laundry! He listened to this unholy female and took me into his office and closed the door. He did not fold me lovingly in his arms and say, "Darling! I understand. You did it all for me." No! The blind fool lifted up my skirt in the rear and spanked a prospective tall, beautiful lady's pants. So improper, to say the least! I made up my mind to get even. I *wouldn't* marry him now, no matter how hard he begged me. Insult me, would he? Turning up *my* dress just like I was some child! Ah, he would pine for my love and never get it. In addition to letting him starve for my love, I was going off and die in a pitiful way. Very lonely and dramatic at the same time, however.

The whole thing was so unjust. She did *not* see me put that brick in her bed. And if the duty-girl did look back over her shoulder and see me coming down the hall with the brick in my hand, what kind of a decent person is that? Going around and looking backwards at people! When I would be grown and sit up in my fine palace eating beef stew and fried chicken, that duty-girl was going to be out in my backyard gnawing door-knobs.

Time passed. Spring came up the St. John's River from down the Everglades way, and school closed in a blaze of programs, cantatas and speeches, and trunks went bumping downstairs. My brother hurried off to take a job. I was to stay there and Papa would send for me.

I kept looking out of the window so that I could see Papa when he came up the walk to the office. But nobody came for me. Weeks passed, and then a letter came. Papa said that the school could adopt me. The Second in Command sent for me and told me about it. She said that she had no place for a girl so young, and besides she was too busy to bring up any children.

It was crumbling news for me. It impressed every detail of the office and her person on my mind. I noted more clearly than ever the thick gray-black ropes of her half-Negro, half-white hair, her thin lips, and white-folks-looking nose. All in all, her yellow skin browned down by age looked like it had been dried between the leaves of a book. I had always been afraid of her sharp tongue and quick hand, but this day she seemed to speak a little softer than usual, and in half-finished sentences, as if she had her tender parts to hide. She took out her purse and handed me some money. She was going to pay my way home by the boat, and I must tell my father to send her her dollar and a half.

The boat trip was thrilling on the side-wheeler *City of Jacksonville*. The water life, the smothering foliage that draped the river banks, the miles of purple hyacinths, all thrilled me anew. The wild thing was back in the jungle.

The curtain of trees along the river shut out the world so that it seemed that the river and the chugging boat was all that there was, and that pleased me a lot. Inside, the boat was glittering with shiny brass.

White-clad waiters dashed about with trays for the

first class upstairs. There was an almost ceaseless rattle of dishes. Red carpet underfoot. Big, shiny lights overhead. White men in greasy overalls popping up from down below now and then to lean on the deck rail for a breath of air. A mulatto waiter with a patch over one eye who kept bringing me slabs of pie and cake and chicken and steak sandwiches, and sent me astern to eat them. Things clattered up the gang plank, and then more things rumbled down into the hold. People on the flimsy docks waving goodbye to anybody who wanted to wave back. Wild hogs appearing now and then along the shore. 'Gators, disturbed by the wash, slipping off of palm logs into the stream. Schools of mullet breaking water now and then. Flocks of waterfowl disturbed at the approach of the steamer, then settling back again to feed. Catfish as long as a man pacing the boat like porpoises for kitchen scraps. A group of turpentine hands with queer haircuts, in blue overalls with red handkerchiefs around their necks, who huddled around a tall, black man with a guitar round his neck. They ate out of shoe-boxes and sang between drinks out of a common bottle. A stocking-foot woman was with them with a dirk in her garter. Her new shoes were in a basket beside her. She dipped snuff and kept missing the spittoon. The glitter of brass and the red carpet made her nervous. The captain kept passing through and pulling my hair gently and asking me to spell something, and kept being surprised when I did. He called out "separate" when I was getting off at Sanford, and I spelled it back at him as I went down the gangplank. I left him leaning on the rail and looking like he had some more words he wanted spelled. Then he threw a half dollar that fell just ahead of me and smiled goodbye.

The day after I started from Jacksonville, the boat docked at Sanford, with the town of Enterprise a shadowy suspicion across the five miles of Lake Monroe. I had to go to the railroad station to take the train for the fifteen miles to Maitland.

The conductor and the whole crew knew me from seeing me with my father so often. They remembered me for another reason, too, which embarrassed me a lot. This very train and crew had been my first experience with railroads. I had seen trains often, but never up so close as that day about four years before when Papa had decided to take me up to Sanford with him. Then I was at the station with Papa and my two oldest brothers. We heard the train blow, leaving Winter Park, three miles south. So we picked up our things and moved down from the platform to a spot beside the track. The train came thundering around Lake Lily, and snorted up to the station. I was there looking the thing dead in the face, and it was fixing its one big, mean-looking eye on me. It looked fit to gnaw me right up. It was truly a most fearsome thing!

The porter swung down and dropped his stool. The conductor in his eyeglasses stood down, changing greetings with Papa, Mr. Wescott, the station-agent, and all of the others whom he knew from long association.

"All aboard!" The train only hesitated at Maitland. It didn't really stop.

This thing was bad, but I saw a chance to save myself yet and still. It did not just have to get me if I moved fast enough.

My father swung up to the platform, and turned around. My brother Bob had me by the hand and prepared to hand me up. This was the last safe moment I had. I tore loose from Bob and dashed under the train and out again. I was going home.

Everybody yelled. The conductor louder than anybody else. "Catch her! Head her off over there!" The engineer held down his whistle. The fireman jumped off and took after me. Everybody was after me. It looked as if the whole world had turned into my enemies. I didn't have a friend to my name.

"There she goes! Hem her up! Head her off from that barbed-wire fence!" My own big brother was chasing me as hard as anybody else. My legs were getting tired and I was winded, but I was running for my life. Brother Bob headed me off from home, so I doubled back into Galloway's store and ran behind the counter. Old Harry, Galloway's son, about Bob's age, grabbed me and pulled me out. I was hauled on board kicking and screaming to the huge amusement of everybody but me. As soon as I saw the glamor of the plush and metal of the inside of that coach, I calmed down. The conductor gave the engineer the high ball and the train rolled. It didn't hurt a bit. Papa laughed and laughed. The porter passed through holding his sides. The conductor came to take Papa's ticket and kept on teasing me about hurting the train's feelings. In a little while he was back with a glass pistol filled with candy. By the time I got to Sanford, I was crazy about the train. I just wished they would quit laughing at me. The inside of that train was too pretty for words. It took years for me to get over loving it.

So when I climbed on board that morning—some four years later, I had that look of "Get away from me, porter! Don't you see I'm too big to be helped on trains"—they all smiled in memory of our first meeting, and let it go at that. The porter was a member of Papa's church in Sanford, and sat beside me when he was not busy.

So I came back to my father's house which was no longer home. The very walls were gummy with gloom. Too much went on to take the task of telling it. Papa's children were in his way, because they were too much trouble to his wife. Ragged, dirty clothes and hit-and-miss meals. The four older children were definitely gone for good. One by one, we four younger ones were shifted to the homes of Mama's friends.

Perhaps it could be no other way. Certainly no other way was open to a man who loved peace and ease the way my father did.

My stepmother was sleeping in Mama's featherbed. The one thing which Mama had brought from her father's house. She had said it must be mine. To see this interloper piled up in my mother's bed was too much for me to bear. I had to do something. The others had been miserable about it all along. I rallied my brother Joel to my aid and we took the mattress off of the bed.

Papa had told her that it was his, so he was faced with the dilemma. I stood my ground, and the other children present backed me. She thought a good beating for me ought to settle the ownership once and for all. John took my part, he was always doing that, dear John, and physical violence, yes actual bloodshed seemed inevitable for a moment. John and Papa stood face to face, and Papa had an open knife in his hand.

Then he looked his defiant son in the eyes and dropped his hand. He just told John to leave home. However, my stepmother had lost her point. She never was pleasured to rack her bones on Mama's feather-bed again. Though there were plenty of beds for her to sleep in, she hated to take any dictation at all from us, especially me.

But Papa's shoulders began to get tired. He didn't rear back and strut like he used to. His well-cut broadcloth, Stetson hats, hand-made alligator-skin shoes and walking-stick had earned him the title of Big Nigger with his children. Behind his back, of course.

He didn't put and take with his cane any more. He just walked along. It didn't take him near so long to put on his hat.

So my second vision picture came to be. I had seen myself homeless and uncared for. There was a chill about that picture which used to wake me up shivering. I had always thought I would be in some lone, arctic wasteland with no one under the sound of my voice. I found the cold, the desolate solitude, and earless silences, but I discovered that all that geography was within me. It only needed time to reveal it.

My vagrancy had begun in reality. I knew that. There was an end to my journey and it had happiness in it for me. It was certain and sure. But the way! Its agony was equally certain. It was before me, and no one could spare me my pilgrimage. The rod of compelment was laid to my back. I must go the way.

VIII
Backstage and the Railroad

There is something about poverty that smells like death. Dead dreams dropping off the heart like leaves in a dry season and rotting around the feet; impulses smothered too long in the fetid air of underground caves. The soul lives in a sickly air. People can be slave-ships in shoes.

This wordless feeling went with me from the time I was ten years old until I achieved a sort of competence around twenty. Naturally, the first five years were the worst. Things and circumstances gave life a most depressing odor.

The five years following my leaving the school at Jacksonville were haunted. I was shifted from house to house of relatives and friends and found comfort nowhere. I was without books to read most of the time, except where I could get hold of them by mere chance. That left no room for selection. I was miserable, and no doubt made others miserable around me, because they could not see what was the matter with me, and I had no part in what interested them.

I was in school off and on, which gave me vagrant peeps into the light, but these intervals lacked peace because I had no guarantee that they would last. I was growing and the general thought was that I could bring in something. This book-reading business was a hold-back and an unrelieved evil. I could not do very much, but look at so-and-so. She was nursing for some good white people. A dollar a week and most of her clothes. People who had no parents could not afford to sit around on school benches wearing out what clothes they had.

One of the most serious objections to me was that having nothing, I still did not know how to be humble. A child in my place ought to realize I was lucky to have a roof over my head and anything to eat at all. And from their point of view, they were right. From mine, my stomach pains were the least of my sufferings. I wanted what they could not conceive of. I could not reveal myself for lack of expression, and then for lack of hope of understanding, even if I could have found the words. I was not comfortable to have around. Strange things must have looked out of my eyes like Lazarus after his resurrection.

So I was forever shifting. I walked by my corpse. I smelt it and felt it. I smelt the corpses of those among whom I must live, though they did not. They were as much at home with theirs as death in a tomb.

Gradually, I came to the point of attempting self-support. It was a glorious feeling when it came to me. But the actual working out of the thing was not so simple as the concept. I was about fourteen then.

For one thing, I really was young for the try. Then my growth was retarded somewhat so that I looked younger than I really was. Housewives would open the door at my ring and look me over. No, they wanted someone old enough to be responsible. No, they wanted someone strong enough to do the work, and so on like that. Did my mother know I was out looking for work? Sometimes in bed at night I would ask myself that very question and wonder.

But now and then someone would like my looks and give me a try. I did very badly because I was interested in the front of the house, not the back. No matter how I resolved, I'd get tangled up with their reading matter, and lose my job. It was not that I was lazy, I just was not interested in dusting and dishwashing. But I always made friends with the children if there were any. That was not intentional. We just got together somehow. That would be fun, but going out to play did not help much on jobs.

One woman liked me for it. She had two little girls, seven and five. I was hired as an upstairs maid. For two or three days things went on very well. The president of the kitchen was a fat, black old woman who had nursed the master of the house and was a fixture. Nobody is so powerful in a Southern family as one of these family fixtures. No matter who hires you, the fixture can fire you. They roam all over the house bossing everybody from the boss on down. Nobody must upset Cynthia or Rhoda or Beckey. If you can't get along with the house president you can't keep the job.

And Miz Cally was President in Full in this house. She looked at me cut-eye first thing because the madam had hired me without asking her about it. She went into her grumble just as soon as I stuck my head in the kitchen door. She looked at me for a moment with her hands on her hips and burst out, "Lawd a'mercy! Miz Alice must done took you to raise! She don't need no more young'uns round de place. Dis house needs a woman to give aid and assistance."

She showed her further disapproval by vetoing every move I made. She was to show me where to find the aprons, and she did. Just as soon as I pulled open the drawer, she bustled me right away from it with her hips.

"Don't you go pulling and hauling through *my* drawers! I keeps things in they place. You take de apron I give you and git on up dem stairs."

I didn't get mad with her. I took the apron and put it on with quite a bit of editing by Sister Cally, and went on up the back stairs. As I emerged on the upper floor, two pairs of gray-blue eyes were ranged on me.

"Hello!" said the two little girls in chorus.

"Hello!" I answered back.

"You going to work for us?" the taller one asked, and fell in beside me.

"Yeah." Maybe I cracked a smile or something, for both of them took a hand on either side and we went on into the room where Mrs. Alice was waiting for me to show me what to do and how to do it.

She was a very beautiful woman in her middle twenties, and she was combing out her magnificent hair. She looked at me through the looking-glass, and we both started to grin for some reason or another.

She showed me how to make beds and clean up. There were three rooms up there, but she told me not to try to do too much at a time. Just keep things looking sort of neat. Then she dressed and left the house. I got things straightened out with Helen and Genevieve acting as convoy at every step. Things went all right till I got to the bathroom, then somehow or other we three found ourselves in a tussle. Screaming, laughing, splashing water and tussling, when a dark shadow filled up the door. Heinz could have wrung enough vinegar out of Cally's look to run his pickle works.

"You going 'way from here!" she prophesied, and shook her head so vigorously that her head rag wagged. She was going to get me gone from there!

"No!" screamed Helen, the littlest girl, and held on to me.

"No! No! No!" Genevieve shrieked.

"Humph! You just wait till yo' daddy come home!" Cally gloomed. "I ain't never seen no sich caper like dis since I been borned in dis world." Then she stumped on back downstairs.

"Don't you go," Genevieve begged. "I like you."

"Me too, I like you too," Helen chorused. "If you go home, we'll go with you."

I had to wait on the table at dinner that night, with my apron too long for me. Mrs. Alice and the children were giving a glowing account of me. The boss glanced at me tolerantly a time or two. Helen would grab hold of my clothes every time I passed her chair, and play in the vegetable dishes when I offered them to her, until her father threatened to spank her hands, but he looked up at me and smiled a little. He looked to me like an aged old soul of thirty-five or so.

Cally kept on cracking the kitchen door to see how I was getting along in there, and I suspect to give the boss a view of her disapproving face.

Things rocked on for a week or two. Mrs. Alice went out more and more to bridge clubs and things like that. She didn't care whether I made up the rooms or not so long as the children were entertained. She would come in late in the afternoon and tell Cally to run upstairs and straighten up a bit.

"What's dat gal been doing?" Cally would growl. Dat gal she was talking about had been off to the park with the children, or stretched out on the floor telling stories or reading aloud from some of their story books. Their mother had been free to go about her business, and a good time was had by all—except Cally.

Before a month passed, things came to a head: Cally burst into the dining-room one night and flew all over the place. The boss had to get somebody to do his cooking. She was tired of doing all the work. She just wasn't going to cook and look after things downstairs and then troop upstairs and do the work somebody else was getting paid for. She was old. Her joints hurt her so bad till she couldn't rest of nights. They really needed to get somebody to help.

Mrs. Alice sat there stark, still and quiet. The boss looked at her, then at old Cally, and then at me.

Finally, he said, "I never meant for you to work yourself down like that, Aunt Cally. You've done more than your share."

" 'Deed, Gawd knows I is!" Cally agreed belligerently, rolling her white eyeballs in my direction.

"Isn't Zora taking care of the upstairs? I thought that was what she was hired for," the boss asked, and looked at his wife.

"Taking care of what?" Cally snorted. " 'Deed, I ain't lying, Mr. Ed. I wouldn't tell a lie on nobody—"

"I know you wouldn't, Auntie," he soothed.

"Dat gal don't do a living thing round dis house but play all day long wid these young 'uns. Den I has to scuffle up dem stairs and do round, cause effen I didn't, dis here place would be like a hawg-pen. Dat's what it would. I *has* to go and do it, Mr. Ed, else it wouldn't never git done. And I'm sick and *tired*. I'm gwine 'way from here!"

"Naw, Cally, you can't do it. You been with me all my life, and I don't aim to let you go. Zora will have to go. These children are too big now to need a nurse."

What did he say that for? My public went into sound and action. Mrs. Alice was letting a tear or two slip. Otherwise she was as still as stone. But Helen scrambled out of her chair with her jaws latched back to the last notch. She stumbled up against me and swung on. Genevieve screamed "No!" in a regular chant like a cheer leader, and ran to me, too. Their mother never raised her head. The boss turned to her.

"Darling, why don't you quiet these children?" he asked gently.

"No! No! No! Zora can't go!" my cheering squad yelled, slinging tears right and left.

"Shut up!" the boss grated at the children and put his hand on the table and scuffled his feet as if he meant to rush off for the hairbrush. "I'll be on you in one more minute! Hush!"

It was easy to see that his heart was not in any spanking. His frown was not right for it. The yelling kept right on. Cally flounced on back to the kitchen, and he got up and hauled the children upstairs. In a minute he called his wife and shut the bedroom door.

Well, then, I didn't have a job any more. I didn't have money either, but I had bought a pair of shoes.

But I was lucky in a way. Somebody told the woman I was staying with about another job, so I went to see about it, and the lady took me. She was sick in the bed, and she had a little girl three years old, but this child did not shine like Helen and Genevieve. She was sort of old-looking in the face.

I didn't like that house. It frowned at me just as soon as I crossed the doorsill. It was a big house with plenty of things in it but the rooms just sat across the hall from each other and made gloomy faces back and forth.

I was soon out of a job again. I got out of many more. Sometimes I didn't suit the people. Sometimes the people didn't suit me. Sometimes my insides tortured me so that I was restless and unstable. I just was not the type. I was doing none of the things I wanted to do. I had to do numerous uninteresting things I did not want to do, and it was tearing me to pieces.

I wanted family love and peace and a resting place. I wanted books and school. When I saw more fortunate people of my own age on their way to and from school, I would cry inside and be depressed for days, until I learned how to mash down on my feelings and numb them for a spell. I felt crowded in on, and hope was beginning to waver.

The third vision of aimless wandering was on me as I had seen it. My brother Dick had married and

sent for me to come to Sanford and stay with him. I
got hopeful for school again. He sent me a ticket, and
I went. I didn't want to go, though. As soon as I got
back to Sanford, my father ordered me to stay at his
house.

It was no more than a month after I got there before my stepmother and I had our fight.

I found my father a changed person. The bounce
was gone from the man. The wreck of his home and
the public reaction to it was telling on him. In spite
of all, I was sorry for him and that added to my resentment towards his wife.

In all fairness to her, she probably did the best she
could, according to her lights. It was just tragic that
her light was so poor. A little more sense would have
told her that the time and manner of her marriage
to my father had killed any hope of success from the
start. No warning bell inside of her caused her to
question the wisdom of an arrangement made over
so many fundamental stumbling stones. My father
certainly could not see the consequences, for he had
never had to consider them too seriously. Mama had
always been there to do that. Suddenly he must have
realized with inward terror that Lucy was not there
any more. This was not just another escapade which
Mama would knot his head for in private and smooth
out publicly. It had rushed him along to where he
did not want to go already and the end was not in
sight. This new wife had wormed her way out of her

little crack in the world to become what looked to her like a great lady, and the big river was too much for her craft. Instead of the world dipping the knee to the new-made Mrs. Reverend, they were spitting on her intentions and calling her a storm-buzzard. Certainly if my father had not built up a strong following years before, he could not have lasted three months. As it was, his foundations rotted from under him, and seven years saw him wrecked. He did not defend her and establish her. It might have been because he was not the kind of a man who could live without his friends, and his old friends, male and female, were the very ones who were leading the attack to disestablish her. Then, too, a certain amount of the prestige every wife enjoys arises out of where the man got her from and how. She lacked the comfort of these bulwarks too. She must have decided that if she could destroy his children she would be safe, but the opposite course would have been the only extenuating circumstance in the eyes of the public. The failure of the project would have been obvious in a few months or even weeks if Papa had been the kind of man to meet the conflict with courage. As it was, the misery of the situation continued for years. He was dragging around like a stepped-on worm. My brief appearance on the scene acted like a catalyzer. A few more months and the thing fell to pieces for good.

I could not bear the air for miles around. It was

too personal and pressing, and humid with memories of what used to be.

So I went off to another town to find work. It was the same as at home so far as the dreariness and lack of hope and blunted impulses were concerned. But one thing did happen that lifted me up. In a pile of rubbish I found a copy of Milton's complete works. The back was gone and the book was yellowed. But it was all there. So I read Paradise Lost and luxuriated in Milton's syllables and rhythms without ever having heard that Milton was one of the greatest poets of the world. I read it because I liked it.

I worked through the whole volume and then I put it among my things. When I was supposed to be looking for work, I would be stretched out somewhere in the woods reading slowly so that I could understand the words. Some of them I did not. But I had read so many books that my reading vocabulary at least was not too meager.

A young woman who wanted to go off on a trip asked me to hold down her job for two months. She worked in a doctor's office and all I had to do was to answer the telephone and do around a little.

The doctor thought that I would not be suitable at first, but he had to have somebody right away so he took a deep breath and said he'd try me. We got along very well indeed after the first day. I became so interested and useful that he said if his old girl did not come back when she promised, he was going to see to it that I was trained for a practical nurse when I was a bit older.

But just at that time I received a letter from Bob, my oldest brother. He had just graduated from Medicine and said that he wanted to help me to go to school. He was sending for me to come to him right away. His wife sent love. He knew that I was going to love his children. He had married in his Freshman year in college and had three of them.

Nothing can describe my joy. I was going to have a home again. I was going to school. I was going to be with my brother! He had remembered me at last. My five haunted years were over!

I shall never forget the exaltation of my hurried packing. When I got on the train, I said goodbye— not to anybody in particular, but to the town, to loneliness, to defeat and frustration, to shabby living, to sterile houses and numbed pangs, to the kind of people I had no wish to know; to an era. I waved it goodbye and sank back into the cushions of the seat.

It was near night. I shall never forget how the red ball of the sun hung on the horizon and raced along with the train for a short space, and then plunged below the belly-band of the earth. There have been other suns that set in significance for me, but *that* sun! It was a book-mark in the pages of a life. I remember the long, strung-out cloud that measured it for the fall.

But I was due for more frustration. There was to be no school for me right away. I was needed around the house. My brother took me for a walk and explained to me that it would cause trouble if he put me in school at once. His wife would feel that he was pampering me. Just work along and be useful around the house and he would work things out in time.

This did not make me happy at all. I wanted to get through high school. I had a way of life inside me and I wanted it with a want that was twisting me. And now, it seemed I was just as far off as before. I was not even going to get paid for working this time, and no time off. But on the other hand, I was with my beloved brother, and the children were adorable! I was soon wrapped up in them head over heels.

It was get up early in the morning and make a fire in the kitchen range. Don't make too much noise and wake up my sister-in-law. I must remember that she was a mother and needed the rest. She had borne my brother's children and deserved the best that he could do for her, and so on. It didn't sound just right. I was not the father of those children, and several months later I found out what was wrong. It came to me in a flash. She had never borne a child for me, so I did not owe her a thing. Maybe somebody did, but it certainly wasn't I. My brother was acting as if I were the father of those children, instead of himself. There was much more, but my brother is dead and I do not wish even to risk being unjust to his memory, or unkind to the living. My sister-in-law is one of the most devoted mothers in the world. She was brave and loyal to my brother when it took courage to be that way. After all she was married to him, not I.

But I made an unexpected friend. She was a white woman and poor. She had children of my own age. Her husband was an electrician. She began to take an interest in me and to put ideas in my head. I will not go so far as to say that I was poorly dressed, for that would be bragging. The best I can say is that I could not be arrested for indecent exposure. I remember wanting gloves. I had never had a pair, and one of my friends told me that I ought to have on gloves when I went anywhere. I could not have them and I was most unhappy. But then, I was not in a position to buy a handkerchief.

This friend slipped me a message one day to come to her house. We had a code. Her son would pass and whistle until I showed myself to let him know I heard. Then he would go on and as soon as I could I would follow. This particular day, she told me that she had a job for me. I was delighted beyond words.

"It's a swell job if you can get it, Zora. I think you can. I told my husband to do all he can, and he thinks he's got it hemmed up for you."

"Oooh! What is it?"

"It is a lady's maid job. She is a singer down at the theater where he is electrician. She brought a maid with her from up North, but the maid met up with a lot of colored people and looks like she's going to get married right off. She don't want the job no more. The lady asked the men around the theater to get her somebody, and my husband thought about you and I told him to tell the rest of the men he had just the right girl for a maid. It seems like she is a mighty nice person."

I was too excited to sit still. I was frightened too, because I did not know the first thing about being a lady's maid. All I hoped was that the lady would overlook that part and give me a chance to catch on.

"You got to look nice for that. So I sent Valena down to buy you a little dress." Valena was her daughter. "It's cheap, but it's neat and stylish. Go inside Valena's room and try it on."

The dress was a navy blue poplin with a boxpleated skirt and a little round, white collar. To my own self, I never did look so pretty before. I put on the dress, and Valena's dark blue felt hat with a rolled brim. She saw to it that I shined my shoes, and then gave me car-fare and sent me off with every bit of advice she could think of.

My feet mounted up the golden stairs as I entered the stage door of that theater. The sounds, the smells, the backstage jumble of things were all things to bear me up into a sweeter atmosphere. I felt like dancing towards the dressing-room when it was pointed out to me. But my friend was walking with me, coaching me how to act, and I had to be as quiet and sober as could be.

The matinee performance of H. M. S. Pinafore was on, so I was told to wait. In a little while a tenor and a soprano voice quit singing a duet and a beautiful blond girl of about twenty-two came hurrying into the dressing-room. I waited until she went inside and closed the door, then I knocked and was told to come in.

She looked at me and smiled so hard till she almost laughed.

"Hello, little girl," she chanted. "Where did you come from?"

"Home. I come to see you."

"Oh, you did? That's fine. What did you come to see me about?"

"I come to work for you."

"Work for me?" She threw back her head and laughed. That frightened me a great deal. Maybe it was all a joke and there was no job after all. "Doing what?" she caroled on.

"Be your lady's maid."

"You? Why, how old are you?"

"Twenty," I said, and tried to look serious as I had been told. But she laughed so hard at that, till I forgot and laughed too.

"Oh, no, you are not twenty." She laughed some

more, but it was not scornful laughter. Just bubbling fun.

"Well, eighteen, then," I compromised.

"No, not eighteen, either."

"Well, then, how about sixteen?"

She laughed at that. Instead of frowning in a sedate way as I had been told, here I was laughing like a fool myself.

"I don't believe you are sixteen, but I'll let it go at that," she said.

"Next birthday. Honest."

"It's all right; you're hired. But let's don't bring this age business up again. I think I'm going to like you. What is your name?"

I told her, fearing all the time she was going to ask questions about my family; but she didn't.

"Well, Zora, I pay ten dollars a week and expenses. You think that will do?"

I almost fell over. Ten dollars each and every week! Was there that much money in the world sure enough? Com-press-ti-bility! ! It wouldn't take long for me to own a bank at that rate.

"Yes, ma'am!" I shouted.

"Well, change my shoes for me."

She stuck out her foot, and pointed at the pair she wanted to put on. I got them on with her tickling me in the back. She showed me a white dress she wanted to change into and I jumped to get it and hook it up.

She touched up her face laughing at me in the mirror and dashed out. I was crazy about her right then. I washed out her shoelaces from a pair of white shoes and her stockings, which were on the back of a chair, and wrung them out in a bath towel for quick drying, and sat down before the mirror to look at myself. It was truly wonderful!

So I had to examine all the curious cosmetics on the table. I was sort of trying them out when she came in.

That night, she let me stand in the wings and hear her sing her duet with the tenor, "Farewell, my own! Light of my life, farewell!" It was so beautiful to me that she seemed more than human. Everything was pleasing and exciting. If there was any more to Heaven than this, I didn't want to see it.

I did not go back home, that is to my brother's house, at all. I was afraid he would try to keep me. I slept on a cot in the room with Valena. She was almost as excited as I was, had come down to see me every night and had met the cast. We were important people, she and I. Her mother had to make us shut up talking and go to sleep every night.

The end of the enchanted week came and the company was to move on. Miss M—— whom I was serving asked me about my clothes and luggage. She told me not to come down to the train with an old dilapidated suitcase for that would make her ashamed. So the upshot of it was that she advanced me the money to buy one, and then paid me for the week. I paid my friend the six dollars which she had spent for my new dress. Valena gave me the hat, an extra pair of panties and stockings. I bought a comb and brush and toothbrush, paste, and two handkerchiefs. Miss M—— did not know when I came down to the station that morning that my new suitcase was stuffed with newspapers to keep my things from rattling.

The company, a Gilbert and Sullivan repertoire, had its own coach. That was another glory to dazzle my eyes. The leading man had a valet, and the contralto had an English maid, both white. I was the only Negro around. But that did not worry me in the least. I had no chance to be lonesome, because the company welcomed me like, or as, a new play-pretty. It did not strike me as curious then. I never even thought about it. Now, I can see the reason for it.

In the first place, I was a Southerner, and had the map of Dixie on my tongue. They were all Northerners except the orchestra leader, who came from Pensacola. It was not that my grammar was bad, it was the idioms. They did not know of the way an average Southern child, white or black, is raised on simile and invective. They know how to call names. It is an everyday affair to hear somebody called a mullet-headed, mule-eared, wall-eyed, hog-nosed, 'gator-faced, shad-mouthed, screw-necked, goat-bellied, puzzle-gutted, camel-backed, butt-sprung, battle-hammed, knock-kneed, razor-legged, box-ankled, shovel-footed, unmated so-and-so! Eyes looking like skint-ginny nuts, and mouth looking like a dish-pan full of broke-up crockery! They can tell you in simile exactly how you walk and smell. They can furnish a picture gallery of your ancestors, and a notion of what your children will be like. What ought to happen to you is full of images and flavor. Since that stratum of the Southern population is not given to book-reading, they take their comparisons right out of the barnyard and the woods. When they get through with you, you and your whole family look like an acre of totem-poles.

First thing, I was young and green, so the baritone started out teasing me the first day. I jumped up and told him to stop trying to run the hog over me! That set everybody off. They teased me all the time just to hear me talk. But there was no malice in it. If I got mad and spoke my piece, they liked it even better. I was stuffed with ice-cream sodas and Coca-cola.

Another reason was that it was fun to them to get hold of somebody whom they could shock. I was hurt to my heart because the company manager called me into his dressing-room and asked me how I liked my job. After I got through telling him how pleased I was, he rushed out with his face half-made up scream-ing, "Stop, oh, Zora! Please stop! Shame on you! Tell-ing me a dirty story like that. Oh! I have never been so shocked in all my life!"

Heads popped out of dressing-rooms all over.

Groans, sad head-shakings and murmurs of outrage. Sad! Sad! They were glad I had not told them such a thing. Too bad! Too bad! Not a smile in the crowd. The more I tried to explain the worse it got. Some locked their doors to shield their ears from such contamination. Finally Miss M—— broke down and laughed and told me what the gag was. For a long while nobody could get me inside a dressing-room outside of Miss M——'s. But that didn't stop the teasing. They would think up more, like having one of the men contrive to walk down the aisle with me and then everybody lift shocked eyebrows, pretend to blush and wink at each other and sigh, "Zora! Zora! What would your mother say?" I would be so upset that I wouldn't know what to do. Maybe they really believed I wasn't nice!

Another sly trick they played on my ignorance was that some of the men would call me and with a very serious face send me to some of the girls to ask about the welfare and condition of cherries and spangles. They would give me a tip and tell me to hurry back with the answer. Some of the girls would send back word that the men need not worry their heads at all. They would never know the first thing about the condition of their cherries and spangles. Some of the girls sent answers full of double talk which went over my head. The soubrette spoke her mind to the men about that practice and it stopped.

But none of this had malice in it. Just their idea of

good backstage gags. By the time they stopped, it seemed that I was necessary to everybody. I was continually stuffed with sweets, nut meats, and soft-drinks. I was welcome in everybody's coach seat and the girls used to pitch pennies to see who carried me off to their hotel rooms. We played games and told stories. They often ordered beer and pretzels, but nobody offered me a drink. I heard all about their love affairs and troubles. They were all looking forward to playing or singing leads some day. Some great personage had raved about all of their performances. The dirty producers and casting directors just hadn't given them their chance. Miss M—— finally put a stop to my going off with the others as soon as she was ready for bed. I had to stay wherever she stayed after that. She had her own affairs to talk about.

She paid for a course for me in manicuring and I practiced on everybody until I became very efficient at it. That course came in handy to me later on.

With all this petting, I became as cocky as a sparrow on Fifth Avenue. I got a scrapbook, and everybody gave me a picture to put in it. I pasted each one on a separate page and wrote comments under each picture. This created a great deal of interest, because some of the comments were quite pert. They egged me on to elaborate. Then I got another idea. I would comment on daily doings and post the sheets on the call-board. This took on right away. The result stayed strictly mine less than a week because members of the cast began to call me aside and tell me things to put in about others. It got to be so general that everybody was writing it. It was just my handwriting, mostly. Then it got beyond that. Most of the cast ceased to wait for me. They would take a pencil to the board and set down their own item. Answers to the wisecracks would appear promptly and often cause uproarious laughter. They always started off with either "Zora says" or "The observant reporter of the Callboard asserts"—Lord, Zora said more *things!* I was continually astonished, but always amused. There were, of course, some sly digs at supposedly secret love affairs at times, but no vicious thrusts. Everybody enjoyed it, even the victims.

When the run came to an end, Miss M—— had a part in another show all set, but rehearsals would not start for two weeks, so she took me to her home in Boston and I found out some things which I did not want to know, particularly.

At times she had been as playful as a kitten. At others, she would be solemn and moody. She loved her mother excessively, but when she received those long, wordy letters from her, she read them with a still face, and tore them up carefully. Then she would be gloomy, and keep me beside her every minute. Sometimes she would become excessively playful. It was puzzling to see a person cry awhile and then commence to romp like a puppy and keep it up for hours. Sometimes she had to have sherry before she went to

bed after a hard romp with me. She invented a game
for us to play in our hotel room. It was known as
"Jake." She would take rouge and paint her face all
over a most startling red. Then I must take eye-
shadow and paint myself blue. Blue Jake and Red
Jake would then chase each other into closets, across
beds, into bathrooms, with our sheet-robes trailing
around us and tripping us up at odd moments. We
crouched and growled and ambushed each other and
laughed and yelled until we were exhausted.

Then maybe next day she hardly said a word.

While I was with her, she met a wealthy business man of Newark, and I could tell that she was
sunk. It all happened very suddenly, but gloriously.
She told me that now that she was going to be married
and leave the stage, she did not want me to work for
anyone else in the business. In fact, she thought that
I should not be working at all. I ought to be in school.
She said she thought I had a mind, and that it would
be a shame for me not to have any further training.
She wished that she herself could go abroad to study,
but that was definitely out of the question, now. The
deep reservoir of things inside her gave off a sigh.

We were in northern Virginia then, and moving
towards Baltimore. When we got there, she inquired
about schools, gave me a big bearful hug, and what
little money she could spare and told me to keep in
touch with her. She would do whatever she could
to help me out.

That was the way we parted. I had been with her
for eighteen months and though neither of us realized
it, I had been in school all that time. I had loosened
up in every joint and expanded in every direction.

I had done some reading. Not as much as before,
but more discriminate reading. The tenor was a Harvard man who had traveled on the Continent. He always had books along with him, and offered them to
me more and more. The first time I asked to borrow
one, he looked at me in a way that said "What for?"
But when he found that I really read it and enjoyed
it, he relaxed and began to hand them to me gruffly.
He never acted as if he liked it, but I knew better.
That was just the Harvard in him.

Then there was the music side. They broke me in
to good music, that is, the classics, if you want to put
it that way. There was no conscious attempt to do this.
Just from being around, I became familiar with Gilbert and Sullivan, and the best parts of the light-opera
field. Grand opera too, for all of the leads had back-
grounds of private classical instruction as well as conservatory training. Even the bit performers and the
chorus had some kind of formal training in voice,
and most of them played the piano. It was not unusual
for some of the principals to drop down at the piano
after a matinee performance and begin to sing arias
from grand opera. Sing them with a wistfulness. The
arias which they would sing at the Metropolitan or
La Scala as they had once hoped actively, and still

hoped passively even as the hair got thinner and the hips got heavier. Others, dressed for the street, would drift over and ease into the singing. Thus I would hear solos, duets, quartets and sextets from the best-known operas. They would eagerly explain to me what they were when I asked. They would go on to say how Caruso, Farrar, Mary Garden, Trentini, Schumann-Heink, Matzenauer and so forth had interpreted this or that piece, and demonstrate it by singing. Perhaps that was their trouble. They were not originators, but followers of originators. Anyway, it was perfectly glorious for me, though I am sure nobody thought of it that way. I just happened to be there while they released their inside dreams.

The experience had matured me in other ways. I had seen, I had been privileged to see folks substituting love for failure of career. I would listen to one and another pour out their feelings sitting on a stool backstage between acts and scenes. Then too, I had seen careers filling up the empty holes left by love, and covering up the wreck of things internal. Those experiences, though vicarious, made me see things and think.

And now, at last it was all over. It was not at all clear to me how I was going to do it, but I was going back to school.

One minute I felt brave and fine about it all. The wish to be back in school had never left me. But alone by myself and feeling it over, I was scared. Before this job I had been lonely; I had been bare and bony of comfort and love. Working with these people I had been sitting by a warm fire for a year and a half and gotten used to the feel of peace. Now, I was to take up my pilgrim's stick and go outside again. Maybe it would be different now. Six of my unhappy visions had passed me and bowed. The seventh one, the house that needed paint, that had threatened me with so much suffering that I used to sit up in bed sodden with agony, had passed. I had fled from it to put on the blue poplin dress. At least that was not before me any more. I took a firm grip on the only weapon I had—hope—and set my feet. Maybe everything would be all right from now on. Maybe. Well, I put on my shoes and I started.

IX
School Again

Back, out walking on fly-paper again. Money was what I needed to get back in school. I could have saved a lot of money if I had received it. But theatrical salaries being so uncertain, I did not get mine half the time. I had it when I had it, but when it was not paid I never worried. But now I needed it. Miss M—— was having her troubles, trying to help her folks she informed me by mail, so I never directly asked her for anything more. I had no resentment, either. It had all been very pleasant.

I tried waiting on table, and made a good waitress when my mind was on it, which was not often. I resented being patronized, more than the monotony of the job; those presumptuous cut-eye looks and supposed-to-be accidental touches on the thigh to see how I took to things. Men at the old game of "stealing a feel." People who paid for a quarter meal, left me a nickel tip, and then stood outside the door and nodded their heads for me to follow on and hear the rest of the story. But I was lacking in curiosity. I was not worrying so much about virtue. The thing just did not call me. There was neither the beauty of love, nor material advantage in it for me. After all, what is the use in having swine without pearls? Some educated men sat and talked about the things I was interested in, but if I seemed to listen, looked at me as much to say, "What would that mean to you?"

Then in the midst of other difficulties, I had to get sick. Not a sensible sickness for poor folks to have. No, I must get down with appendicitis and have to have an operation right away. So it was the free ward of the Maryland General Hospital for me.

When I was taken up to the amphitheatre for the operation I went up there placing a bet with God. I did not fear death. Nobody would miss me very much, and I had no treasures to leave behind me, so I would not go out of life looking backwards on that account. But I bet God that if I lived, I would try to find out the vague directions whispered in my ears and find the road it seemed that I must follow. How? When? Why? What? All those answers were hidden from me.

So two o'clock that day when they dressed me for surgery and took me up there in that room with the northern light and many windows, I stepped out of the chair before the nurse could interfere. walked to a window and took a good look out over Baltimore and the world as far as I could see, resigned myself to fate and, unaided, climbed upon the table, and breathed deeply when the ether cone was placed over my nose.

I scared the doctor and the nurses by not waking up until nine o'clock that night, but otherwise I was all right. I was alive, so I had to win my bet with God.

Soon, I had another waitress's job, trying to save money again, but I was only jumping up and down in my own foot-tracks.

I tried several other things but always I had that feeling that you have in a dream of trying to run, and sinking to your knees at every step in soft sticky mud. And this mud not only felt obscure to my feet, it smelled filthy to my nose. How to pull out?

How then did I get back to school? I just went. I got tired of trying to get the money to go. My clothes were practically gone. Nickeling and dimering along was not getting me anywhere. So I went to the night high school in Baltimore and that did something for my soul.

There I met the man who was to give me the key to certain things. In English, I was under Dwight O. W. Holmes. There is no more dynamic teacher anywhere under any skin. He radiates newness and nerve and says to your mind, "There is something wonderful to behold just ahead. Let's go see what it is." He is a pilgrim to the horizon. Anyway, that is the way he struck me. He made the way clear. Something about his face killed the drabness and discouragement in me. I felt that the thing could be done.

I turned in written work and answered questions like everybody else, but he took no notice of me particularly until one night in the study of English poets he read Kubla Khan. You must get him to read it for you sometime. He is not a pretty man, but he has the face of a scholar, not dry and set like, but fire flashes from his deep-set eyes. His high-bridged, but sort of bent nose over his thin-lipped mouth . . . well, the whole thing reminds you of some old Roman like Cicero, Cæsar or Virgil in tan skin.

That night, he liquefied the immortal brains of Coleridge, and let the fountain flow. I do not know whether something in my attitude attracted his attention, or whether what I had done previously made him direct the stream at me. Certainly every time he lifted his eyes from the page, he looked right into my eyes. It did not make me see him particularly, but it made me see the poem. That night seemed queer, but I am so visual-minded that all the other senses induce pictures in me. Listening to Coleridge's poem for the first time, I saw all that the writer had meant for me to see with him, and infinite cosmic things besides. I was not of the work-a-day world for days after Mr. Holmes's voice had ceased.

This was my world, I said to myself, and I shall be in it, and surrounded by it, if it is the last thing I do on God's green dirt-ball.

But he did something more positive than that. He stopped me after class and complimented me on my work. He did something else. He never asked me anything about myself, but he looked at me and toned his voice in such a way that I felt he knew all about me. His whole manner said, "No matter about the difficulties past and present, step on it!"

I went back to class only twice after that. I did not say a word to him about my resolve. But the next week, I went out to Morgan College to register in the high-school department.

William Pickens, a Negro, was the Dean there, and he fooled me too. I was prepared to be all scared of him and his kind. I had no money and no family to refer to. I just went and he talked to me. He gave me a brief examination and gave me credit for two years' work in high school and assigned me to class. He was just as understanding as Dwight Holmes in a way.

Knowing that I had no money, he evidently spoke to his wife, because she sent for me a few days later and told me enthusiastically that she had a job for me that would enable me to stay in school. Dr. Baldwin, a white clergyman, and one of the trustees of Morgan, had a wife with a broken hip. He wanted a girl to stay at the house, help her dress in the morning, undress at night and generally look after her. There was no need for anyone except in the morning and at night. He would give me a home and two dollars a week. The way Mrs. Pickens described the work to me, I could tell she knew I would be glad to accept the job, and I was.

So I went to live with the Baldwins. The family consisted of the Minister, his wife and his daughter, Miss Maria, who seemed to be in her thirties and un-married.

They had a great library, and I waded in. I acted as if the books would run away. I remember commit-ting to memory, overnight—lest I never get a chance to read it again—Gray's Elegy in a Country Church-yard. Next I learned the Ballad of Reading Gaol and started on the Rubaiyat.

It would be dramatic in a Cinderella way if I were to say that the well-dressed students at school snubbed me and shoved me around, but that I studied hard and triumphed over them. I did study hard because I realized that I was three years behind schedule, and then again study has never been hard to me. Then too, I had hundreds of books under my skin already. Not selected reading, all of it. Some of it could be called trashy. I had been through Nick Carter, Hora-tio Alger, Bertha M. Clay and the whole slew of dime novelists in addition to some really constructive read-ing. I do not regret the trash. It has harmed me in no way. It was a help, because acquiring the reading habit early is the important thing. Taste and natural development will take care of the rest later on.

Nobody shoved me around. There were eighteen people in my class. Six of them were boys. Good-look-ing, well-dressed girls from Baltimore's best Negro families were classmates of mine: Ethel Cummings, the daughter of a very successful lawyer, Bernice Naylor, whose father was a big preacher, the Hughes girls, Bernice and Gwendolyn, who were not only beautiful, but whose family is distinguished in the professions all over America, Mary Jane Watkins of New York, now a dentist, and considered the most sex-appealing thing, with her lush figure and big eyes and soft skin—all of the girls in my class passed for pretty. It was said to be, not only the best-looking class on the campus, college or prep, but about the best-looking group ever to happen to come together. Rosa Brown was in that class too. She had not only lovely eyes set in a cameo-like face, but shining, beautiful black curls that fell easily to her waist. She has done well by herself, too. She is now married to Tanner Moore, a prosperous lawyer of Philadelphia. Town house, cars and country place, and things like that.

Well, here was this class of pretty girls and snappy boys. The girls were in the majority, but what we had of boys were in demand in town and on campus. The class knew it caused a lot of trouble too, as the college girls were always growling about "that prep class" grabbing off the college men. They passed a rule about it, but it did not help matters. They, the college girls, just got left out of things, themselves, while the prep girls romped on.

And here I was, with my face looking like it had been chopped out of a knot of pine wood with a hatchet on somebody's off day, sitting up in the middle of all this pretty. To make things worse, I had only one dress, a change of underwear and one pair of tan oxfords.

Therefore, I did not rush up to make friends, but neither did I shrink away. My second day at school, I had to blow my nose and I had no handkerchief with me. Mary Jane Watkins was sitting next to me, so she quickly shoved her handkerchief in my hand without saying a word. We were in chapel and Dr. Spencer was up speaking. So she kept her eyes front. I nodded my thanks and so began a friendship.

One day, after about a week in school, Bernice Hughes, whose father, Dr. W. A. C. Hughes, was somebody important in the Methodist Episcopal Church, and a trustee of the College, sat watching me. Her gray eyes were fixed on me, and her red lips were puckered in a frown. I did not know what to think. But it was in English History which I liked very much and I was not doing badly in recitation. When the period was over and the class passed on to the next room, she fell in beside me and said, "If you ain't one knowing fool! I'm naming you old Knowledge Bug." Then she laughed that kind of a laugh she has to cover up her feelings and I laughed too. Bernice can register something that makes you look at her and like her no matter what she does.

"I'm sitting by you tomorrow, fool, and from now on. You hear me?" She went on with her catching laugh. "No use in both of us studying like a fool. You can just study for both of us."

So from then on I was knee deep in the Hughes family. There is more looks and native ability in the Hughes clan to the square child than any I can think of offhand. If they do not always make a brilliant showing, it is not because they can't do it. Their looks and charm interfere with their brain-work, that is all. And you are not going to forget them either. If a Hughes is in town, you are going to know it in one way or another.

It soon became apparent that my lack of clothes was no drawback to my getting along. Sometimes somebody would ask me, "Zora, what do you think you'll wear to school tomorrow?" I'd humor the joke and describe what I was going to wear. But let a program or a get-together come along, and all the girls in the class would be backing me off in a corner, or writing me notes offering to lend me something to wear. I would have to take it in rotation to keep from causing hard feelings.

I got on with the boys, too. In no time I made Stanley James, a varsity football man. Then it was Douglas Camper, a senior college man. His brother was a football star at Howard University in Washington. Our class had cornered all of the college seniors so that not one college girl was escorted to the senior prom. We just couldn't see how functions like that could go on without our gang. Mary Jane had cornered Ed Wilson, the Clark Gable of the campus, for the occasion, so the marines had landed.

Whenever Miss Clarke, our English teacher, was absent, I was put in charge of the class. This happened time and time again, sometimes for a whole week at a time. With history it was the same. Once I had the history classes for nearly a month and had to be excused from my other classes. At times like that, my classmates were perfectly respectful to me until the bell rang. Then how they would poke fun at my serious face while I was teaching!

With Dean Pickens to coach me, I placed second in the school oratorical contest. Rosa Brown placed first and Bernice Hughes third, indicating that our class was determined to be head muck-de-muck in everything that went on.

My first publication was on the blackboard in the assembly hall at Morgan. I decided to write an allegory using the faculty members as characters. Most of my classmates were in the know.

I went to school extra early that morning and when the bell rang for assembly, the big board was covered with the story. Dr. Spencer, the President of Morgan, had a great shock of curly white hair. He was the kindly "Great Gray Bear" of the story. Dean Pickens was the "Ferocious Pick." Practically every faculty member was up there, to the great entertainment of the student body. Furthermore, we could see the various members of the faculty sneaking peeps at the board over their shoulders from time to time as the service went on.

When Dr. Spencer rose to read from the Bible, his face was as red as a beet under all that white hair. He ran his fingers through his hair two or three times as he kept looking back at the board.

After the short service was over, he commented on it and actually burst out laughing. Then, of course, everybody else could laugh. All except one man who was there to succeed Dean Pickens, who was going to New York to work for the N.A.A.C.P. This man clouded up and tried to rain. He was up there in the character of "Pocket Tooth" and he didn't like it. He had earned that name because his two canine teeth were extra long, but sort of square at the ends. My class decided that they looked like the pockets on my dress. So far as we were concerned, he was Pocket Tooth, and he stayed Pocket Tooth for the duration. He led devotions next morning and dared everybody to write anything like that on that board again. Dean Pickens, for all his ferocious official frown and hot temper, was full of boy. Down in his apartment, Mrs. Pickens ran things, and he played with his three children. Ruby, the youngest, seemed to have the inside track with him. I was in and out of the Pickens home every day. I actually heard him discussing with Ruby her chances of licking Harriet, her older sister. She had tried it, and failed. Dean Pickens was full of sympathy, but he told her he was afraid Harriet was too tough for her. She had better get even with Harriet some other way. If she felt she must fight, hit Harriet one quick lick and run. That was the best advice he could give her. Mrs. Pickens put down her book and looked at her husband just as she would have at Bill, her son.

My two years at Morgan went off very happily indeed. The atmosphere made me feel right. I was at last doing the things I wanted to do. Every new thing I learned in school made me happy. The science courses were tremendously interesting to me. Perhaps it was because Professor Calloway was such an earnest teacher. I did not do well in Mathematics. Why should A be minus B? Who the devil was X anyway? I could not even imagine. I still do not know. I passed the courses because Professor Johnson, knowing that I did well in everything else, just made it a rule to give me a C. He probably understood that I am one of those people who have no number sense. I have been told that you can never factor A — B to the place where it comes out even. I wouldn't know because I never tried to find out.

When it came time to consider college, I planned to stay on at Morgan. But that was changed by chance. Mae Miller, daughter of the well-known Dr. Kelly Miller of Howard University, came over to Morgan to spend the week-end with her first cousins, Bernice and Gwendolyn Hughes. So we were thrown together.

After a few hours of fun and capers, she said, "Zora, you are Howard material. Why don't you come to Howard?"

Now as everyone knows, Howard University is the capstone of Negro education in the world. There gather Negro money, beauty, and prestige. It is to the Negro what Harvard is to the whites. They say the same thing about a Howard man that they do about Harvard—you can tell a Howard man as far as you can see him, but you can't tell him much. He listens to the doings of other Negro schools and their graduates with bored tolerance. Not only is the scholastic rating at Howard high, but tea is poured in the manner!

I had heard all about the swank fraternities and sororities and the clothes and everything, and I knew I could never make it. I told Mae that.

"You can come and live at our house, Zora," Bernice offered. At the time, her parents were living in Washington, and Bernice and Gwendolyn were in the boarding department at Morgan. "I'll ask Mama the next time she comes over. Then you won't have any room and board to pay. We'll all get together and rustle you up a job to make your tuition."

So that summer I moved on to Washington and got a job. First, as a waitress in the exclusive Cosmos Club downtown, and later as a manicurist in the G Street shop of Mr. George Robinson. He is a Negro who has a chain of white barber shops in downtown Washington. I managed to scrape together money for my first quarter's tuition, and went up to register.

Lo and behold, there was Dwight Holmes sitting up there at Howard! He saved my spirits again. I was short of money, and Morgan did not have the class-A rating that it now has. There was trouble for me and I was just about to give up and call it a day when I had a talk with Dwight Holmes. He encouraged me all he could, and so I stuck and made up all of those hours I needed.

I shall never forget my first college assembly, sitting there in the chapel of that great university. I was so exalted that I said to the spirit of Howard, "You have taken me in. I am a tiny bit of your greatness. I swear to you that I shall never make you ashamed of me."

It did not wear off. Every time I sat there as part and parcel of things, looking up there at the platform crowded with faculty members, the music, the hundreds of students about me, it would come down on me again. When on Mondays we ended the service by singing Alma Mater, I felt just as if it were the Star Spangled Banner:

> Reared against the eastern sky
> Proudly there on hill-top high
> Up above the lake so blue
> Stands Old Howard brave and true.
> There she stands for truth and right,

Sending forth her rays of light,
Clad in robes of majesty
Old Howard! We sing of thee.

My soul stood on tiptoe and stretched up to take in all that it meant. So I was careful to do my classwork and be worthy to stand there under the shadow of the hovering spirit of Howard. I felt the ladder under my feet.

Mr. Robinson arranged for me to come to work at 3:30 every afternoon and work until 8:30. In that way, I was able to support myself. Soon, most of the customers knew I was a student, and tipped me accordingly. I averaged twelve to fifteen dollars a week.

Mr. Robinson's 1410 G Street shop was frequented by bankers, Senators, Cabinet Members, Congressmen, and gentlemen of the Press. The National Press Club was one block down the same street, the Treasury Building was one block up the street and the White House not far away.

I learned things from holding the hands of men like that. The talk was of world affairs, national happenings, personalities, the latest quips from the cloakrooms of Congress and such things. I heard many things from the White House and the Senate before they appeared in print. They probably were bursting to talk to somebody, and I was safe. If I told, nobody would have believed me anyway. Besides, I was much flattered by being told and warned not to repeat what I had heard. Sometimes a Senator, a banker, a newspaper correspondent attached to the White House would all be sitting around my table at one time. While I worked on one, the others waited, and they all talked. Sometimes they concentrated on teasing me. At other times they talked about what had happened, or what they reasoned was bound to happen. Intimate stories about personalities, their secret love affairs, cloakroom retorts, and the like. Soon they took me for granted and would say, "Zora knows how to keep a secret. She's all right." Now, I know that my discretion really didn't matter. They were relieving their pent-up feelings where it could do no harm.

Some of them meant more to me than others because they paid me more attention. Frederick William Wile, White House correspondent, used to talk to me at times quite seriously about life and opportunities and things like that. He had seen three presidents come and go. He had traveled with them, to say nothing of his other traveling to and fro upon the earth. He had read extensively. Sometimes he would be full of stories and cracks, but at other times he would talk to me quite seriously about attitudes, points of view, why one man was great and another a mere facile politician, and so on.

There were other prominent members of the press who would sit and talk longer than it took me to do their hands. One of them, knowing that certain others sat around and talked, wrote out questions two or three times for me to ask and tell him what was said.

Each time the questions were answered, but I was told to keep that under my hat, and so I had to turn around and lie and say the man didn't tell me. I never realized how serious it was until he offered me twenty-five dollars to ask a certain Southern Congressman something and let him know as quickly as possible. He sent out and bought me a quart of French ice cream to bind the bargain. The man came in on his regular time, which was next day, and in his soft voice, began to tell me how important it was to be honorable at all times and to be trustworthy. How could I ask him then? Besides, he was an excellent Greek scholar and translated my entire lesson for me, which was from Xenophon's *Cyropædeia,* and talked at length on the ancient Greeks and Persians. The news man was all right. He had to get his information the best way he could, but, for me, it would have been terrible to do that nice man like that. I told the reporter how it was and he understood and never asked me again.

Mr. Johns, a pressman, big, slow, with his eternal walking-stick, was always looking for a laugh. Logan, our head-porter, was his regular meat. Logan had a long head, so flat on each side that it looked like it had been pressed between two planks. His toes turned in and his answers were funny.

One day, while shining Mr. Johns's shoes, he told him what a fighter he was. He really was tough when he got mad, according to himself. According to Logan, Logan was mean! Just couldn't help it. He had

Indian blood in him. Just mean and strong. When he straightened out his African soup-bone (arm), something was just bound to fall. If a man didn't fall when *he* hit him, he went around behind him to see what was propping him up. Yassuh! Mr. Johns listened at Logan and smiled. He egged him on to tell more of his powers. The very next day Mr. Johns came in and announced that they had a bear up at Keith's theater, and they needed somebody to wrestle with him. There was good money in it for the man who would come right forward and wrestle with that bear, and knowing that Logan needed money and that he was fearless, he had put Logan's name down. He liked Logan too well to let him get cheated out of such a swell chance to get rich and famous. All Logan needed to do was to go to the theater and tell them that Mr. Johns sent him.

"Naw sir, Mr. Johns," Logan said, "I ain't wrestling no bear. Naw sir!"

"But Logan, you told me—everybody in here heard you—that when you get mad, you go bear-hunting with your fist. You don't even have to hunt this bear. He's right up there on the corner waiting for you. You can't let me down like this. I've already told the man you would be glad to wrestle his old bear!"

"How big is dat bear, Mister Johns?"

"Oh, he is just a full-grown bear, Logan. Nothing to worry about at all. He wouldn't weigh more than two hundred pounds at the outside. Soft snap for a man like you, and you weigh about that yourself, Logan."

"Naw sir! Not no big bear like that. Naw sir!"

"Well, Logan, what kind of a bear would you consider? You just tell me, and I'll fix it up with the man."

"Git me a little bitty baby bear, Mr. Johns, 'bout three months old. Dats de kind of bear I wants to wrestle wid. Yassuh!"

An incident happened that made me realize how theories go by the board when a person's livelihood is threatened. A man, a Negro, came into the shop one afternoon and sank down in Banks's chair. Banks was the manager and had the first chair by the door. It was so surprising that for a minute Banks just looked at him and never said a word. Finally, he found his tongue and asked, "What do you want?"

"Hair-cut and shave," the man said belligerently.

"But you can't get no hair-cut and shave here. Mr. Robinson has a fine shop for Negroes on U Street near Fifteenth," Banks told him.

"I know it, but I want one here. The Constitution of the United States—"

But by that time, Banks had him by the arm. Not roughly, but he was helping him out of his chair, nevertheless.

"I don't know how to cut your hair," Banks objected. "I was trained on straight hair. Nobody in here knows how."

"Oh, don't hand me that stuff!" the crusader snarled. "Don't be such an Uncle Tom."

"Run on, fellow. You can't get waited on in here."

"I'll stay right here until I do. I know my rights. Things like this have got to be broken up. I'll get waited on all right, or sue the place."

"Go ahead and sue," Banks retorted. "Go on up-town, and get your hair cut, man. Don't be so hard-headed for nothing."

"I'm getting waited on right here!"

"You're next, Mr. Powell," Banks said to a waiting customer. "Sorry, mister, but you better go on up-town."

"But I have a right to be waited on wherever I please," the Negro said, and started towards Updyke's chair which was being emptied. Updyke whirled his chair around so that he could not sit down and stepped in front of it. "Don't you touch *my* chair!" Updyke glared. "Go on about your business."

But instead of going, he made to get into the chair by force.

"Don't argue with him! Throw him out of here!" somebody in the back cried. And in a minute, barbers, customers all lathered and hair half cut, and porters, were all helping to throw the Negro out.

The rush carried him way out into the middle of G

Street and flung him down. He tried to lie there and be a martyr, but the roar of oncoming cars made him jump up and scurry off. We never heard any more about it. I did not participate in the mêlée, but I wanted him thrown out, too. My business was threatened.

It was only that night in bed that I analyzed the whole thing and realized that I was giving sanction to Jim Crow, which theoretically, I was supposed to resist. But here were ten Negro barbers, three porters and two manicurists all stirred up at the threat of our living through loss of patronage. Nobody thought it out at the moment. It was an instinctive thing. That was the first time it was called to my attention that self-interest rides over all sorts of lines. I have seen the same thing happen hundreds of times since, and now I understand it. One sees it breaking over racial, national, religious and class lines. Anglo-Saxon against Anglo-Saxon, Jew against Jew, Negro against Negro, and all sorts of combinations of the three against other combinations of the three. Offhand, you might say that we fifteen Negroes should have felt the racial thing and served him. He was one of us. Perhaps it would have been a beautiful thing if Banks had turned to the shop crowded with customers and announced that this man was going to be served like everybody else even at the risk of losing their patronage, with all of the other employees lined up in the center of the floor shouting, "So say we all!" It would have been a stirring gesture, and made the headlines for a day. Then we could all have gone home to our unpaid rents and bills and things like that. I could leave school and begin my wanderings again. The "militant" Negro who would have been the cause of it all, would have perched on the smuddled-up wreck of things and crowed. Nobody ever found out who or what he was. Perhaps he did what he did on the spur of the moment, not realizing that serving him would have ruined Mr. Robinson, another Negro who had got what he had the hard way. For not only would the G Street shop have been forced to close, but the F Street shop and all of his other six downtown shops. Wrecking George Robinson like that on a "race" angle would have been ironic tragedy. He always helped out any Negro who was trying to do anything progressive as far as he was able. He had no education himself, but he was for it. He would give any Howard University student a job in his shops if they could qualify, even if it was only a few hours a week.

So I do not know what was the ultimate right in this case. I do know how I felt at the time. There is always something fiendish and loathsome about a person who threatens to deprive you of your way of making a living. That is just human-like, I reckon.

At the University, I got on well both in class-work and the matter of making friends. I could take in but so many social affairs because I had to work, and then I had to study my lessons after work hours at night, and I was carrying a heavy program.

The teacher who most influenced me was Dr. Lorenzo Dow Turner, head of the English department. He was tall, lean, with a head of wavy black hair above his thin, æsthetic, tan-colored face. He was a Harvard man and knew his subject. His delivery was soft and restrained. The fact that he looked to be in his late twenties or early thirties at most made the girls conscious of shiny noses before they entered his classroom.

Listening to him, I decided that I must be an English teacher and lean over my desk and discourse on the eighteenth-century poets, and explain the roots of the modern novel. Children just getting born were going to hear about Addison, Poe, DeQuincey, Steele, Coleridge, Keats and Shelley from me, leaning nonchalantly over my desk. Defoe, Burns, Swift, Milton and Scott were going to be sympathetically, but adequately explained, with just that suspicion of a smile now and then before I returned to my notes.

The man who seemed to me to be most overpowering was E. C. Williams, Librarian and head of the Romance Language department. He was cosmopolitan and world-traveled. His wit was instant and subtle. He was so inaccessible in a way, too. He told me once that a flirtation with a co-ed was to him like playing with a teething-ring. He liked smart, sophisticated women. He used to lunch every day with E. D. Davis, head of the Greek and German department. Davis was just the antithesis of Williams, so shy, in the Charles S. Johnson manner, in spite of his erudition. They would invite me to come along and would pay for my milk and pie. Williams did most of the talking. I put in something now and then. Davis sat and smiled. Professor Williams egged me on to kiss him. He said that Davis would throw a fit, and he wanted to be present to see it. He whispered that Davis liked to have me around, but from what he ever said, I couldn't notice. When I was sick, Professor Davis came to see me and brought an arm-load of roses, but he sat there half an hour and scarcely said a word. He just sat there and smiled now and then.

All in all, I did a year and a half of work at Howard University. I would have done the two full years, but I was out on account of illness, and by the time that was over, I did not have the money for my tuition.

I joined the Zeta Phi Beta Sorority, took part in all the literary activities on the campus, and made The Stylus, the small literary society on the hill. I named the student paper *The Hill Top*. The Stylus was limited to nineteen members, two of them being faculty members. Dr. Alain Leroy Locke was the presiding genius and we had very interesting meetings.

My joining The Stylus influenced my later moves. On account of a short story which I wrote for The Stylus, Charles S. Johnson, who was just then founding *Opportunity Magazine,* wrote to me for material. He explained that he was writing to all of the Negro colleges with the idea of introducing new writers and new material to the public. I sent on *Drenched in Light* and he published it. Later, he published my second story *Spunk*. He wrote me a kind letter and said something about New York. So, beginning to feel the urge to write, I wanted to be in New York.

This move on the part of Dr. Johnson was the root of the so-called Negro Renaissance. It was his work, and only his hush-mouth nature has caused it to be attributed to many others. The success of *Opportunity* Award dinners was news. Later on, the best of this material was collected in a book called *The New Negro* and edited by Dr. Alain Locke, but it was the same material, for the most part, gathered and published by Dr. Charles Spurgeon Johnson, now of the Department of Social Sciences, Fisk University, Nashville.

Being out of school for lack of funds, and wanting to be in New York, I decided to go there and try to get back in school in that city. So the first week of January, 1925, found me in New York with $1.50, no job, no friends, and a lot of hope.

The Charles Johnsons befriended me as best they could. I could always find something to eat out at their house. Mrs. Johnson would give me carfare and encouragement. I came to worship them really.

So I came to New York through *Opportunity,* and through *Opportunity* to Barnard. I won a prize for a short story at the first Award dinner, May 1, 1925, and

Fannie Hurst offered me a job as her secretary, and Annie Nathan Meyer offered to get me a scholarship to Barnard. My record was good enough, and I entered Barnard in the fall, graduating in 1928.

I have no lurid tales to tell of race discrimination at Barnard. I made a few friends in the first few days. Eleanor Beer, who lived on the next chair to me in Economics, was the first. She was a New York girl with a sumptuous home down in West 71st Street, near the Hudson. She invited me down often, and her mother set out to brush me up on good manners. I learned a lot of things from them. They were well traveled and cosmopolitan. I found out about forks, who entered a room first, sat down first, and who offered to shake hands. A great deal more of material like that. These people are still lying very close to my heart. I was invited to Eleanor's wedding when she married Enzo de Chetalat, a Swiss mining engineer, but I was down in Florida at the time. So I sent her a hat-box full of orange blossoms for the occasion, so she could know how I felt.

The Social Register crowd at Barnard soon took me up, and I became Barnard's sacred black cow. If you had not had lunch with me, you had not shot from taw. I was secretary to Fannie Hurst and living at her 67th Street duplex apartment, so things were going very well with me.

Because my work was top-heavy with English, Political Science, History and Geology, my adviser at

Barnard recommended Fine Arts, Economics, and Anthropology for cultural reasons. I started in under Dr. Gladys Reichard, had a term paper called to the attention of Dr. Franz Boas and thereby gave up my dream of leaning over a desk and explaining Addison and Steele to the sprouting generations.

I began to treasure up the words of Dr. Reichard, Dr. Ruth Benedict, and Dr. Boas, the king of kings.

That man can make people work the hardest with just a look or a word, than anyone else in creation. He is idolized by everybody who takes his orders. We all call him Papa, too. One day, I burst into his office and asked for "Papa Franz" and his secretary gave me a look and told me I had better not let him hear me say that. Of course, I knew better, but at a social gathering of the Department of Anthropology at his house a few nights later, I brought it up.

"Of course, Zora is my daughter. Certainly!" he said with a smile. "Just one of my missteps, that's all." The sabre cut on his cheek, which it is said he got in a duel at Heidelberg, lifted in a smile.

Away from his office, Dr. Boas is full of youth and fun, and abhors dull, stodgy arguments. Get to the point is his idea. Don't raise a point which you cannot defend. He wants facts, not guesses, and he can pin you down so expertly that you soon lose the habit of talking all over your face. Either that, or you leave off Anthropology.

I had the same feeling at Barnard that I did at Howard, only more so. I felt that I was highly privileged and determined to make the most of it. I did not resolve to be a grind, however, to show the white folks that I had brains. I took it for granted that they knew that. Else, why was I at Barnard? Not everyone who cries, "Lord! Lord!" can enter those sacred iron gates. In her high scholastic standards, equipment, the quality of her student-body and graduates, Barnard has a right to the first line of Alma Mater. "Beside the waters of the Hudson, Our Alma Mater stands serene!" Dean Gildersleeve has that certain touch. We know there are women's colleges that are older, but not better ones.

So I set out to maintain a good average, take part in whatever went on, and just be a part of the college like everybody else. I graduated with a *B* record, and I am entirely satisfied.

Mrs. Meyer, who was the moving spirit in founding the college and who is still a trustee, did nobly by me in getting me in. No matter what I might do for her, I would still be in her debt.

Two weeks before I graduated from Barnard, Dr. Boas sent for me and told me that he had arranged a fellowship for me. I was to go south and collect Negro folklore. Shortly before that, I had been admitted to the American Folk-Lore Society. Later, while I was in the field, I was invited to become a member of the American Ethnological Society, and shortly after the American Anthropological Society.

Booker T. Washington said once that you must not judge a man by the heights to which he has risen, but by the depths from which he came. So to me these honors meant something, insignificant as they might appear to the world. It was a long step for the waif of Eatonville. From the depth of my inner heart I appreciated the fact that the world had not been altogether unkind to Mama's child.

While in the field, I drove to Memphis, and had a beautiful reconciliation with Bob, my oldest brother, and his family. We had not seen each other since I ran off to be a lady's maid. He said that it had taken him a long time to realize what I was getting at. He regretted deeply that he had not been of more service to me on the way. My father had been killed in an automobile accident during my first year at Morgan, and Bob talked to me about his last days. In reality, my father was the baby of the family. With my mother gone and nobody to guide him, life had not hurt him, but it had turned him loose to hurt himself. He had been miserable over the dispersion of his children when he came to realize that it was so. We were all so sorry for him, instead of feeling bitter as might have been expected. Old Maker had left out the steering gear when He gave Papa his talents.

In Memphis, my brother Ben was doing well as a pharmacist and owner of the East Memphis Drug Store. Between his dogs, his wife, his store, and his car, he was quite the laughing, witty person and I was glad that he was. We talked about Clifford Joel, who had become, and still is, principal of the Negro High School in Decatur, Alabama, and I told him about seeing John in Jacksonville, Florida, where he was doing well with his market. I had the latest news for them on Everett, Mama's baby child, in the Post Office in Brooklyn, New York. Dick, the lovable, the irresponsible, was having a high-heel time up and down the east coast of the United States. He had never cared about school, but he had developed into a chef cook and could always take care of himself. Sarah was struggling along with a husband for whom we all wished a short sickness and a quick funeral.

It was a most happy interval for me. I drove back to New Orleans to my work in a glowing aura. I felt the warm embrace of kin and kind for the first time since the night after my mother's funeral, when we had huddled about the organ all sodden and bewildered, with the walls of our home suddenly blown down. On September 18th, that house had been a hovering home. September 19th, it had turned into a bleak place of desolation with unknown dangers creeping upon us from unseen quarters that made of us a whimpering huddle, though then we could not see why. But now, that was all over. We could touch each other in the spirit if not in the flesh.

X
Research

Research is formalized curiosity. It is poking and prying with a purpose. It is a seeking that he who wishes may know the cosmic secrets of the world and they that dwell therein.

I was extremely proud that Papa Franz felt like sending me on that folklore search. As is well known, Dr. Franz Boas of the Department of Anthropology of Columbia University, is the greatest anthropologist alive, for two reasons. The first is his insatiable hunger for knowledge and then more knowledge; and the second is his genius for pure objectivity. He has no pet wishes to prove. His instructions are to go out and find what is there. He outlines his theory, but if the facts do not agree with it, he would not warp a jot or dot of the findings to save his theory. So knowing all this, I was proud that he trusted me. I went off in a vehicle made out of corona stuff.

My first six months were disappointing. I found out later that it was not because I had no talents for research, but because I did not have the right approach. The glamor of Barnard College was still upon me. I dwelt in marble halls. I knew where the material was all right. But, I went about asking, in carefully accented Barnardese, "Pardon me, but do you know any folk-tales or folk-songs?" The men and women who had whole treasuries of material just seeping through their pores looked at me and shook their heads. No, they had never heard of anything like that around there. Maybe it was over in the next county. Why didn't I try over there? I did, and got the selfsame answer. Oh, I got a few little items. But compared with what I did later, not enough to make a flea a waltzing jacket. Considering the mood of my going south, I went back to New York with my heart beneath my knees and my knees in some lonesome valley.

I stood before Papa Franz and cried salty tears. He gave me a good going over, but later I found that he was not as disappointed as he let me think. He knew I was green and feeling my oats, and that only bitter disappointment was going to purge me. It did.

What I learned from him then and later, stood me in good stead when Godmother, Mrs. R. Osgood Mason, set aside two hundred dollars a month for a two-year period for me to work.

My relations with Godmother were curious. Laugh if you will, but there was and is a psychic bond between us. She could read my mind, not only when I was in her presence, but thousands of miles away. Both Max Eastman and Richmond Barthe have told me that she could do the same with them. But, the thing that delighted her was the fact that I was her only Godchild who could read her thoughts at a distance. Her old fingers were cramped and she could not write, but in her friend Cornelia Chapin's exact script, a letter would find me in Alabama, or Florida, or in the Bahama Islands and lay me by the heels for what I was *thinking*. "You have broken the law," it would accuse sternly. "You are dissipating your powers in things that have no real meaning," and go on to lacerate me. "Keep silent. Does a child in the womb speak?"

She was just as pagan as I. She had lived for years among the Plains Indians and had collected a beautiful book of Indian lore. Often when she wished to impress upon me my garrulity, she would take this book from the shelf and read me something of Indian beauty and restraint. Sometimes, I would feel like a rabbit at a dog convention. She would invite me to dinner at her apartment, 399 Park Avenue, and then she, Cornelia Chapin, and Miss Chapin's sister, Mrs. Katherine Garrison Biddle would all hem me up and give me what for. When they had given me a proper straightening, and they felt that I saw the light, all the sternness would vanish, and I would be wrapped in love. A present of money from Godmother, a coat from Miss Chapin, a dress from Mrs. Biddle. We had a great deal to talk about because Cornelia Chapin was a sculptor, Katherine Biddle, a poet, and Godmother, an earnest patron of the arts.

Then too, she was Godmother to Miguel Covarrubias and Langston Hughes. Sometimes all of us were there. She has several paintings by Covarrubias on her walls. She summoned us when one or the other of us returned from our labors. Miguel and I would exhibit our movies, and Godmother and the Chapin family, including brother Paul Chapin, would praise us and pan us, according as we had done. Godmother could be as tender as mother-love when she felt that you had been right spiritually. But anything in you, however clever, that felt like insincerity to her, called forth her well-known "That is nothing! It has no soul in it. You have broken the law!" Her tongue was a knout, cutting off your outer pretenses, and bleeding your vanity like a rusty nail. She was merciless to a lie, spoken, acted or insinuated.

She was extremely human. There she was sitting up there at the table over capon, caviar and gleaming silver, eager to hear every word on every phase of life on a saw-mill "job." I must tell the tales, sing the songs, do the dances, and repeat the raucous sayings and doings of the Negro farthest down. She is altogether in sympathy with them, because she says truthfully they are utterly sincere in living.

My search for knowledge of things took me into many strange places and adventures. My life was in danger several times. If I had not learned how to take care of myself in these circumstances, I could have been maimed or killed on most any day of the several years of my research work. Primitive minds are quick to sunshine and quick to anger. Some little word, look or gesture can move them either to love or to sticking a knife between your ribs. You just have to sense the delicate balance and maintain it.

In some instances, there is nothing personal in the killing. The killer wishes to establish a reputation as a killer, and you'll do as a sample. Some of them go around, making their announcements in singing:

> I'm going to make me a graveyard of my own,
> I'm going to make me a graveyard of my own,
> Oh, carried me down on de smoky road,
> Brought me back on de coolin' board,
> But I'm going to make me a graveyard of my own.

And since the law is lax on these big saw-mill, turpentine and railroad "jobs," there is a good chance that they never will be jailed for it. All of these places have plenty of men and women who are fugitives from justice. The management asks no questions. They need help and they can't be bothered looking for a bug under every chip. In some places, the "law" is forbidden to come on the premises to hunt for malefactors who did their malefacting elsewhere. The wheels of industry must move, and if these men don't do the work, who is there to do it?

So if a man, or a woman, has been on the gang for petty-thieving and mere mayhem, and is green with jealousy of the others who did the same amount of time for a killing and had something to brag about, why not look around for an easy victim and become a hero, too? I was nominated like that once in Polk County, Florida, and the only reason that I was not elected, was because a friend got in there and staved off old club-footed Death.

> Polk County! Ah!
> Where the water tastes like cherry wine.
> Where they fell great trees with axe and muscle.

These poets of the swinging blade! The brief, but infinitely graceful, dance of body and axe-head as it lifts over the head in a fluid arc, dances in air and rushes down to bite into the tree, all in beauty. Where the logs march into the mill with its smokestacks disputing with the elements, its boiler room reddening the sky, and its great circular saw screaming arrogantly as it attacks the tree like a lion making its kill. The log on the carriage coming to the saw. A growling grumble. Then contact! Yeelld-u-u-ow! And a board is laid shining and new on a pile. All day, all night. Rumble, thunder and grumble. Yee-ee-ow! Sweating black bodies, muscled like gods, working to feed the hunger of the great tooth. Polk County!

Polk County. Black men laughing and singing. They go down in the phosphate mines and bring up the wet dust of the bones of pre-historic monsters, to make rich land in far places, so that people can eat.

But, all of it is not dust. Huge ribs, twenty feet from belly to backbone. Some old-time sea monster caught in the shallows in that morning when God said, "Let's make some more dry land. Stay there, great Leviathan! Stay there as a memory and a monument to Time." Shark-teeth as wide as the hand of a working man. Joints of backbone three feet high, bearing witness to the mighty monster of the deep when the Painted Land rose up and did her first dance with the morning sun. Gazing on these relics, forty thousand years old and more, one visualizes the great surrender to chance and change when these creatures were rocked to sleep and slumber by the birth of land.

Polk County. Black men from tree to tree among the lordly pines, a swift, slanting stroke to bleed the trees for gum. Paint, explosives, marine stores, flavors, perfumes, tone for a violin bow, and many other things which the black men who bleed the trees never heard about.

Polk County. The clang of nine-pound hammers on railroad steel. The world must ride.

Hah! A rhythmic swing of the body, hammer falls, and another spike driven to the head in the tie.

> Oh, Mobile! Hank!
> Oh, Alabama! Hank!
> Oh, Fort Myers! Hank!
> Oh, in Florida! Hank!
> Oh, let's shake it! Hank!
> Oh, let's break it! Hank!

Oh, let's shake it! Hank!
Oh, just a hair! Hank!

The singing-liner cuts short his chant. The straw-boss relaxes with a gesture of his hand. Another rail spiked down. Another offering to the soul of civilization whose other name is travel.

Polk County. Black men scrambling up ladders into orange trees. Singing, laughing, cursing, boasting of last night's love, and looking forward to the darkness again. They do not say embrace when they mean that they slept with a woman. A behind is a behind and not a form. Nobody says anything about incompatibility when they mean it does not suit. No bones are made about being fed up.

I got up this morning, and I knowed I didn't want it,
Yea! Polk County!
You don't know Polk County like I do
Anybody been there, tell you the same thing, too.
Eh, rider, rider!
Polk County, where the water tastes like cherry wine.

Polk County. After dark, the jooks. Songs are born out of feelings with an old beat-up piano, or a guitar for a mid-wife. Love made and unmade. Who put out dat lie, it was supposed to last forever? Love is when it is. No more here? Plenty more down the road. Take you where I'm going, woman? Hell no! Let every town furnish its own. Yeah, I'm going. Who care anything about no train fare? The railroad track is there, ain't it? I can count tires just like I been doing. I can ride de blind, can't I?

> Got on de train didn't have no fare
> But I rode some
> Yes I rode some
> Got on de train didn't have no fare
> Conductor ast me what I'm doing there
> But I rode some.
> Yes I rode some.
>
> Well, he grabbed me by de collar and he led me to de
>   door
> But I rode some
> Yes I rode some.
> Well, he grabbed me by de collar and he led me to de
>   door
> He rapped me over de head with a forty-four
> But I rode some
> Yes I rode some.

Polk County in the jooks. Dancing the square dance. Dancing the scronch. Dancing the belly-rub. Knocking the right hat off the wrong head, and backing it up with a switch-blade.

"Fan-foot, what you doing with my man's hat cocked on *your* nappy head? I know you want to see your Jesus. Who's a whore? Yeah I sleeps with my mens, but they pays me. I wouldn't be a fan-foot like you—just on de road somewhere. Runs up and down de road from job to job making pay-days. Don't nobody hold her! Let her jump on me! She pay her way on me, and I'll pay it off. Make time in old Bartow jail for her."

Maybe somebody stops the fight before the two switch-blades go together. Maybe nobody can. A short, swift dash in. A lucky jab by one opponent and the other one is dead. Maybe one gets a chill in the feet and leaps out of the door. Maybe both get cut badly and back off. Anyhow, the fun of the place goes on. More dancing and singing and buying of drinks, parched peanuts, fried rabbit. Full drummy bass from the piano with weepy, intricate right-hand stuff. Singing the memories of Ella Wall, the Queen of love in the jooks of Polk County. Ella Wall, Planchita, Trottin' Liza.

It is a sad, parting song. Each verse ends up with:

Quarters Boss! High Sheriff? Lemme git gone from
    here!
Cold, rainy day, some old cold, rainy day
I'll be back, some old cold, rainy day.
Oh de rocks may be my pillow, Lawd!
De sand may be my bed
I'll be back some old cold, rainy day.

"Who run? What you running from the man for, nigger? Me, I don't aim to run a step. I ain't going to run unless they run me. I'm going to live anyhow until I die. Play me some music so I can dance! Aw, spank dat box, man! ! Them white folks don't care nothing bout no nigger getting cut and kilt, nohow.

They ain't coming in here. I done kilt me four and they ain't hung me yet. Beat dat box!"

"Yeah, but you ain't kilt no women, yet. They's mighty particular 'bout you killing up women."

"And I ain't killing none neither. I ain't crazy in de head. Nigger woman can kill all us men she wants to and they don't care. Leave us kill a woman and they'll run you just as long as you can find something to step on. I got good sense. I know I ain't got no show. De white mens and de nigger women is running this thing. Sing about old Georgy Buck and let's dance off of it. Hit dat box!"

> Old Georgy Buck is dead
> Last word he said
> I don't want no shortening in my bread.
> Rabbit on de log
> Ain't got no dog
> Shoot him wid my rifle, bam! bam!

And the night, the pay night rocks on with music and gambling and laughter and dancing and fights. The big pile of cross-ties burning out in front simmers down to low ashes before sun-up, so then it is time to throw up all the likker you can't keep down and go somewhere and sleep the rest off, whether your knife has blood on it or not. That is, unless some strange, low member of your own race has gone and pimped to the white folks about something getting hurt. Very few of those kind are to be found.

That is the primeval flavor of the place, and as I said before, out of this primitive approach to things, I all but lost my life.

It was in a saw-mill jook in Polk County that I almost got cut to death.

Lucy really wanted to kill me. I didn't mean any harm. All I was doing was collecting songs from Slim, who used to be her man back up in West Florida before he ran off from her. It is true that she found out where he was after nearly a year, and followed him to Polk County and he paid her some slight attention. He was knocking the pad with women, all around, and he seemed to want to sort of free-lance at it. But what he seemed to care most about was picking his guitar, and singing.

He was a valuable source of material to me, so I built him up a bit by buying him drinks and letting him ride in my car.

I figure that Lucy took a pick at me for three reasons. The first one was, her vanity was rubbed sore at not being able to hold her man. That was hard to own up to in a community where so much stress was laid on suiting. Nobody else had offered to shack up with her either. She was getting a very limited retail trade and Slim was ignoring the whole business. I had store-bought clothes, a lighter skin, and a shiny car, so she saw wherein she could use me for an alibi. So in spite of public knowledge of the situation for a year or more before I came, she was telling it around that I came and broke them up. She was going to cut everything off of me but "quit it."

Her second reason was, because of my research methods I had dug in with the male community. Most of the women liked me, too. Especially her sworn enemy, Big Sweet. She was scared of Big Sweet, but she probably reasoned that if she cut Big Sweet's protégée it would be a slam on Big Sweet and build up her own reputation. She was fighting Big Sweet through me.

Her third reason was, she had been in little scraps and been to jail off and on, but she could not swear that she had ever killed anybody. She was small potatoes and nobody was paying her any mind. I was easy. I had no gun, knife or any sort of weapon. I did not even know how to do that kind of fighting.

Lucky for me, I had friended with Big Sweet. She came to my notice within the first week that I arrived on location. I heard somebody, a woman's voice "specifying" up this line of houses from where I lived and asked who it was.

"Dat's Big Sweet" my landlady told me. "She got her foot up on somebody. Ain't she specifying?"

She was really giving the particulars. She was giving a "reading," a word borrowed from the fortune-tellers. She was giving her opponent lurid data and bringing him up to date on his ancestry, his looks, smell, gait, clothes, and his route through Hell in the hereafter. My landlady went outside where nearly everybody else of the four or five hundred people on the "job" were to listen to the reading. Big Sweet broke the news to him, in one of her mildest bulletins that his pa was a double-humpted camel and his ma was a grass-gut cow, but even so, he tore her wide open in the act of getting born, and so on and so forth. He was a bitch's baby out of a buzzard egg.

My landlady explained to me what was meant by "putting your foot up" on a person. If you are sufficiently armed—enough to stand off a panzer division —and know what to do with your weapons after you get 'em, it is all right to go to the house of your enemy, put one foot up on his steps, rest one elbow on your knee and play in the family. That is another way of saying play the dozens, which also is a way of saying low-rate your enemy's ancestors and him, down to the present moment for reference, and then go into his future as far as your imagination leads you. But if you have no faith in your personal courage and confidence in your arsenal, don't try it. It is a risky pleasure. So then I had a measure of this Big Sweet.

"Hurt who?" Mrs. Bertha snorted at my fears. "Big Sweet? Humph! Tain't a man, woman nor child on this job going to tackle Big Sweet. If God send her a pistol she'll send him a man. She can handle a knife with anybody. She'll join hands and cut a duel. Dat Cracker Quarters Boss wears two pistols round his waist and goes for bad, but he won't break a breath with Big Sweet lessen he got his pistol in his hand. Cause if he start anything with her, he won't never get a chance to draw it. She ain't mean. She don't bother nobody. She just don't stand for no foolishness, dat's all."

Right away, I decided that Big Sweet was going to be my friend. From what I had seen and heard in the short time I had been there, I felt as timid as an egg without a shell. So the next afternoon when she was pointed out to me, I waited until she was well up the sawdust road to the Commissary, then I got in my car and went that way as if by accident. When I pulled up beside her and offered her a ride, she frowned at me first, then looked puzzled, but finally broke into a smile and got in.

By the time we got to the Commissary post office we were getting along fine. She told everybody I was her friend. We did not go back to the Quarters at once. She carried me around to several places and showed me off. We made a date to go down to Lakeland come Saturday, which we did. By the time we sighted the Quarters on the way back from Lakeland, she had told me, "You sho is crazy!" Which is a way of saying I was witty. "I loves to friend with somebody like you. I aims to look out for you, too. Do your fighting for you. Nobody better not start nothing with you, do I'll get my switch-blade and go round de ham-bone looking for meat."

We shook hands and I gave her one of my bracelets. After that everything went well for me. Big Sweet helped me to collect material in a big way. She had no idea what I wanted with it, but if I wanted it, she meant to see to it that I got it. She pointed out people who knew songs and stories. She wouldn't stand for balkiness on their part. We held two lying contests, story-telling contests to you, and Big Sweet passed on who rated the prizes. In that way, there was no argument about it.

So when the word came to Big Sweet that Lucy was threatening me, she put her foot up on Lucy in a most particular manner and warned her against the try. I suggested buying a knife for defense, but she said I would certainly be killed that way.

"You don't know how to handle no knife. You ain't got dat kind of a sense. You wouldn't even know how to hold it to de best advantage. You would draw your arm way back to stop her, and whilst you was doing all dat, Lucy would run in under your arm and be done; cut you to death before you could touch her. And then again, when you sure 'nough fighting, it ain't enough to just stick 'em wid your knife. You got to ram it in to de hilt, then you pull *down*. They ain't no more trouble after dat. They's *dead*. But don't you bother 'bout no fighting. You ain't like me. You don't even sleep with no mens. I wanted to be a virgin one time, but I couldn't keep it up. I needed the money too bad. But I think it's nice for you to be like that. You just keep on writing down them lies. I'll take care of all de fighting. Dat'll make it more better, since we done made friends."

She warned me that Lucy might try to "steal" me. That is, ambush me, or otherwise attack me without warning. So I was careful. I went nowhere on foot without Big Sweet.

Several weeks went by, then I ventured to the jook alone. Big Sweet let it be known that she was not going. But later she came in and went over to the coon-can game in the corner. Thinking I was alone, Lucy waited until things were in full swing and then came in with the very man to whom Big Sweet had given the "reading." There was only one door. I was far from it. I saw no escape for me when Lucy strode in, knife in hand. I saw sudden death very near that moment. I was paralyzed with fear. Big Sweet was in a crowd over in the corner, and did not see Lucy come in. But the sudden quiet of the place made her look around as Lucy charged. My friend was large and portly, but extremely light on her feet. She sprang like a lioness and I think the very surprise of Big Sweet being there when Lucy thought she was over at another party at the Pine Mill unnerved Lucy. She stopped abruptly as Big Sweet charged. The next moment, it was too late for Lucy to start again. The man who came in with Lucy tried to help her out, but two other men joined Big Sweet in the battle. It took on amazingly. It seemed that anybody who had any fighting to do, decided to settle-up then and there. Switch-blades, ice-picks and old-fashioned razors were out. One or two razors had already been bent back and thrown across the room, but our fight was the main attraction. Big Sweet yelled to me to run. I really ran, too. I ran out of the place, ran to my room, threw my things in the car and left the place. When the sun came up I was a hundred miles up the road, headed for New Orleans.

In New Orleans, I delved into Hoodoo, or sympathetic magic. I studied with the Frizzly Rooster, and all of the other noted "doctors." I learned the routines for making and breaking marriages; driving off and punishing enemies; influencing the minds of judges and juries in favor of clients; killing by remote control and other things. In order to work with these "two-headed" doctors, I had to go through an initiation with each. The routine varied with each doctor.

In one case it was not only elaborate, it was impressive. I lay naked for three days and nights on a couch, with my navel to a rattlesnake skin which had been dressed and dedicated to the ceremony. I ate no food in all that time. Only a pitcher of water was on a little table at the head of the couch so that my soul would not wander off in search of water and be attacked by evil influences and not return to me. On the second day, I began to dream strange exalted dreams. On the third night, I had dreams that seemed real for weeks. In one, I strode across the heavens with lightning flashing from under my feet, and grumbling thunder following in my wake.

In this particular ceremony, my finger was cut and I became blood brother to the rattlesnake. We were to aid each other forever. I was to walk with the storm and hold my power, and get my answers to life and things in storms. The symbol of lightning was painted on my back. This was to be mine forever.

In another ceremony, I had to sit at the crossroads at midnight in complete darkness and meet the Devil, and make a compact. That was a long, long hour as I sat flat on the ground there alone and invited the King of Hell.

The most terrifying was going to a lonely glade in the swamp to get the black cat bone. The magic circle was made and all of the participants were inside. I was told that anything outside that circle was in deadly peril. The fire was built inside, the pot prepared and the black cat was thrown in with the proper ceremony and boiled until his bones fell apart. Strange and terrible monsters seemed to thunder up to that ring while this was going on. It took months for me to doubt it afterwards.

When I left Louisiana, I went to South Florida again, and from what I heard around Miami, I decided to go to the Bahamas. I had heard some Bahaman music and seen a Jumping Dance out in Liberty City and I was entranced.

This music of the Bahaman Negroes was more original, dynamic and African, than American Negro songs. I just had to know more. So without giving

Godmother a chance to object, I sailed for Nassau.

I loved the place the moment I landed. Then, that first night as I lay in bed, listening to the rustle of a cocoanut palm just outside my window, a song accompanied by string and drum broke out in full harmony. I got up and peeped out and saw four young men and they were singing Bellamina, led by Ned Isaacs. I did not know him then, but I met him the next day. The song has a beautiful air, and the oddest rhythm.

> Bellamina, Bellamina!
> She come back in the harbor
> Bellamina, Bellamina
> She come back in the harbor
> Put Bellamina on the dock
> And paint Bellamina black! Black!
> Oh, put the Bellamina on the dock
> And paint Bellamina, black! Black!

I found out later that it was a song about a rum-running boat that had been gleaming white, but after it had been captured by the United States Coast Guard and released, it was painted black for obvious reasons.

That was my welcome to Nassau, and it was a beautiful one. The next day I got an idea of what prolific song-makers the Bahamans are. In that West African accent grafted on the English of the uneducated Bahaman, I was told, "You do anything, we put you in sing." I walked carefully to keep out of "sing."

This visit to Nassau was to have far-reaching effects. I stayed on, ran to every Jumping Dance that I heard of, learned to "jump," collected more than a hundred tunes and resolved to make them known to the world.

On my return to New York in 1932, after trying vainly to interest others, I introduced Bahaman songs and dances to a New York audience at the John Golden Theater, and both the songs and the dances took on. The concert achieved its purpose. I aimed to show what beauty and appeal there was in genuine Negro material, as against the Broadway concept, and it went over.

Since then, there has been a sharp trend towards genuine Negro material. The dances aroused a tremendous interest in primitive Negro dancing. Hall Johnson took my group to appear with his singers at the Lewisohn Stadium that summer and built his "Run Lil' Chillun" around them and the religious scene from my concert, "From Sun to Sin." That was not all, the dramatized presentation of Negro work-songs in that same concert aroused interest in them and they have been exploited by singers ever since.

I had no intention of making concert my field. I wanted to show the wealth and beauty of the material to those who were in the field and therefore I felt that my job was well done when it took on.

My group was invited to perform at the New School

of Social Research; in the folk-dance carnival at the
Vanderbilt Hotel in New York; at Nyack; at St.
Louis; Chicago; Rollins College in Winter Park,
Florida; Lake Wales; Sanford; Orlando; Constitu-
tion Hall, Washington, D.C.; and Daytona Beach,
Florida.

Besides the finding of the dances and the music,
two other important things happened to me in Nassau. One was, I lived through that terrible five-day
hurricane of 1929. It was horrible in its intensity and
duration. I saw dead people washing around on the
streets when it was over. You could smell the stench
from dead animals as well. More than three hundred
houses were blown down in the city of Nassau alone.

Then I saw something else out there. I met Leon
Walton Young. He is a grizzly, stocky black man, who
is a legislator in the House. He represented the first
district in the Bahamas and had done so for more
than twenty years when I met him.

Leon Walton Young was either a great hero, or a
black bounder, according to who was doing the talking. He was a great champion and a hero in the
mouths of the lowly blacks of the islands and to a
somewhat lesser degree to the native-born whites. He
was a Bahaman for the Bahaman man and a stout fellow along those lines. To the English, who had been
sent out to take the jobs of the natives, white and
black, he was a cheeky dastard of a black colonial who
needed to be put in his place. He was also too much

for the mixed-blood Negroes of education and property, who were as prejudiced against his color as the English. What was more, Leon Walton Young had no formal education, though I found him like George Schuyler of New York to be better read than most people with college degrees. But did he, because of his lack of schooling, defer to the Negroes who had journeyed to London and Edinburgh? He most certainly did not, and what was more, he more than held his own in the hustings.

There was a much felt need for him to be put down, but those who put on the white armor of St. George to go out and slay the dragon always came back—not honorably dead on their shields—but splattered all over with mud and the seat of their pants torn and missing. A peasant mounted on a mule had unhorsed a cavalier and took his pants. The dance drums of Grantstown and Baintown would throb and his humbled opponents would be "put in sing."

He so humbled a governor, who tried to overawe Young by reminding him that he was "His Majesty's representative in these Islands" that the governor was recalled and sent to some peaceful spot in West Africa. Young had replied to that pompous statement with, "Yes, but if you continue your tactics out here you will make me forget it."

That was one of his gentlest thumps on the Governor's pride and prestige. His Majesty's Representative accused Young of having said publicly that he, the Governor, was a bum out of the streets of London, and to his eternal rage, Young more than admitted the statement. The English appointees and the high yellows shuddered at such temerity, but the local whites and the working blacks gloried in his spunk.

The humble Negroes of America are great song-makers, but the Bahaman is greater. He is more prolific and his tunes are better. Nothing is too big, or little, to be "put in sing." They only need discovery. They are much more original than the Calypso singers of Trinidad, as will be found the moment you put it to the proof.

I hear that now the Duke of Windsor is their great hero. To them, he is "Our King." I would love to hear how he and his Duchess have been put in sing.

I enjoyed collecting the folk-tales and I believe the people from whom I collected them enjoyed the telling of them, just as much as I did the hearing. Once they got started, the "lies" just rolled and story-tellers fought for a chance to talk. It was the same with the songs. The one thing to be guarded against, in the interest of truth, was over-enthusiasm. For instance, if a song was going good, and the material ran out, the singer was apt to interpolate pieces of other songs into it. The only way you can know when that happens, is to know your material so well that you can sense the violation. Even if you do not know the song that is being used for padding, you can tell the change in rhythm and tempo. The words do not count. The subject matter in Negro folk-songs can be anything and go from love to work, to travel, to food, to weather, to fight, to demanding the return of a wig by a woman who has turned unfaithful. The tune is the unity of the thing. And you have to know what you are doing when you begin to pass on that, because Negroes can fit in more words and leave out more and still keep the tune better than anyone I can think of.

One bit of research I did jointly for the Journal of Negro History and Columbia University, was in Mobile, Alabama. There I went to talk to Cudjo Lewis. That is the American version of his name. His African name was Kossola-O-Lo-Loo-Ay.

He arrived on the last load of slaves run into the United States and was the only Negro alive that came over on a slave ship. It happened in 1859 just when the fight between the South and the Abolitionists was moving toward the Civil War. He has died since I saw him.

I found him a cheerful, poetical old gentleman in his late nineties, who could tell a good story. His interpretation of the story of Jonah was marvelous.

He was a good Christian and so he pretended to have forgotten all of his African religion. He turned me off with the statement that his Nigerian religion was the same as Christianity. "We know it a God, you unner'stand, but we don't know He got a Son."

He told me in detail of the circumstances in Africa that brought about his slavery here. How the powerful Kingdom of Dahomey, finding the slave trade so profitable, had abandoned farming, hunting and all else to capture slaves to stock the barracoons on the beach at Dmydah to sell to the slavers who came from across the ocean. How quarrels were manufactured by the King of Dahomey with more peaceful agricultural nations in striking distance of Dahomey in Nigeria and Gold Coast; how they were assaulted, completely wiped off the map, their names never to appear again, except when they were named in boastful chant before the King at one of his "customs" when his glory was being sung. The able-bodied who were captured were marched to Abomey, the capital city of Dahomey and displayed to the King, then put into the barracoons to await a buyer. The too old, the too young, the injured in battle were instantly beheaded and their heads smoked and carried back to the King. He paid off on heads, dead or alive. The skulls of the slaughtered were not wasted either. The King had his famous Palace of Skulls. The Palace grounds had a massive gate of skull-heads. The wall surrounding the grounds were built of skulls. You see, the Kings of Dahomey were truly great and mighty and a lot of skulls were bound to come out of their ambitions. While it looked awesome and splendid to him and his warriors, the sight must have been most grewsome and crude to Western eyes.

One thing impressed me strongly from this three months of association with Cudjo Lewis. The white people had held my people in slavery here in America. They had bought us, it is true and exploited us. But the inescapable fact that stuck in my craw, was: my people had *sold* me and the white people had bought me. That did away with the folklore I had been brought up on—that the white people had gone to Africa, waved a red handkerchief at the Africans and lured them aboard ship and sailed away. I know that civilized money stirred up African greed. That wars between tribes were often stirred up by white traders to provide more slaves in the barracoons and all that. But, if the African princes had been as pure and as innocent as I would like to think, it could not have happened. No, my own people had butchered and killed, exterminated whole nations and torn families apart, for a profit before the strangers got their chance at a cut. It was a sobering thought. What is more, all that this Cudjo told me was verified from other historical sources. It impressed upon me the universal nature of greed and glory. Lack of power and opportunity passes off too often for virtue. If I were King, let us say, over the Western Hemisphere tomorrow, instead of who I am, what would I consider right and just? Would I put the cloak of Justice on my ambition and send her out a-whoring after conquests? It is something to ponder over with fear.

Cudjo's eyes were full of tears and memory of fear

when he told me of the assault on his city and its capture. He said that his nation, the Takkoi, lived "three sleeps" from Dahomey. The attack came at dawn as the Takkoi were getting out of bed to go to their fields outside the city. A whooping horde of the famed Dahoman women warriors burst through the main gate, seized people as they fled from their houses and beheaded victims with one stroke of their big swords.

"Oh, oh! I runnee this way to that gate, but they there. I runnee to another one, but they there, too. All eight gates they there. Them women, they very strong. I nineteen years old, but they too strong for me. They take me and tie me. I don't know where my people at. I never see them no more."

He described the awful slaughter as the Amazons sacked the city. The clusters of human heads at their belts. The plight of those who fled through the gates to fall into the hands of the male warriors outside. How his King was finally captured and carried before the King of Dahomey, who had broken his rule and come on this expedition in person because of a grudge against the King of Takkoi, and how the vanquished monarch was led before him, bound.

"Now, that you have dared to send impudent words to me," the King of Dahomey said, "your country is conquered and you are before me in chains. I shall take you to Abomey."

"No," the King of Takkoi answered. "I am King in Takkoi. I will not go to Dahomey." He knew that he would be killed for a spectacle in Dahomey. He chose to die at home.

So two Dahoman warriors held each of his hands and an Amazon struck off his head.

Later, two representatives of a European power attended the customs of the King at Abomey, and told of seeing the highly polished skull of the King of Takkoi mounted in a beautiful ship-model. His name and his nation were mentioned in the chant to the glory of Dahomey. The skull was treated with the utmost respect, as the King of Dahomey would expect his to be treated in case he fell in battle. That was the custom in West Africa. For the same reason, no one of royal blood was sold into slavery. They were killed. There are no descendants of royal African blood among American Negroes for that reason. The Negroes who claim that they are descendants of royal African blood have taken a leaf out of the book of the white ancestor-hounds in America, whose folks went to England with William the Conqueror, got restless and caught the *Mayflower* for Boston, then feeling a romantic lack, rushed down the coast and descended from Pocahontas. From the number of her children, one is forced to the conclusion that that Pocahontas wasn't so poky, after all.

Kossola told me of the March to Abomey after the fall of Takkoi. How they were yoked by forked sticks and tied in a chain. How the Dahomans halted the march the second day in order to smoke the heads of the victims because they were spoiling. The prisoners had to watch the heads of their friends and relatives turning on long poles in the smoke. Abomey and the palace of the King and then the march to the coast and the barracoons. They were there sometime before a ship came to trade. Many, many tribes were there, each in a separate barracoon, lest they war among themselves. The traders could choose which tribe they wanted. When the tribe was decided upon, he was carried into the barracoon where that tribe was confined, the women were lined up on one side and the men on the other. He walked down between the lines and selected the individuals he wanted. They usually took an equal number.

He described the embarcation and the trip across the ocean in the *Chlotilde,* a fast sailing vessel built by the Maher brothers of Maine, who had moved to Alabama. They were chased by a British man-of-war on the lookout for slavers, but the *Chlotilde* showed her heels. Finally the cargo arrived in Mobile. They were unloaded up the river, the boat sunk, and the hundred-odd Africans began a four-year life of slavery.

"We so surprised to see mule and plow. We so surprised to see man pushee and mule pullee."

After the war, these Africans made a settlement of their own at Plateau, Alabama, three miles up the river from Mobile. They farmed and worked in the lumber mills and bought property. The descendants of these people are still there.

Kossola's great sorrow in America was the death of his favorite son, David, killed by a train. He refused to believe it was his David when he saw the body. He refused to let the bell be tolled for him.

"If dat my boy, where his head? No, dat not my David. Dat not my boy. My boy gone to Mobile. No, No! Don't ringee de bell for David. Dat not him."

But, finally his wife persuaded him that the headless body on the window blind was their son. He cried hard for several minutes and then said, "Ringee de bell."

His other great sorrow was that he had lost track of his folks in Africa.

"They don't know what become of Kossola. When you go there, you tellee where I at." He begged me. He did not know that his tribe was no more upon this earth, except for those who reached the barracoon at Dmydah. None of his family was in the barracoon. He had missed seeing their heads in the smoke, no doubt. It is easy to see how few would have looked on that sight too closely.

"I lonely for my folks. They don't know. Maybe they ask everybody go there where Kossola. I know they hunt for me." There was a tragic catch in his voice like the whimper of a lost dog.

After seventy-five years, he still had that tragic sense of loss. That yearning for blood and cultural ties. That sense of mutilation. It gave me something to feel about.

Of my research in the British West Indies and Haiti, my greatest thrill was coming face to face with a Zombie and photographing her. This act had never happened before in the history of man. I mean the taking of the picture. I have said all that I know on the subject in the book, "Tell My Horse," which has been published also in England under the title "Voodoo Gods." I have spoken over the air on We the People on the subject, and the matter has been so publicized that I will not go into details here. But, it was a tremendous thrill, though utterly macabre.

I went Canzo in Voodoo ceremonies in Haiti and the ceremonies were both beautiful and terrifying.

I did not find them any more invalid than any other religion. Rather, I hold that any religion that satisfies the individual urge is valid for that person. It does satisfy millions, so it is true for its believers. The Sect Rouge, also known as the Cochon Gris (gray pig) and Ving Bra-Drig (from the sound of the small drum), a cannibalistic society there, has taken cover under the name of Voodoo, but the two things are in no wise the same. What is more, if science ever gets to the bottom of Voodoo in Haiti and Africa, it will be found that some important medical secrets, still unknown to medical science, give it its power, rather than the gestures of ceremony.

XI
Books and Things

While I was in the research field in 1929, the idea of "Jonah's Gourd Vine" came to me. I had written a few short stories, but the idea of attempting a book seemed so big, that I gazed at it in the quiet of the night, but hid it away from even myself in daylight.

For one thing, it seemed off-key. What I wanted to tell was a story about a man, and from what I had read and heard, Negroes were supposed to write about the Race Problem. I was and am thoroughly sick of the subject. My interest lies in what makes a man or a woman do such-and-so, regardless of his color. It seemed to me that the human beings I met reacted pretty much the same to the same stimuli. Different idioms, yes. Circumstances and conditions having power to influence, yes. Inherent difference, no. But I said to myself that that was not what was expected of me, so I was afraid to tell a story the way I wanted, or rather the way the story told itself to me. So I went on that way for three years.

Something else held my attention for a while. As I told you before, I had been pitched head-foremost into the Baptist Church when I was born. I had heard the singing, the preaching and the prayers. They were a part of me. But on the concert stage, I always heard songs called spirituals sung and applauded as Negro music, and I wondered what would happen if a white audience ever heard a real spiritual. To me, what the Negroes did in Macedonia Baptist Church was finer than anything that any trained composer had done to the folk-songs.

I had collected a mass of work-songs, blues and spirituals in the course of my years of research. After offering them to two Negro composers and having them refused on the ground that white audiences would not listen to anything but highly arranged spirituals, I decided to see if that was true. I doubted it because I had seen groups of white people in my father's church as early as I could remember. They had come to hear the singing, and certainly there was no distinguished composer in Zion Hope Baptist Church. The congregation just got hold of the tune and arranged as they went along as the spirit moved them. And any musician, I don't care if he stayed at a conservatory until his teeth were gone and he smelled like old-folks, could never even approach what those untrained singers could do. LET THE PEOPLE SING, was and is my motto, and finally I resolved to see what would happen.

So on money I had borrowed, I put on a show at the John Golden Theater on January 10, 1932, and tried out my theory. The performance was well received by both the audience and the critics. Because I know that music without motion is not natural with my people, I did not have the singers stand in a stiff group and reach for the high note. I told them to just imagine that they were in Macedonia and go ahead. One critic said that he did not believe that the concert was rehearsed, it looked so natural. I had dramatized a working day on a railroad camp, from the shack-rouser waking up the camp at dawn until the primitive dance in the deep woods at night.

While I did not lose any money, I did not make much. But I am satisfied that I proved my point. I have seen the effects of that concert in all the Negro singing groups since then. Primitive Negro dancing has been given tremendous impetus. Work-songs have taken on. In that performance I introduced West Indian songs and dances and they have come to take an important place in America. I am not upset by the fact that others have made something out of the things I pointed out. Rather I am glad if I have called any beauty to the attention of those who can use it.

In May, 1932, the depression did away with money for research so far as I was concerned. So I took my nerve in my hand and decided to try to write the story I had been carrying around in me. Back in my native village, I wrote first "Mules and Men." That is, I edited the huge mass of material I had, arranged it in some sequence and laid it aside. It was published after my first novel. Mr. Robert Wunsch and Dr. John Rice were both on the faculty at Rollins College, at Winter Park, which is three miles from Eatonville. Dr. Edwin Osgood Grover, Dr. Hamilton Holt, President of Rollins, together with Rice and Wunsch, were interested in me. I gave three folk concerts at the college under their urging.

Then I wrote a short story, "The Gilded Six-Bits," which Bob Wunsch read to his class in creative writing before he sent it off to *Story Magazine*. Thus I came to know Martha Foley and her husband, Whit Burnett, the editors of *Story*. They bought the story and it was published in the August issue, 1933. They never told me, but it is my belief that they did some missionary work among publishers in my behalf, because four publishers wrote me and asked if I had anything of book-length. One of the editors of the J. B. Lippincott Company, was among these. He wrote a gentle-like letter and so I was not afraid of him. Exposing my efforts did not seem so rash to me after reading his letter. I wrote him and said that I was writing a book. Mind you, not the first word was on paper when I wrote him that letter. But the very next week I moved up to Sanford where I was not so much at home as at Eatonville, and could concentrate more and sat down to write "Jonah's Gourd Vine."

I rented a house with a bed and stove in it for $1.50 a week. I paid two weeks and then my money ran out. My cousin, Willie Lee Hurston, was working and making $3.50 per week, and she always gave me the fifty cents to buy groceries with. In about three months, I finished the book. The problem of getting it typed was then upon me. Municipal Judge S. A. B. Wilkinson asked his secretary, Mildred Knight, if she would not do it for me and wait on the money. I explained to her that the book might not even be taken by Lippincott. I had been working on a hope. She took the manuscript home with her and read it. Then she offered to type it for me. She said, "It is going to be accepted, all right. I'll type it. Even if the first publisher does not take it, somebody will." So between them, they bought the paper and carbon and the book was typed.

I took it down to the American Express office to mail it and found that it cost $1.83 cents to mail, and I did not have it. So I went to see Mrs. John Leonardi, a most capable woman lawyer, and wife of the County Prosecutor. She did not have the money at the moment, but she was the treasurer of the local Daughter Elks. She "borrowed" $2.00 from the treasury and gave it to me to mail my book. That was on October 3, 1933. On October 16th, I had an acceptance by wire.

But it did not come so simply as that. I had been hired by the Seminole County Chamber of Commerce to entertain the business district of Sanford with my concert group for that day. I was very glad to get the work, because my landlord was pressing me for the back rent. I now owed $18. I was to receive $25 for the day, so I saw my way clear to pay up my rent, and have a little over. It was not to be that way, however. At eight o'clock of October 16th, my landlady came and told me to get out. I told her that I could pay her that day, but she said she didn't believe that I would ever have that much money. No, she preferred the house. So I took my card table and my clothes up to my Uncle Isaiah's house and went off to entertain the city at eleven o'clock. The sound truck went up and down the streets and my boys sang. That afternoon while I was still on the sound truck, a Western Union messenger handed me a wire. Naturally I did not open it there. We were through at three o'clock. The Chamber of Commerce not only paid us, we were all given an order which we could take to any store we wanted and get what we chose. I needed shoes, so I took mine to a shoe store. My heart was weighing as much as cord-wood, and so I forgot the wire until I was having the shoes fitted. When I opened it and read that "Jonah's Gourd Vine" was accepted and that Lippincott was offering me $200 advance, I tore out of that place with one old shoe and one new one on and ran to the Western Union office. Lippincott had asked for an answer by wire and they got it! Terms accepted. I never expect to have a greater thrill than that wire gave me. You know the feeling when you found your first pubic hair. Greater than that. When Producer Arthur Hornblow took me to lunch at Lucey's and hired me at Paramount, it was nice—very nice. I was most elated. But I had had five books accepted then, been a Guggenheim Fellow twice, spoken at three book fairs with all the literary greats of America and some from abroad, and so I was a little more used to things. So you see why that editor is *Colonel* to me. When the Negroes in the South name a white man a colonel, it means CLASS. Something like a monarch, only bigger and better. And when the colored population in the South confer a title, the white people recognize it because the Negroes are never wrong. They may flatter an ordinary bossman by calling him "Cap'n" but when they say "Colonel," "General" and "Governor" they are recognizing something internal. It is there, and it is accepted because it can be seen.

I wrote "Their Eyes Were Watching God" in Haiti. It was dammed up in me, and I wrote it under internal pressure in seven weeks. I wish that I could write it again. In fact, I regret all of my books. It is one of the tragedies of life that one cannot have all the wisdom one is ever to possess in the beginning. Perhaps, it is just as well to be rash and foolish for a while. If writers were too wise, perhaps no books would be written at all. It might be better to ask yourself "Why?" afterwards than before. Anyway, the force from somewhere in Space which commands you to write in the first place, gives you no choice. You take up the pen when you are told, and write what is commanded. There is no agony like bearing an untold story inside you. You have all heard of the Spartan youth with the fox under his cloak.

"Dust Tracks on a Road" is being written in California where I did not expect to be at this time.

I did not come out here to California to write about the state. I did not come to get into the movies. I came because my good friend, Katharane Edson Mershon, invited me out here to rest and have a good time. However, I have written a book here, and gone to work in the movies. This surprises me because I did not think that I would live long enough to do anything out here but die. Friend Katharane Mershon is a mountain goat while I am a lowland turtle. I want to rock along on level ground. She can't look at a mountain without leaping on it. I think she is ashamed if she ever catches both of her feet on the same level. She cries "Excelsior!" in her sleep. Jack, her husband, told me that the reason he has that sort of smoothed-off look was because she dragged him up a mountain the next day after they got married and he has never been able to get his right shape back again. Well, 1941 was a hard year for me, too. She showed me California. Before it was over, I felt like I had spent two months walking a cross-cut saw. The minute I get to be governor of California, I mean to get me an over-sized plane and a spirit-level and fix this state so it can be looked at without rearing back. EPIC nothing! LEVEL! Level California! And I do mean L E V E L ! ! !

XII
My People! My People!

"My people! My people!" From the earliest rocking of my cradle days, I have heard this cry go up from Negro lips. It is forced outward by pity, scorn and hopeless resignation. It is called forth by the observations of one class of Negro on the doings of another branch of the brother in black. For instance, well-mannered Negroes groan out like that when they board a train or a bus and find other Negroes on there with their shoes off, stuffing themselves with fried fish, bananas and peanuts, and throwing the garbage on the floor. Maybe they are not only eating and drinking. The offenders may be "loud-talking" the place, and holding back nothing of their private lives, in a voice that embraces the entire coach. The well-dressed Negro shrinks back in his seat at that, shakes his head and sighs, "My people! My people!"

Now, the well-mannered Negro is embarrassed by the crude behavior of the others. They are not friends, and have never seen each other before. So why should he or she be embarrassed? It is like this: the well-bred Negro has looked around and seen America with his eyes. He or she has set himself to measure up to what he thinks of as the white standard of living. He is conscious of the fact that the Negro in America needs more respect if he expects to get any acceptance at all. Therefore, after straining every nerve to get an education, maintain an attractive home, dress decently, and otherwise conform, he is dismayed at the sight of other Negroes tearing down what he is trying to build up. It is said every day, "And that good-for-nothing, trashy Negro is the one the white people judge us all by. They think we're all just alike. My people! My people!"

What that educated Negro knows further is that he can do very little towards imposing his own viewpoint on the lowlier members of his race. Class and culture stand between. The humble Negro has a built-up antagonism to the "Big Nigger." It is a curious thing that he does not resent a white man looking down on him. But he resents any lines between himself and the wealthy and educated of his own race. "He's a nigger just like us," is the sullen rejoinder. The only answer to this is "My people! My people!"

So the quiet-spoken Negro man or woman who finds himself in the midst of one of these "broadcasts" as on the train, cannot go over and say, "Don't act like that, brother. You're giving us all a black eye." He or she would know better than to try that. The performance would not only go on, it would get better with the "dicky" Negro as the butt of all the quips. The educated Negro may know all about differential calculus and the theory of evolution, but he is fighting entirely out of his class when he tries to quip with the underprivileged. The bookless may have difficulty in reading a paragraph in a newspaper, but when they get down to "playing the dozens" they have no equal in America, and, I'd risk a sizable bet, in the whole world. Starting off in the first by calling you a seven-sided son-of-a-bitch, and pausing to name the sides, they proceed to "specify" until the tip-top branch of your family tree has been "given a reading." No profit in that to the upper-class Negro, so he minds his own business and groans, "My people! My people!"

It being a traditional cry, I was bound to hear it often and under many circumstances. But it is not the only folk label that I heard. "Race Pride"—"Race Prejudice"—"Race Man"—"Race Solidarity"— "Race Consciousness"—"Race."

"Race Prejudice" I was instructed was something bad that white people used on us. It seemed that white people felt superior to black ones and would not give Negroes justice for that reason. "Race Pride" was something that, if we had it, we would feel ourselves superior to the whites. A black skin was the greatest honor that could be blessed on any man. A "Race Man" was somebody who always kept the glory and honor of his race before him. Must stand ever ready to defend the Negro race from all hurt, harm and danger. Especially if a white person said "Nigger," "You people," "Negress" or "Darkies." It was a mark of shame if somebody accused: "Why, you are not a Race Man (or woman)." People made whole careers of being "Race" men and women. They were champions of the race.

"Race Consciousness" is a plea to Negroes to bear their color in mind at all times. It was just a phrase to me when I was a child. I knew it was supposed to mean something deep. By the time I got grown I saw that it was only an imposing line of syllables, for no Negro in America is apt to forget his race. "Race Solidarity" looked like something solid in my childhood, but like all other mirages, it faded as I came close enough to look. As soon as I could think, I saw that there is no such thing as Race Solidarity in America with any group. It is freely admitted that it does not exist among Negroes. Our so-called Race Leaders cry over it. Others accept it as a natural thing that Negroes should not remain an unmelting black knot in the body politic. Our interests are too varied. Personal benefits run counter to race lines too often for it to hold. If it did, we could never fit into the national pattern. Since the race line has never held any other group in America, why expect it to be effective with us? The upper-class Negroes admit it in their own phrases. The lower-class Negroes say it with a tale.

It seems that a Negro was asked to lead the congregation in prayer. He got down on his knees and began, "Oh, Lawd, I got something to ask You, but I know You can't do it."

"Go on, Brother Isham and ask Him."

"Lawd," Brother Isham began again, "I really want to ask You something but I just know You can't do it."

"Aw, Brother Isham, go on and tell the Lawd what you want. He's the Lawd! Ain't nothing He can't do! He can even lead a butt-headed cow by the horns. You're killing up time. Go 'head on, Brother Isham, and let the church roll on."

"Well then, Lawd, I ask You to get these Negroes together, but I know You can't do it." Then there is laughter and "My people! My people!"

Hearing things like this from my childhood, sooner or later I was bound to have some curiosity about my race of people.

What fell into my ears from time to time tended more to confuse than to clarify. One thing made a liar out of the one that went before and the thing that came after. At different times I heard opposite viewpoints expressed by the same person or persons.

For instance, come school-closing time and like formal occasions, I heard speeches which brought thunderous applause. I did not know the word for it at the time, but it did not take me long to know the material was traditional. Just as folk as the songs in church. I knew that because so many people got up and used the same, identical phrases: (*a*) The Negro had made the greatest progress in fifty years of any race on the face of the globe. (*b*) Negroes composed the most *beautiful* race on earth, being just like a flower garden with every color and kind. (*c*) Negroes were the bravest men on earth, facing every danger like lions, and fighting with demons. We must remember with pride that the first blood spilled for American Independence was that of the brave and daring Crispus Attucks, a Negro who had bared his black breast to the bullets of the British tyrants at Boston, and thus struck the first blow for American liberty. They had marched with Colonel Shaw during the Civil War and hurled back the forces of the iniquitous South, who sought to hold black men in bondage. It was a Negro named Simon who had been the only one with enough pity and compassion in his heart to help the Savior bear His cross upon Calvary. It was the Negro troops under Teddy Roosevelt who won the battle of San Juan Hill.

It was the genius of the Negro which had invented the steam engine, the cotton gin, the airbrake, and numerous other things—but conniving white men had seen the Negro's inventions and run off and put them into practice before the Negro had a chance to do anything about it. Thus the white man got credit for what the genius of the Negro brain had produced. Were it not for the envy and greed of the white man, the Negro would hold his rightful place—the noblest and the greatest man on earth.

The people listening would cheer themselves hoarse and go home feeling good. Over the fences next day it would be agreed that it was a wonderful speech, and nothing but the God's truth. What a great people we would be if we only had our rights!

But my own pinnacle would be made to reel and rock anyway by other things I heard from the very people who always applauded "the great speech," when it was shouted to them from the schoolhouse rostrum. For instance, let some member of the community do or say something which was considered either dumb or underhand: the verdict would be "Dat's just like a nigger!" or "Nigger from nigger leave nigger"—("Nothing from nothing leave nothing"). It was not said in either admiration or pity. Utter scorn was in the saying. "Old Cuffy just got to cut de fool, you know. Monkey see, monkey do. Nigger see de white man do something, he jump in and try to do like de white man, and make a great big old mess."

"My people! My people!"

"Yeah, you's mighty right. Another monkey on de line. De white man, you understand, he was a railroad engineer, so he had a pet monkey he used to take along wid him all de time. De monkey, he set up there in de cab wid de engineer and see what he do to run de train. Way after while, figger he can run de train just as good as de engineer his own self. He was just itching to git at dat throttle and bust dat main line wide open. Well, one day de engineer jumped down at de station to git his orders and old monkey seen his chance. He just jumped up in de engineer's seat, grabbed a holt of dat throttle, and dat engine was splitting de wind down de track. So de engineer sent a message on ahead, say 'Clear de track. Monkey on de line!' Well, Brer Monk he was holding de throttle wide open and jumping up and down and laughing fit to kill. Course, he didn't know nothing about no side tracks and no switches and no schedules, so he was making a mile a minute when he hit a open switch and a string of box cars was standing on de siding. Ker-blam-er-lam-er-lam! And dat was de last of Brer Engine-driving Monk. Lovely monkey he was, but a damned poor engineer." "My people! My people!"

Everybody would laugh at that, and the laughter puzzled me some. Weren't Negroes the smartest people on earth, or something like that? Somebody ought to remind the people of what we had heard at the schoolhouse. Instead of that, there would be more monkey stories.

There was the one about the white doctor who had a pet monkey who wanted to be a doctor. Kept worrying his master to show him how, and the doctor had other troubles, too. Another man had a bulldog who used to pass the doctor's gate every day and pick a fight with the monkey. Finally, the doctor saw a way to stop the monkey from worrying him about showing him how to be a doctor. "Whip that bulldog until he evacuates, then bring me some of it, monkey. I'll take it and show you how to be a doctor, and then I'll treat it in a way so as to ruin that bulldog for life. He won't be no more trouble to you."

"Oh, I'll git it, boss. Don't you worry. I sho' wants to be a doctor, and then again, dat old bulldog sho' is worrisome."

No sooner did the bulldog reach the gate that day, than the monkey, which could not wait for the bulldog to start the fight as usual, jumped on the dog. The monkey was all over him like gravy over rice. He put all he had into it and it went on until the doctor came out and drove the dog off and gave the monkey a chance to bolt into the office with what he had been fighting for.

"Here 'tis, boss. It was a tight fight, but I got it."

"Fine! Fine!" the doctor told him. "Now, gimme that bottle over there. I'll fix that bulldog so he'll never be able to sit down again. When I get through with this, he'll be ruined for life."

"Hold on there, boss! Hold on there a minute! I wish you wouldn't do dat, boss."

"How come? You want to get rid of that old bulldog, don't you?"

"Dat's right, I sho' do."

"Well, why don't you want me to fix him, then?"

"Well, boss, you see it's like dis. Dat was a tight fight, a mighty tight fight. I could have been mistaken about dat bulldog, boss, we was all tangled up to-gether so bad. You better leave dat fixing business alone, boss. De wrong man might git hurt."

There were many other tales, equally ludicrous, in which the Negro, sometimes symbolized by the monkey, and sometimes named outright, ran off with the wrong understanding of what he had seen and heard. Several white and Negro proposals of marriage were compared, and the like. The white suitor had said his love had dove's eyes. His valet had hurried to compliment his girl by saying she had dog's eyes, and so on.

There was a general acceptance of the monkey as kinfolks. Perhaps it was some distant memory of tribal monkey reverence from Africa which had been forgotten in the main, but remembered in some vague way. Perhaps it was an acknowledgment of our talent for mimicry with the monkey as a symbol.

The classic monkey parable, which is very much alive wherever the Negroes congregate in America, is the one about "My people!"

It seems that a monkey squatted down in the middle of a highway to play. A Cadillac full of white people came along, saw the monkey at play and carefully drove around him. Then came a Buick full of more white people and did the same. The monkey kept right on playing. Way after a while a T-model Ford came along full of Negroes. But instead of driving around the monkey, the car headed straight for him. He only saved his life by a quick leap to the shoulder of the road. He sat there and watched the car rattle off in the distance and sighed "My people! My people!"

A new addition to the tale is that the monkey has quit saying "My people!" He is now saying, "Those people! Those people!"

I found the Negro, and always the blackest Negro, being made the butt of all jokes,—particularly black women.

They brought bad luck for a week if they came to your house of a Monday morning. They were evil. They slept with their fists balled up ready to fight and squabble even while they were asleep. They even had evil dreams. White, yellow and brown girls dreamed about roses and perfume and kisses. Black gals dreamed about guns, razors, ice-picks, hatchets and hot lye. I heard men swear they had seen women dreaming and knew these things to be true.

"Oh, gwan!" somebody would chide, laughing. You know dat ain't so."

"Oh, now, he ain't lying," somebody else would take up the theme. "I know for my own self. I done slept wid yaller women and I done slept wid black ones. They *is* evil. You marry a yaller or a brown woman and wake her up in de night and she will sort of stretch herself and say, 'I know what I was dreaming when you woke me up. I was dreaming I had done baked you a chicken and cooked you a great big old cake, and we was at de table eating our dinner out of de same plate, and I was sitting on your lap and we was just enjoying ourselves to death!' Then she will kiss you more times than you ask her to, and go on back to sleep. But you take and wake up a black gal, now! First thing she been sleeping wid her fists balled up, and you shake her, she'll lam you five or six times before you can get her awake. Then when she do git wake she'll have off and ast you, 'Nigger, what you wake me up for? Know what I was dreaming when you woke me up? I dreamt dat you shook your old rusty black fist under my nose and I split your head open wid a axe.' Then she'll kick your feets away from hers, snatch de covers all over on her side, ball up her fists agin, and gwan back to sleep. You can't tell me nothing. I know." "My people!"

This always was, and is still, good for a raucous burst of laughter. I listened to this talk and became more and more confused. If it was so honorable and glorious to be black, why was it the yellow-skinned people among us had so much prestige? Even a child in the first grade could see that this was so from what happened in the classroom and on school programs. The light-skinned children were always the angels, fairies and queens of school plays. The lighter the girl, the more money and prestige she was apt, and expected, to marry. So on into high-school years, I was asking myself questions. Were Negroes the great heroes I heard about from the platform, or were they the ridiculous monkeys of everyday talk? Was it really honorable to be black? There was even talk that it was no use for Negro boys and girls to rub all the hair off of their heads against college walls. There was no place for them to go with it after they got all this education. Some of the older heads held that it was too much for Negroes to handle. Better leave such things for the white folks, who knew what to do with it. But there were others who were all for pushing ahead. I saw the conflict in my own home between my parents. My mother was the one to dare all. My father was satisfied.

This Negro business came home to me in incidents and ways. There was the time when Old Man Bronner was taken out and beaten. Mr. Bronner was a white man of the poor class who had settled in aristocratic Maitland. One night just after dark, we heard terrible cries back in the woods behind Park Lake. Sam Moseley, his brother Elijah, and Ike Clarke, hurried up to our gate and they were armed. The howls of pain kept up. Old fears and memories must have stirred inside of the grown folks. Many people closed and barred their doors. Papa and the men around our gate were sullen and restless as the cries churned over the woods and lake.

"Who do you reckon it is?" Sam Moseley asked.

"I don't know for sure, but some thinks it's Jim Watson. Anyhow, he ain't home yet," Clarke said, and all of them looked at each other in an asking way.

Finally Papa said, "Well, hold on a minute till I go get my rifle."

" 'Tain't no ifs and buts about it," Elijah Moseley

said gravely, "We can't leave Jim Watson be beat to death like that."

Papa had sensed that these armed men had not come to merely stand around and talk. They had come to see if he would go with the rest. When he came out shoving the sixteen bullets into his rifle, and dropping more into his pocket, Mama made no move to stop him. "Well, we all got families," he said with an attempt at lightness. "Shoot off your gun, somebody, so de rest will know we ready."

Papa himself pointed his Winchester rifle at the sky and fired a shot. Another shot answered him from around the store and a huddle of figures came hurrying up the road in the dark.

"It's Jim Watson. Us got to go git him!" and the dozen or more men armed with double-barreled shotguns, breech-loaders, pistols and Papa's repeating Winchester hurried off on their grim mission. Perhaps not a single one of them expected to return alive. No doubt they hoped. But they went.

Mama gasped a short sentence of some sort and herded us all into the house and barred the door. Lights went out all over the village and doors were barred. Axes had been dragged in from woodpiles, grass-hooks, pitch-forks and scythes were ranked up in corners behind those barred doors. If the men did not come back, or if they only came back in part, the women and children were ready to do the best they could. Mama spoke only to say she wished Hezekiah

and John, the two biggest boys, had not gone to Maitland late in the afternoon. They were not back and
she feared they might start home and— But she did
not cry. Our seven hounds with big, ferocious Ned
in the lead, barked around the house. We huddled
around Mama in her room and kept quiet. There was
not a human sound in all the village. Nothing had
ever happened before in our vicinity to create such
tension. But people had memories and told tales of
what happened back there in Georgia, and Alabama
and West Florida that made the skin of the young
crawl with transmitted memory, and reminded the
old heads that they were still flinchy.

The dark silence of the village kept up for an hour
or more. The once loud cries fell and fell until our
straining ears could no longer find them. Strangest
of all, not a shot was fired. We huddled in the dark
and waited, and died a little, and waited. The silence
was ten times more punishing than the cries.

At long last, a bubble of laughing voices approached our barn from the rear. It got louder and
took on other dimensions between the barn and the
house. Mama hissed at us to shut up when, in fact,
nobody was saying a thing.

"Hey, there Little-Bits," Papa bellowed. "Open
up!"

"Strike a light, Daught," Mama told my sister, feeling around in the dark to find Sarah's hand to give
her the matches which I had seen clutched in her

fingers before she had put out the light. Mama had said very little, and I could not see her face in the dark; somehow she could not scratch a match now that Papa was home again.

All of the men came in behind Papa, laughing and joking, perhaps more from relief than anything else.

"Don't stand there grinning like a chessy cat, Mr. Hurston," Mama scolded. "You ain't told me a thing."

"Oh, it wasn't Jim Watson at all, Lulu. You remember 'bout a week ago Old Man Bronner wrote something in de Orlando paper about H.'s daughter and W.B.G.'s son being seen sitting around the lakes an awful lot?"

"Yeah, I heard something about it."

"Well, you know those rich white folks wasn't going to 'low nothing like dat. So some of 'em waylaid him this evening. They pulled him down off of a load of hay he was hauling and drug him off back there in de woods and tanned his hide for him."

"Did y'all see any of it?"

"Nope, we could hear him hollering for a while, though. We never got no further than the lake. A white man, one of the G— boys was standing in the bushes at de road. When we got ready to turn off round de lake he stepped out and spoke to us and told us it didn't concern us. They had Bronner down there tied down on his all-fours, and de men was taking turns wid dat bull whip. They must have been standing on tip-toes to do it. You could hear them licks clear out to de road."

The men all laughed. Somebody mocked Bronner's cries and moans a time or two and the crowd laughed immoderately. They had gone out to rescue a neighbor or die in the attempt, and they were back with their families. So they let loose their insides and laughed. They resurrected a joke or two and worried it like a bone and laughed some more. Then they just laughed. The men who spoke of members of their race as monkeys had gone out to die for one. The men who were always saying, "My skin-folks, but not kin-folks; my race but not my taste," had rushed forth to die for one of these same contemptibles. They shoved each other around and laughed. So I could see that what looked like ridicule was really the Negro poking a little fun at himself. At the same time, just like other people, hoping and wishing he was what the orators said he was.

My mother eased back in her chair and took a dip of snuff. Maybe she did not feel so well, for she didn't get tickled at all. After a while, she ordered us off to bed in a rough voice. Time was, and the men scattered. Mama sat right where she was until Hezekiah and John came home around ten o'clock. She gave them an awful going over with her tongue for staying out late, and then she eased to bed.

I was dredged up inside that night, so I did not think about the incident's general connection with race. Besides I had to go to sleep. But days later, it was called to my recollection again. There was a program at the Methodist Church, and Mrs. Mattie Moseley, it was announced, was to have a paper. She was also going to have a fine new dress to read it in. We all wanted to see the dress.

The time came and she had the dress on. The subject of her paper was, "What will the Negroes do with the whites?" I do not know what she decided was to be done. It seemed equally unimportant to the rest of the town. I remember that everybody said it was a fine subject. But the next week, the women talked about nothing else but the new wrist-watch she had on. It was the first one ever seen in our town.

But in me, the affair stirred up more confusion. Why bring the subject up? Something was moving around me which I had no hooks to grasp. What was this about white and black people that was being talked about?

Certainly nothing changed in the village. The townspeople who were in domestic service over in Maitland or Winter Park went to work as usual. The white people interested in Eatonville came and went as before. Mr. Irving Bacheller, the author, who had a show place in Winter Park, petted up Willie Sewell, who was his head gardener, in the same old way. Bishop Whipple petted Elijah Moseley, and Mrs. Mars, who was his sister, did lots of things for Lulu Moseley, Elijah's wife. What was all the talk about? It certainly was puzzling to me.

As time went on, the confusion grew. By the time that I got to high school, I was conscious of a group that was neither the top nor the bottom of Negrodom. I met the type which designates itself as "the better-thinking Negro." I was thrown off my stride by finding that while they considered themselves Race Champions, they wanted nothing to do with anything frankly Negroid. They drew color lines within the race. The Spirituals, the Blues, *any* definitely Negroid thing was just not done. They went to the trouble at times to protest the use of them by Negro artists. Booker T. Washington was absolutely vile for advocating industrial education. There was no analysis, no seeking for merits. If it was old cuffy, down with it! "My People! My People!"

This irritated me until I got to the place where I could analyze. The thing they were trying to do went wrong because it lacked reason. It lacked reason because they were attempting to stand equal with the best in America without having the tools to work with. They were attempting a flight away from Negrodom because they felt that there was so much scorn for black skin in the nation that their only security was in flight. They lacked the happy carelessness of a class beneath them and the understanding of the top-flight Negro above them. Once, when they used to set their mouths in what they thought was the Boston Crimp, and ask me about the great differences between the ordinary Negro and "the better-thinking Negro," I used to show my irritation by saying I did not know who the better-thinking Negro was. I knew who the think-they-are-better Negroes were, but who were the better-thinkers was another matter. But when I came to understand what made them make their useless motions, and saw them pacing a cage that wasn't there, I felt more sympathy than irritation. If they want to establish a sort of fur-coat peerage, let 'em! Since they can find no comfort where they happened to be born, no especial talents to lift them, and other doors are closed to them, they have to find some pleasure somewhere in life. They have to use whatever their mentality provides. "My People! My People!"

But one thing and another kept the conflict going on inside me, off and on for years. Sometimes I was sure that the Negro race was all that the platform speakers said. Then I would hear so much self-deprecation that I would be deflated. Over and over I heard people shake their heads and explain us by the supposed prayer of a humble Negro, who got down on his knees and said: "Lawd, you know I ain't nothing. My wife, she ain't nothing. My chillun ain't nothing, and if you fool 'round us, Lawd, you won't be nothing neither."

So I sensed early, that the Negro race was not one band of heavenly love. There was stress and strain inside as well as out. Being black was not enough. It took more than a community of skin color to make your love come down on you. That was the beginning of my peace.

Light came to me when I realized that I did not have to consider any racial group as a whole. God made them duck by duck and that was the only way I could see them. I learned that skins were no measure of what was inside people. So none of the Race clichés meant anything any more. I began to laugh at both white and black who claimed special blessings on the basis of race. Therefore I saw no curse in being black, nor no extra flavor by being white. I saw no benefit in excusing my looks by claiming to be half Indian. In fact, I boast that I am the only Negro in the United States whose grandfather on the mother's side was *not* an Indian chief. Neither did I descend from George Washington, Thomas Jefferson, or any Governor of a Southern state. I see no need to manufacture me a legend to beat the facts. I do not coyly admit to a touch of the tarbrush to my Indian and white ancestry. You can consider me Old Tar-Brush in person if you want to. I am a mixed-blood, it is true, but I differ from the party line in that I neither consider it an honor nor a shame. I neither claim Jefferson as my grandpa, nor exclaim, "Just look how that white man took advantage of my grandma!" It does not matter in the first place, and then in the next place, I do not know how it came about. Since nobody ever told me, I give my ancestress the benefit of the doubt. She probably ran away from him just as fast as she could. But if that white man could run faster than my grandma, that was no fault of hers. Anyway, you must remember, he didn't have a thing to do but to keep on running forward. She, being the pursued, had to look back over her shoulder every now and then to see how she was doing. And you know your ownself, how looking backwards slows people up.

In this same connection, I have been told that God meant for all the so-called races of the world to stay just as they are, and the people who say that may be right. But it is a well-known fact that no matter where two sets of people come together, there are bound to be some in-betweens. It looks like the command was given to people's heads, because the other parts don't seem to have heard tell. When the next batch is made up, maybe Old Maker will straighten all that out. Maybe the men will be more tangle-footed and the women a whole lot more faster around the feet. That will bring about a great deal more of racial and other kinds of purity, but a somewhat less exciting world. It might work, but I doubt it. There will have to be something harder to get across than an ocean to keep East and West from meeting. But maybe Old Maker will have a remedy. Maybe even He has given up. Perhaps in a moment of discouragement He turned the job over to Adolf Hitler and went on about His business of making more beetles.

I do not share the gloomy thought that Negroes in

America are doomed to be stomped out bodaciously, nor even shackled to the bottom of things. Of course some of them will be tromped out, and some will always be at the bottom, keeping company with other bottom-folks. It would be against all nature for all the Negroes to be either at the bottom, top, or in between. It has never happened with anybody else, so why with us? No, we will go where the internal drive carries us like everybody else. It is up to the individual. If you haven't got it, you can't show it. If you have got it, you can't hide it. That is one of the strongest laws God ever made.

I maintain that I have been a Negro three times—a Negro baby, a Negro girl and a Negro woman. Still, if you have received no clear cut impression of what the Negro in America is like, then you are in the same place with me. There is no *The Negro* here. Our lives are so diversified, internal attitudes so varied, appearances and capabilities so different, that there is no possible classification so catholic that it will cover us all, except My people! My people!

XIII
Two Women in Particular

Two women, among the number whom I have known intimately force me to keep them well in mind. Both of them have rare talents, are drenched in human gravy, and both of them have meant a great deal to me in friendship and inward experience. One, Fannie Hurst, because she is so young for her years, and Ethel Waters because she is both so old and so young for hers.

Understand me, their ages have nothing to do with their birthdays. Ethel Waters is still a young woman. Fannie Hurst is far from old.

In my undergraduate days I was secretary to Fannie Hurst. From day to day she amazed me with her moods. Immediately before and after a very serious moment you could just see her playing with her dolls. You never knew where her impishness would break out again.

One day, for instance, I caught her playing at keeping house with company coming to see her. She told me not to leave the office. If the doorbell rang, Clara, her cook, was to answer it. Then she went downstairs and told Clara that I was to answer the doorbell. Then she went on to another part of the house. Presently I heard the bell, and it just happened that I was on my way downstairs to get a drink of water. I wondered why Clara did not go to the door. What was my amazement to see Miss Hurst herself open the door and come in, greet herself graciously and invite herself to have some tea. Which she did. She went into that huge duplex studio and had toasted English muffins and played she had company with her for an hour or more. Then she came on back up to her office and went to work.

I knew that she was an only child. She did not even have cousins to play with. She was born to wealth. With the help of images, I could see that lonely child in a big house making up her own games. Being of artistic bent, I could see her making up characters to play with. Naturally she had to talk for her characters, or they would not say what she wanted them to. Most children play at that at times. I had done that extensively so I knew what she was doing when I saw her with the door half open, ringing her own doorbell and inviting herself to have some tea and muffins. When she was tired of her game, she just quit and was a grown woman again.

She likes for me to drive her, and we have made several tours. Her impishness broke out once on the road. She told me to have the car all serviced and ready for next morning. We were going up to Belgrade Lakes in Maine to pay Elizabeth Marbury a visit.

So soon next day we were on the road. She was Fannie Hurst, the famous author as far as Saratoga Springs. As we drove into the heart of town, she turned to me and said, "Zora, the water here at Saratoga is marvelous. Have you ever had any of it?"

"No, Miss Hurst, I never did."

"Then we must stop and let you have a drink. It would never do for you to miss having a drink of Saratoga water."

We parked near the famous United States Hotel and got out.

"It would be nice to stop over here for the night," she said. "I'll go see about the hotel. There is a fountain over there in the park. Be sure and get yourself a drink! You can take Lummox for a run while you get your water."

I took Lummox out of the car. To say I took Lummox for a run would be merely making a speech-figure. Lummox weighed about three pounds, and with his short legs, when he thought that he was running he was just jumping up and down in the same place. But anyway, I took him along to get the water. It was so-so as far as the taste went.

When I got back to the car, she was waiting for me. It was too early in the season for the hotel to be open. Too bad! She knew I would have enjoyed it so much. Well, I really ought to have some pleasure. Had I ever seen Niagara Falls?

"No, Miss Hurst. I always wanted to see it, but I never had a chance."

"Zora! You mean to tell me that you have never seen Niagara Falls?"

"No." I felt right sheepish about it when she put it that way.

"Oh, you must see the Falls. Get in the car and let's go. You must see those Falls right now." The way she sounded, my whole life was bare up to then and wrecked for the future unless I saw Niagara Falls.

The next afternoon around five o'clock, we were at Niagara Falls. It had been a lovely trip across Northern New York State.

"Here we are, now, Zora. Hurry up and take a good look at the Falls. I brought you all the way over here so that you could see them."

She didn't need to urge me. I leaned on the rail and looked and looked. It was worth the trip, all right. It was just like watching the Atlantic Ocean jump off Pike's Peak.

In ten minutes or so, Miss Hurst touched me and I turned around.

"Zora, have you ever been across the International Bridge? I think you ought to see the Falls from the Canadian side. Come on, so you can see it from over there. It would be too bad for you to come all the way over here to see it and not see it from the Bridge."

So we drove across the Bridge. A Canadian Customs

Official tackled us immediately. The car had to be registered. How long did we intend to stay?

"You'd better register it for two weeks," Miss Hurst answered and it was done. The sun was almost down.

"Look, Zora, Hamilton is only a short distance. I know you want to see it. Come on, let's drive on, and spend the night at Hamilton."

We drove on. I was surprised to see that everything in Canada looked so much like everything in the United States. It was deep twilight when we got into Hamilton.

"They tell me Kitchener is a most interesting little place, Zora. I know it would be fun to go on there and spend the night." So on to Kitchener we went.

Here was Fannie Hurst, a great artist and globe famous, behaving like a little girl, teasing her nurse to take her to the zoo, and having a fine time at it.

Well, we spent an exciting two weeks motoring over Ontario, seeing the countryside and eating at quaint but well-appointed inns. She was like a child at a circus. She was a run-away, with no responsibilities.

Fannie Hurst, the author, and the wife of Jacques Danielson, was not with us again until we hit Westchester on the way home. Then she replaced Mrs. Hurst's little Fannie and began to discuss her next book with me and got very serious in her manner.

While Fannie Hurst brings a very level head to her dressing, she exults in her new things like any debutante. She knows exactly what goes with her very

white skin, black hair and sloe eyes, and she wears it.
I doubt if any woman on earth has gotten better effects than she has with black, white and red. Not only
that, she knows how to parade it when she gets it on.
She will never be jailed for uglying up a town.

THIS ETHEL WATERS

I am due to have this friendship with Ethel Waters,
because I worked for it.

She came to me across the footlights. Not the artist
alone, but the person, and I wanted to know her very
much. I was too timid to go backstage and haunt her,
so I wrote her letters and she just plain ignored me.
But I kept right on. I sensed a great humanness and
depth about her; I wanted to know someone like that.

Then Carl Van Vechten gave a dinner for me. A
great many celebrities were there, including Sinclair
Lewis, Dwight Fiske, Anna May Wong, Blanche
Knopf, an Italian soprano, and my old friend, Jane
Belo. Carl whispered to me that Ethel Waters was
coming in later. He was fond of her himself and he
knew I wanted to know her better, so he had persuaded her to come. Carl is given to doing nice things
like that.

We got to talking, Ethel and I, and got on very well.
Then I found that what I suspected was true. Ethel
Waters is a very shy person. It had not been her intention to ignore me. She felt that I belonged to another

world and had no need of her. She thought that I had been merely curious. She laughed at her error and said, "And here you were just like me all the time." She got warm and friendly, and we went on from there. When she was implored to sing, she asked me first what I wanted to hear. It was "Stormy Weather," of course, and she did it beautifully.

Then I did something for her. She told us that she was going to appear with Hall Johnson's Choir at Carnegie Hall, and planned to do some spirituals. Immediately, the Italian soprano and others present advised her not to do it. The argument was that Marian Anderson, Roland Hayes and Paul Robeson had sung them so successfully that her audience would make comparisons and Ethel would suffer by it. I saw the hurt in Ethel's face and jumped in. I objected that Ethel was not going to do any concertized versions of spirituals. She had never rubbed any hair off her head against any college walls and she was not going to sing that way. She was going to sing those spirituals just the way her humble mother had sung them to her.

She turned to me with a warm, grateful smile on her face, and said, "Thank you."

When she got ready to leave, she got her wraps and said, "Come on, Zora. Let's go on uptown." I went along with her, her husband, and faithful Lashley, a young woman spiritual singer from somewhere in Mississippi, whom Ethel has taken under her wing.

We kept up with each other after that, and I got

to know her very well. We exchanged confidences that really mean something to both of us. I am her friend, and her tongue is in my mouth. I can speak her sentiments for her, though Ethel Waters can do very well indeed in speaking for herself. She has a homely philosophy that reaches all corners of Life, and she has words to fit when she speaks.

She is one of the strangest bundles of people that I have ever met. You can just see the different folks wrapped up in her if you associate with her long. Just like watching an open fire—the color and shape of her personality is never the same twice. She has extraordinary talents which her lack of formal education prevents her from displaying. She never had a chance to go beyond the third grade in school. A terrible fear is in me that the world will never really know her. You have seen her and heard her on the stage, but so little of her capabilities are seen. Her struggle for adequate expression throws her into moods at times. She said to me Christmas Day of 1941, "You have the advantage of me, Zora. I can only show what is on the stage. You can write a different kind of book each time."

She is a Catholic, and deeply religious. She plays a good game of bridge, but no card-playing at her house on Sundays. No more than her mother would have had in her house. Nobody is going to dance and cut capers around her on the Sabbath, either. What she sings about and acts out on the stage, has nothing to do with her private life.

Her background is most humble. She does not mind saying that she was born in the slums of Philadelphia in an atmosphere that smacked of the rural South. She neither drinks nor smokes and is always chasing me into a far corner of the room when I light a cigarette. She thanks God that I don't drink.

Her religious bent shows in unexpected ways. For instance, we were discussing her work in "Cabin in the Sky." She said, "When we started to rehearse the spirituals, some of those no-manners people started to swinging 'em, and get smart. I told 'em they better not play with God's music like that. I told 'em if I caught any of 'em at it, I'd knock 'em clean over into that orchestra pit." Her eyes flashed fire as she told me about it. Then she calmed down and laughed. "Of course, you know, Zora, God didn't want me to knock 'em over. That was an idea of mine."

And this fact of her background has a great deal to do with her approach to people. She is shy and you must convince her that she is really wanted before she will open up her tender parts and show you. Even in her career, I am persuaded that Ethel Waters does not know that she has arrived. For that reason, she is grateful for any show of love or appreciation. People to whom she has given her love and trust have exploited it heartlessly, like hogs under an acorn tree —guzzling and grabbing with their ears hanging over their eyes, and never looking up to see the high tree that the acorns fell from.

She went on the stage at thirteen and says that she got eight dollars a week for her first salary. She was so frightened that she had to be pushed on to sing her song, and then another member of the cast had to come on with her until she could get started. Then too, they had to place a chair for her to lean on to overcome her nervousness.

At fifteen, she introduced the "St. Louis Blues" to the world. She saw a sheet of the music, had it played for her, then wrote to W. C. Handy for permission to use it. Handy answered on a postal card and told her to go as far as she liked, or words to that effect. If W. C. Handy had only known at that time the importance of his act!

She is gay and sombre by turns. I have listened to her telling a story and noticed her change of mood in mid-story. I have asked her to repeat something particularly pungent that she has said, and had her tell me, "I couldn't say it now. My thoughts are different. Sometime when I am thinking that same way, I'll tell it to you again."

The similes and metaphors just drip off of her lips. One day I sat in her living-room on Hobart Street in Los Angeles, deep in thought. I had really forgotten that others were present. She nudged Archie Savage and pointed at me. "Salvation looking at the temple forlorn," she commented and laughed. "What you doing, Zora? Pasturing in your mind?"

"It's nice to be talking things over with you, Zora," she told me another time. "Conversation is the ceremony of companionship."

Speaking of a man we both know, she said, "The bigger lie he tells, the more guts he tells it with."

"That man's jaws are loaded with big words, but he never says a thing," she said speaking of a mutual friend. "He got his words out of a book. I got mine out of life."

"She shot him lightly and he died politely," she commented after reading in the *Los Angeles Examiner* about a woman killing her lover.

Commenting on a man who had used coarse language, she said, "I'd rather him to talk differently, but you can't hold him responsible, Zora, they are all the words he's got."

Ethel Waters has known great success and terrible personal tragedy, so she knows that no one can have everything.

"Don't care how good the music is, Zora, you can't dance on every set."

I am grateful for the friendship of Fannie Hurst and Ethel Waters. But how does one speak of honest gratitude? Who can know the outer ranges of friendship? I am tempted to say that no one can live without it. It seems to me that trying to live without friends is like milking a bear to get cream for your morning coffee. It is a whole lot of trouble, and then not worth much after you get it.

XIV
Love

What do I really know about love? I have had some experiences and feel fluent enough for my own satisfaction. Love, I find is like singing. Everybody can do enough to satisfy themselves, though it may not impress the neighbors as being very much. That is the way it is with me, but whether I know anything unusual, I couldn't say. Don't look for me to call a string of names and point out chapter and verse. Ladies do not kiss and tell any more than gentlemen do.

I have read many books where the heroine was in love for a long time without knowing it. I have talked with people and they have told me the same thing. So maybe that is the way it ought to be. That is not the way it is with me at all. I have been *out* of love with people for a long time, perhaps without finding it out. But when I fall *in*, I can feel the bump. That is a fact and I would not try to fool you. Love may be a sleepy, creeping thing with some others, but it is a mighty wakening thing with me. I feel the jar, and I know it from my head on down.

Though I started falling in love before I was seven

years old, I never had a fellow until I was nearly grown. I was such a poor picker. I would have had better luck if I had stuck to boys around my own age, but that wouldn't do me. I wanted somebody with long pants on, and they acted as if they didn't know I was even born. The heartless wretches would walk right past my gate with grown women and pay me no attention at all, other than to say hello or something like that. Then I would have to look around for another future husband, only to have the same thing happen all over again.

Of course, in high school I received mushy notes and wrote them. A day or two, a week or month at most would see the end of the affair. Gone without a trace. I was in my Freshman year in college when I first got excited, really.

He could stomp a piano out of this world, sing a fair baritone and dance beautifully. He noticed me, too, and I was carried away. For the first time since my mother's death, there was someone who felt really close and warm to me.

This affair went on all through my college life, with the exception of two fallings-out. We got married immediately after I finished my work at Barnard College, which should have been the happiest day of my life. St. Augustine, Florida, is a beautiful setting for such a thing.

But, it was not my happiest day. I was assailed by doubts. For the first time since I met him, I asked myself if I really were in love, or if this had been a habit. I had an uncomfortable feeling of unreality. The day and the occasion did not underscore any features of nature or circumstance, and I wondered why. Who had canceled the well-advertised tour of the moon? Somebody had turned a hose on the sun. What I had taken for eternity turned out to be a moment walking in its sleep.

After our last falling-out, he asked me please to forgive him, and I said that I did. But now, had I really? A wind full of memories blew out of the past and brought a chilling fog. This was not the expected bright dawn. Rather, some vagrant ray had played a trick on the night. I could not bring myself to tell him my thoughts. I just couldn't, no matter how hard I tried, but there they were crowding me from pillar to post.

Back in New York, I met Mrs. Mason and she offered me the chance to return to my research work, and I accepted it. It seemed a way out without saying anything very much. Let nature take its course. I did not tell him about the arrangement. Rather, I urged him to return to Chicago to continue his medical work. Then I stretched my shivering insides out and went back to work. I have seen him only once since then. He has married again, and I hope that he is happy.

Having made such a mess, I did not rush at any serious affair right away. I set to work and really worked in earnest. Work was to be all of me, so I said. Three years went by. I had finished that phase of research and was considering writing my first book, when I met the man who was really to lay me by the heels. I met A.W.P.

He was tall, dark brown, magnificently built, with a beautifully modeled back head. His profile was strong and good. The nose and lip were especially good front and side. But his looks only drew my eyes in the beginning. I did not fall in love with him just for that. He had a fine mind and that intrigued me. When a man keeps beating me to the draw mentally, he begins to get glamorous.

I did not just fall in love. I made a parachute jump. No matter which way I probed him, I found something more to admire. We fitted each other like a glove. His intellect got me first for I am the kind of a woman that likes to move on mentally from point to point, and I like for my man to be there way ahead of me. Then if he is strong and honest, it goes on from there. Good looks are not essential, just extra added attraction. He had all of those things and more. It seems to me that God must have put in extra time making him up. He stood on his own feet so firmly that he reared back.

To illustrate the point, I got into trouble with him for trying to loan him a quarter. It came about this way.

I lived in the Graham Court at 116th Street and

Seventh Avenue. He lived down in 64th Street, Columbus Hill. He came to call one night and everything went off sweetly until he got ready to leave. At the door he told me to let him go because he was going to walk home. He had spent the only nickel he had that night to come to see me. That upset me, and I ran to get a quarter to loan him until his pay day. What did I do that for? He flew hot. In fact he was the hottest man in the five boroughs. Why did I insult him like that? The responsibility was all his. He had known that he did not have his return fare when he left home, but he had wanted to come, and so he had come. Let him take the consequences for his own acts. What kind of a coward did I take him for? How could he deserve my respect if he behaved like a cream puff? He was a *man!* No woman on earth could either lend him or give him a cent. If a man could not do for a woman, what good was he on earth? His great desire was to do for me. *Please* let him be a *man!*

For a minute I was hurt and then I saw his point. He had done a beautiful thing and I was killing it off in my blindness. If it pleased him to walk all of that distance for my sake, it pleased him as evidence of his devotion. Then too, he wanted to do all the doing, and keep me on the receiving end. He soared in my respect from that moment on. Nor did he ever change. He meant to be the head, *so help him over the fence!*

That very manliness, sweet as it was, made us both suffer. My career balked the completeness of his ideal.

I really wanted to conform, but it was impossible. To me there was no conflict. My work was one thing, and he was all of the rest. But, I could not make him see that. Nothing must be in my life but himself.

But, I am ahead of my story. I was interested in him for nearly two years before he knew it. A great deal happened between the time we met and the time we had any serious talk.

As I said, I loved, but I did not say so, because nobody asked me. I made up my mind to keep my feelings to myself since that they did not seem to matter to anyone else but me.

I went South, did some more concert work and wrote "Jonah's Gourd Vine" and "Mules and Men," then came back to New York.

He began to make shy overtures to me. I pretended not to notice for a while so that I could be sure and not be hurt. Then he gave me the extreme pleasure of telling me right out loud about it. It seems that he had been in love with me just as long as I had been with him, but he was afraid that I didn't mean him any good, as the saying goes. He had been trying to make me tell him something. He began by complimenting me on my clothes. Then one night when we had attended the Alpha Phi Alpha fraternity dance —yes, he is an Alpha man—he told me that the white dress I was wearing was beautiful, but I did not have on an evening wrap rich enough to suit him. He had in mind just the kind he wanted to see me in, and when he made the kind of money he expected to, the first thing he meant to do was to buy me a gorgeous evening wrap and everything to go with it. He wanted *his* wife to look swell. He looked at me from under his eyelashes to see how I was taking it. I smiled and so he went on.

"You know, Zora, you've got a real man on your hands. You've got somebody to do for you. I'm tired of seeing you work so hard. I wouldn't want *my* wife to do anything but look after me. Be home looking like Skookums when I got there."

He always said I reminded him of the Indian on the Skookum Apples, so I knew he meant me to understand that he wanted to be coming home to me, and with those words he endowed me with Radio City, the General Motors Corporation, the United States, Europe, Asia and some outlying continents. I had everything!

So actively began the real love affair of my life. He was then a graduate of City College, and was working for his Master's degree at Columbia. He had no money. He was born of West Indian parents in the Columbus Hill district of New York City, and had nothing to offer but what it takes—a bright soul, a fine mind in a fine body, and courage. He is so modest that I do not think that he yet knows his assets. That was to make trouble for us later on.

It was a curious situation. He was so extraordinary that I lived in terrible fear lest women camp on his doorstep in droves and take him away from me. I found out later on that he could not believe that I wanted just him. So there began an agonizing tug of war. Looking at a very serious photograph of me that Carl Van Vechten had made, he told me one night in a voice full of feeling that that was the way he wanted me to look all the time unless I was with him. I almost laughed out loud. That was just the way I felt. I hated to think of him smiling unless he was smiling at me. His grins were too precious to be wasted on ordinary mortals, especially women.

If he could only have realized what a lot he had to offer, he need not have suffered so much through doubting that he could hold me. I was hog-tied and branded, but he didn't realize it. He could make me fetch and carry, but he wouldn't believe it. So when I had to meet people on business, or went to literary parties and things like that, it would drive him into a sulk, and then he would make me unhappy. I, too, failed to see how deeply he felt. I would interpret his moods as indifference and die, and die, and die.

He begged me to give up my career, marry him and live outside of New York City. I really wanted to do anything he wanted me to do, but that one thing I could not do. It was not just my contract with my publishers, it was that I had things clawing inside of me that must be said. I could not see that my work should make any difference in marriage. He was all and everything else to me but that. One did not conflict with the other in my mind. But it was different with him. He felt that he did not matter to me enough. He was the master kind. All, or nothing, for him.

The terrible thing was that we could neither leave each other alone, nor compromise. Let me seem too cordial with any male and something was going to happen. Just let him smile too broad at any woman, and no sooner did we get inside my door than the war was on! One night (I didn't decide this) something primitive inside me tore past the barriers and before I realized it I had slapped his face. That was a mistake. He was still smoldering from an incident a week old. A fellow had met us on Seventh Avenue and kissed me on my cheek. Just one of those casual things, but it had burned up A.W.P. So I had unknowingly given him an opening he had been praying for. He paid me off then and there with interest. No broken bones, you understand, and no black eyes. I realized afterwards that my hot head could tell me to beat him, but it would cost me something. I would have to bring head to get head. I couldn't get his and leave mine locked up in the dresser-drawer.

Then I knew I was too deeply in love to be my old self. For always a blow to my body had infuriated me beyond measure. Even with my parents, that was true. But somehow, I didn't hate him at all. We sat down on the floor and each one of us tried to take all the blame. He went out and bought some pie and I made a pot of hot chocolate and we were more affectionate than ever. The next day he made me a bookcase that I needed and you couldn't get a pin between us.

But fate was watching us and laughing. About a month later when he was with me, the telephone rang. Would I please come down to an apartment in the Fifties and meet an out-of-town celebrity? He was in town for only two days and he wanted to meet me before he left. When I turned from the phone, A.W.P. was changed. He begged me not to go. I reminded him that I had promised, and begged him to come along. He refused and walked out. I went, but I was most unhappy.

This sort of thing kept up time after time. He would not be reconciled to the thing. We were alternately the happiest people in the world, and the most miserable. I suddenly decided to go away to see if I could live without him. I did not even tell him that I was going. But I wired him from some town in Virginia.

Miss Barnicle of New York University asked me to join her and Alan Lomax on a short bit of research. I was to select the area and contact the subjects. Alan Lomax was joining us with a recording machine. So because I was delirious with joy and pain, I suddenly decided to leave New York and see if I could come to some decision. I knew no more at the end than I did when I went South. Six weeks later I was back in New York and just as much his slave as ever.

Really, I never had occasion to doubt his sincerity,

but I used to drag my heart over hot coals by supposing. I did not know that I could suffer so. Then all of my careless words came to haunt me. For theatrical effect, I had uttered sacred words and oaths to others before him. How I hated myself for the sacrilege now! It would have seemed so wonderful never to have uttered them before.

But no matter how soaked we were in ecstasy, the telephone or the doorbell would ring, and there would be my career again. A charge had been laid upon me and I must follow the call. He said once with pathos in his voice, that at times he could not feel my presence. My real self had escaped him. I could tell from both his face and his voice that it hurt him terribly. It hurt me just as much to see him hurt. He really had nothing to worry about, but I could not make him see it. So there we were. Caught in a fiendish trap. We could not leave each other alone, and we could not shield each other from hurt. Our bitterest enemies could not have contrived more exquisite torture for us.

Another phase troubled me. As soon as he took his second degree, he was in line for bigger and better jobs. I began to feel that our love was slowing down his efforts. He had brains and character. He ought to go a long way. I grew terribly afraid that later on he would feel that I had thwarted him in a way and come to resent me. That was a scorching thought. Even if I married him, what about five years from now, the way we were going?

In the midst of this, I received my Guggenheim Fellowship. This was my chance to release him, and fight myself free from my obsession. He would get over me in a few months and go on to be a very big man. So I sailed off to Jamaica. But I freely admit that everywhere I set my feet down, there were tracks of blood. Blood from the very middle of my heart. I did not write because if I had written and he answered my letter, everything would have broken down.

So I pitched in to work hard on my research to smother my feelings. But the thing would not down. The plot was far from the circumstances, but I tried to embalm all the tenderness of my passion for him in "Their Eyes were Watching God."

When I returned to America after nearly two years in the Caribbean, I found that he had left his telephone number with my publishers. For some time, I did not use it. Not because I did not want to, but because the moment when I should hear his voice something would be in wait for me. It might be warm and eager. It might be cool and impersonal, just with overtones from the grave of things. So I went South and stayed several months before I ventured to use it. Even when I returned to New York it took me nearly two months to get up my courage. When I did make the call, I cursed myself for the delay. Here was the shy, warm man I had left.

Then we met and talked. We both were stunned by

the revelation that all along we had both thought and acted desperately in exile, and all to no purpose. We were still in the toils and after all my agony, I found out that he was a sucker for me, and he found out that I was in his bag. And I had a triumph that only a woman could understand. He had not turned into a tramp in my absence, but neither had he flamed like a newborn star in his profession. He confessed that he needed my aggravating presence to push him. He had settled down to a plodding desk job and reconciled himself. He had let his waistline go a bit and that bespoke his inside feeling. That made me happy no end. No woman wants a man all finished and perfect. You have to have something to work on and prod. That waistline went down in a jiffy and he began to discuss work-plans with enthusiasm. He could see something ahead of him besides time. I was happy. If he had been crippled in both legs, it would have suited me even better.

What will be the end? That is not for me to know. Life poses questions and that two-headed spirit that rules the beginning and end of things called Death, has all the answers. And even if I did know all, I am supposed to have some private business to myself. Whatever I do know, I have no intention of putting but so much in the public ears.

Perhaps the oath of Hercules shall always defeat me in love. Once when I was small and first coming upon the story of The Choice of Hercules, I was so impressed that I swore an oath to leave all pleasure and take the hard road of labor. Perhaps God heard me and wrote down my words in His book. I have thought so at times. Be that as it may, I have the satisfaction of knowing that I have loved and been loved by the perfect man. If I never hear of love again, I have known the real thing.

So much for what I know about the major courses in love. However, there are some minor courses which I have not grasped so well, and would be thankful for some coaching and advice.

First is the number of men who pant in my ear on short acquaintance, "You passionate thing! I can see you are just *burning* up! Most men would be disappointing to you. It takes a man like me for you. Ahhh! I know that you will just wreck me! Your eyes and your lips tell me a lot. You are a walking furnace!" This amazes me sometimes. Often when this is whispered gustily into my ear, I am feeling no more amorous than a charter member of the Union League Club. I may be thinking of turnip greens with dumplings, or more royalty checks, and here is a man who visualizes me on a divan sending the world up in smoke. It has happened so often that I have come to expect it. There must be something about me that looks sort of couchy. Maybe it is a birthmark. My mother could have been frightened by a bed. There is nothing to be done about it, I suppose. But, I must say about these mirages that seem to rise around me, that the timing is way off on occasion.

Number two is, a man may lose interest in me and go where his fancy leads him, and we can still meet as friends. But if I get tired and let on about it, he is certain to become an enemy of mine. That forces me to lie like the cross-ties from New York to Key West. I have learned to frame it so that I can claim to be deserted and devastated by him. Then he goes off with a sort of twilight tenderness for me, wondering what it is that he's got that brings so many women down! I do not even have to show real tears. All I need to do is show my stricken face and dash away from him to hide my supposed heartbreak and renunciation. He understands that I am fleeing before his allure so that I can be firm in my resolution to save the pieces. He knew all along that he was a hard man to resist, so he visualized my dampened pillow. It is a good thing that some of them have sent roses as a poultice and stayed away. Otherwise, they might have found the poor, heartbroken wreck of a thing all dressed to kill and gone out for a high-heel time with the new interest, who has the new interesting things to say and do. Now, how to break off without acting deceitful and still keep a friend?

Number three is kin to Number two, in a way. Under the spell of moonlight, music, flowers, or the cut and smell of good tweeds, I sometimes feel the divine urge for an hour, a day or maybe a week. Then it is gone and my interest returns to corn pone and mustard greens, or rubbing a paragraph with a soft cloth. Then my ex-sharer of a mood calls up in a fevered voice and reminds me of every silly thing I said, and eggs me on to say them all over again. It is the third presentation of turkey hash after Christmas. It is asking me to be a seven-sided liar. Accuses me of being faithless and inconsistent if I don't. There is no inconsistency there. I was sincere for the moment in which I said the things. It is strictly a matter of time. It was true for the moment, but the next day or the next week, is not that moment. No two moments are any more alike than two snowflakes. Like snowflakes, they get that same look from being so plentiful and falling so close together. But examine them closely and see the multiple differences between them. Each moment has its own task and capacity; doesn't melt down like snow and form again. It keeps its character forever. So the great difficulty lies in trying to transpose last night's moment to a day which has no knowledge of it. That look, that tender touch, was issued by the mint of the richest of all kingdoms. That same expression of today is utter counterfeit, or at best the wildest of inflation. What could be more zestless than passing out canceled checks? It is wrong to be called faithless under circumstances like that. What to do?

I have a strong suspicion, but I can't be sure, that much that passes for constant love is a golded-up moment walking in its sleep. Some people know that it is the walk of the dead, but in desperation and desolation, they have staked everything on life after death and the resurrection, so they haunt the graveyard. They build an altar on the tomb and wait there like faithful Mary for the stone to roll away. So the moment has authority over all of their lives. They pray constantly for the miracle of the moment to burst its bonds and spread out over time.

But pay no attention to what I say about love, for as I said before, it may not mean a thing. It is my own bathtub singing. Just because my mouth opens up like a prayer book, it does not just have to flap like a Bible. And then again, anybody whose mouth is cut cross-ways is given to lying, unconsciously as well as knowingly. So pay my few scattering remarks no mind as to love in general. I know only my part.

Anyway, it seems to be the unknown country from which no traveler ever returns. What seems to be a returning pilgrim is another person born in the strange country with the same-looking ears and hands. He is a stranger to the person who fared forth, and a stranger to family and old friends. He is clothed in mystery henceforth and forever. So, perhaps nobody knows, or can tell, any more than I. Maybe the old Negro folk rhyme tells all there is to know:

> Love is a funny thing; Love is a blossom;
> If you want your finger bit, poke it at a possum.

XV
Religion

You wouldn't think that a person who was born with God in the house would ever have any questions to ask on the subject.

But as early as I can remember, I was questing and seeking. It was not that I did not hear. I tumbled right into the Missionary Baptist Church when I was born. I saw the preachers and the pulpits, the people and the pews. Both at home and from the pulpit, I heard my father, known to thousands as "Reverend Jno" (an abbreviation for John) explain all about God's habits, His heaven, His ways and means. Everything was known and settled.

From the pews I heard a ready acceptance of all that Papa said. Feet beneath the pews beat out a rhythm as he pictured the scenery of heaven. Heads nodded with conviction in time to Papa's words. Tense snatches of tune broke out and some shouted until they fell into a trance at the recognition of what they heard from the pulpit. Come "love feast" * some of

* The "Love Feast" or "Experience Meeting" is a meeting held either the Friday night or the Sunday morning before Communion. Since no one is supposed to take Communion unless he or she is in harmony

the congregation told of getting close enough to peep
into God's sitting-room windows. Some went further.
They had been inside the place and looked all around.
They spoke of sights and scenes around God's throne.

That should have been enough for me. But somehow it left a lack in my mind. They should have
looked and acted differently from other people after
experiences like that. But these people looked and
acted like everybody else—or so it seemed to me.
They plowed, chopped wood, went possum-hunting,
washed clothes, raked up back yards and cooked
collard greens like anybody else. No more ornaments
and nothing. It mystified me. There were so many
things they neglected to look after while they were
right there in the presence of All-Power. I made up
my mind to do better than that if ever I made the trip.

I wanted to know, for instance, why didn't God
make grown babies instead of those little measly things
that messed up didies and cried all the time? What
was the sense in making babies with no teeth? He
knew that they had to have teeth, didn't He? So why
not give babies their teeth in the beginning instead
of hiding the toothless things in hollow stumps and
logs for grannies and doctors to find and give to people? He could see all the trouble people had with
babies, rubbing their gums and putting wood-lice
around their necks to get them to cut teeth. Why did

with all other members, there are great protestations of love and friendship. It is an opportunity to reaffirm faith plus anything the imagination might dictate.

God hate for children to play on Sundays? If Christ, God's son, hated to die, and God hated for Him to die and have everybody grieving over it ever since, why did He have to do it? Why did people die anyway?

It was explained to me that Christ died to save the world from sin and then too, so that folks did not have to die any more. That was a simple, clear-cut explanation. But then I heard my father and other preachers accusing people of sin. They went so far as to say that people were so prone to sin, that they sinned with every breath they drew. You couldn't even breathe without sinning! How could that happen if we had already been saved from it? So far as the dying part was concerned, I saw enough funerals to know that somebody was dying. It seemed to me that somebody had been fooled and I so stated to my father and two of his colleagues. When they got through with me, I knew better than to say that out loud again, but their shocked and angry tirades did nothing for my bewilderment. My head was full of misty fumes of doubt.

Neither could I understand the passionate declarations of love for a being that nobody could see. Your family, your puppy and the new bull-calf, yes. But a spirit away off who found fault with everybody all the time, that was more than I could fathom. When I was asked if I loved God, I always said yes because I knew that that was the thing I was supposed to say. It was a guilty secret with me for a long time. I did not dare ask even my chums if they meant it when they said they loved God with all their souls and minds and hearts, and would be glad to die if He wanted them to. Maybe they had found out how to do it, and I was afraid of what they might say if they found out I hadn't. Maybe they wouldn't even play with me any more.

As I grew, the questions went to sleep in me. I just said the words, made the motions and went on. My father being a preacher, and my mother superintendent of the Sunday School, I naturally was always having to do with religious ceremonies. I even enjoyed participation at times; I was moved, not by the spirit, but by action, more or less dramatic.

I liked revival meetings particularly. During these meetings the preacher let himself go. God was called by all of His praise-giving names. The scenery of heaven was described in detail. Hallelujah Avenue and Amen Street were paved with gold so fine that you couldn't drop a pea on them but what they rang like chimes. Hallelujah Avenue ran north and south across heaven, and was tuned to sound alto and bass. Amen Street ran east and west and was tuned to "treble" and tenor. These streets crossed each other right in front of the throne and made harmony all the time. Yes, and right there on that corner was where all the loved ones who had gone on before would be waiting for those left behind.

Oh yes! They were all there in their white robes with the glittering crowns on their heads, golden girdles clasped about their waists and shoes of jeweled gold on their feet, singing the hallelujah song and waiting. And as they walked up and down the golden streets, their shoes would sing, "sol me, sol do" at every step.

Hell was described in dramatic fury. Flames of fire leaped up a thousand miles from the furnaces of Hell, and raised blisters on a sinning man's back before he hardly got started downward. Hell-hounds pursued their ever-dying souls. Everybody under the sound of the preacher's voice was warned, while yet they were on pleading terms with mercy, to take steps to be sure that they would not be a brand in that eternal burning.

Sinners lined the mourner's bench from the opening night of the revival. Before the week was over, several or all of them would be "under conviction." People, solemn of face, crept off to the woods to "praying ground" to seek religion. Every church member worked on them hard, and there was great clamor and rejoicing when any of them "come through" religion.

The pressure on the unconverted was stepped up by music and high drama. For instance I have seen my father stop preaching suddenly and walk down to the front edge of the pulpit and breathe into a whispered song. One of his most effective ones was:

Run! Run! Run to the City of Refuge, children!
Run! Oh, run! Or else you'll be consumed.

The congregation working like a Greek chorus behind him, would take up the song and the mood and
hold it over for a while even after he had gone back
into the sermon at high altitude:

Are you ready-ee? Hah!
For that great day, hah!
When the moon shall drape her face in mourning, hah!
And the sun drip down in blood, hah!
When the stars, hah!
Shall burst forth from their diamond sockets, hah!
And the mountains shall skip like lambs, hah!
Havoc will be there, my friends, hah!
With her jaws wide open, hah!
And the sinner-man, hah!
He will run to the rocks, hah!
And cry, Oh rocks! Hah!
Hide me! Hah!
Hide me from the face of an angry God, hah!
Hide me, Ohhhhhh!
But the rocks shall cry, hah!
Git away! Sinner man git away, hah!

(Tense harmonic chant seeps over the audience.)

	You run to de rocks,
CHORUS:	You can't hide
SOLOIST:	Oh, you run to de rocks
CHORUS:	Can't hide
SOLOIST:	Oh, run to de mountain, you can't hide
ALL:	Can't hide sinner, you can't hide.
	Rocks cry " 'I'm burning too, hah!
	In the eternal burning, hah!
	Sinner man! Hah!

Where will you stand? Hah!
In that great gittin'-up morning? Hah!

The congregation would be right in there at the right moment bearing Papa up and heightening the effect of the fearsome picture a hundredfold. The more susceptible would be swept away on the tide and "come through" shouting, and the most reluctant would begin to waver. Seldom would there be anybody left at the mourners' bench when the revival meeting was over. I have seen my father "bring through" as many as seventy-five in one two-week period of revival. Then a day would be set to begin the induction into the regular congregation. The first thing was to hear their testimony or Christian experience, and thus the congregation could judge whether they had really "got religion" or whether they were faking and needed to be sent back to "lick de calf over" again.

It was exciting to hear them tell their "visions." This was known as admitting people to the church on "Christian experience." This was an exciting time.

These visions are traditional. I knew them by heart as did the rest of the congregation, but still it was exciting to see how the converts would handle them. Some of them made up new details. Some of them would forget a part and improvise clumsily or fill up the gap with shouting. The audience knew, but everybody acted as if every word of it was new.

First they told of suddenly becoming conscious that

they had to die. They became conscious of their sins. They were Godly sorry. But somehow, they could not believe. They started to pray. They prayed and they prayed to have their sins forgiven and their souls converted. While they laid under conviction, the hell-hounds pursued them as they ran for salvation. They hung over Hell by one strand of hair. Outside of the meeting, any of the listeners would have laughed at the idea of anybody with hair as close to their heads as ninety-nine is to a hundred hanging over Hell or anywhere else by a strand of that hair. But it was part of the vision and the congregation shuddered and groaned at the picture in a fervent manner. The vision must go on. While the seeker hung there, flames of fire leaped up and all but destroyed their ever-dying souls. But they called on the name of Jesus and immediately that dilemma was over. They then found themselves walking over Hell on a foot-log so narrow that they had to put one foot right in front of the other while the howling hell-hounds pursued them relentlessly. Lord! They saw no way of rescue. But they looked on the other side and saw a little white man and he called to them to come there. So they called the name of Jesus and suddenly they were on the other side. He poured the oil of salvation into their souls and, hallelujah! They never expect to turn back. But still they wouldn't believe. So they asked God, if he had saved their souls, to give them a sign. If their sins were forgiven and their souls set free, please move that big star in the west over to the east. The star moved over. But still they wouldn't believe. If they were really saved, please move that big oak tree across the road. The tree skipped across the road and kept on growing just like it had always been there. Still they didn't believe. So they asked God for one more sign. Would He please make the sun shout so they could be sure. At that God got mad and said He had shown them all the signs He intended to. If they still didn't believe, He would send their bodies to the grave, where the worm never dies, and their souls to Hell, where the fire is never quenched. So then they cried out "I believe! I believe!" Then the dungeon shook and their chains fell off. "Glory! I know I got religion! I know I been converted and my soul set free! I never will forget that day when the morning star bust in my soul. I never expect to turn back!"

The convert shouted. Ecstatic cries, snatches of chants, old converts shouting in frenzy with the new. When the tumult finally died down, the pastor asks if the candidate is acceptable and there is unanimous consent. He or she is given the right hand of fellowship, and the next candidate takes the floor. And so on to the end.

I know now that I liked that part because it was high drama. I liked the baptisms in the lake too, and the funerals for the same reason. But of the inner thing, I was right where I was when I first began to seek answers.

Away from the church after the emotional fire had died down, there were little jokes about some of the testimony. For instance a deacon said in my hearing, "Sister Seeny ought to know better than to be worrying God about moving the sun for her. She asked Him to move de tree to convince her, and He done it. Then she took and asked Him to move a star for her and He done it. But when she kept on worrying Him about moving the sun, He took and told her, says, 'I don't mind moving that tree for you, and I don't mind moving a star just to pacify your mind, because I got plenty of *them*. I aint got but one sun, Seeny, and I aint going to be shoving it around to please you and nobody else. I'd like mighty much for you to believe, but if you can't believe without me moving my sun for you, you can just go right on to Hell.' "

The thing slept on in me until my college years without any real decision. I made the necessary motions and forgot to think. But when I studied both history and philosophy, the struggle began again.

When I studied the history of the great religions of the world, I saw that even in his religion man carried himself along. His worship of strength was there. God was made to look that way too. We see the Emperor Constantine, as pagan as he could lay in his hide, having his famous vision of the cross with the injunction: *"In Hoc Signo Vinces,"* and arising next day not only to win a great battle, but to start out on his missionary journey with his sword. He could not sing like Peter, and he could not preach like Paul. He probably did not even have a good straining voice like my father to win converts and influence people. But he had his good points—one of them being a sword—and a seasoned army. And the way he brought sinners to repentance was nothing short of miraculous. Whole tribes and nations fell under conviction just as soon as they heard he was on the way. They did not wait for any stars to move, nor trees to jump the road. By the time he crossed the border, they knew they had been converted. Their testimony was in on Christian experience and they were all ready for the right hand of fellowship and baptism. It seems that Reverend Brother Emperor Constantine carried the gospel up and down Europe with his revival meetings to such an extent that Christianity really took on. In Rome where Christians had been looked upon as rather indifferent lion-bait at best, and among other things as keepers of virgins in their homes for no real good to the virgins, Christianity mounted. Where before, Emperors could scarcely find enough of them to keep the spectacles going, now they were everywhere, in places high and low. The arrow had left the bow. Christianity was on its way to world power that would last. That was only the beginning. Military power was to be called in time and time again to carry forward the gospel of peace. There is not apt to be any difference of opinion between you and a dead man.

It was obvious that two men, both outsiders, had

given my religion its chances of success. First the Apostle Paul, who had been Saul, the erudite Pharisee, had arisen with a vision when he fell off of his horse on the way to Damascus. He not only formulated the religion, but exerted his brilliant mind to carry it to the most civilized nations of his time. Then Constantine took up with force where Paul left off with persuasion.

I saw the same thing with different details, happen in all the other great religions, and seeing these things, I went to thinking and questing again. I have achieved a certain peace within myself, but perhaps the seeking after the inner heart of truth will never cease in me. All sorts of interesting speculations arise.

So, having looked at the subject from many sides, studied beliefs by word of mouth and then as they fit into great rigid forms, I find I know a great deal about form, but little or nothing about the mysteries I sought as a child. As the ancient tent-maker said, I have come out of the same door wherein I went.

But certain things have seemed to me to be true as I heard the tongues of those who had speech, and listened at the lips of books. It seems to me to be true that heavens are placed in the sky because it is the unreachable. The unreachable and therefore the unknowable always seems divine—hence, religion. People need religion because the great masses fear life and its consequences. Its responsibilities weigh heavy. Feeling a weakness in the face of great forces, men seek an alliance with omnipotence to bolster up their feeling of weakness, even though the omnipotence they rely upon is a creature of their own minds. It gives them a feeling of security. Strong, self-determining men are notorious for their lack of reverence. Constantine, having converted millions to Christianity by the sword, himself refused the consolation of Christ until his last hour. Some say not even then.

As for me, I do not pretend to read God's mind. If He has a plan of the universe worked out to the smallest detail, it would be folly for me to presume to get down on my knees and attempt to revise it. That, to me, seems the highest form of sacrilege. So I do not pray. I accept the means at my disposal for working out my destiny. It seems to me that I have been given a mind and will-power for that very purpose. I do not expect God to single me out and grant me advantages over my fellow men. Prayer is for those who need it. Prayer seems to me a cry of weakness, and an attempt to avoid, by trickery, the rules of the game as laid down. I do not choose to admit weakness. I accept the challenge of responsibility. Life, as it is, does not frighten me, since I have made my peace with the universe as I find it, and bow to its laws. The ever-sleepless sea in its bed, crying out "How long?" to Time; million-formed and never motionless flame; the contemplation of these two aspects alone, affords me sufficient food for ten spans of my expected lifetime. It seems to me that organized creeds are collections of words around a wish. I feel no need for such. However, I would not, by word or deed, attempt to deprive another of the consolation it affords. It is simply not for me. Somebody else may have my rapturous glance at the archangels. The springing of the yellow line of morning out of the misty deep of dawn, is glory enough for me. I know that nothing is destructible; things merely change forms. When the consciousness we know as life ceases, I know that I shall still be part and parcel of the world. I was a part before the sun rolled into shape and burst forth in the glory of change. I was, when the earth was hurled out from its fiery rim. I shall return with the earth to Father Sun, and still exist in substance when the sun has lost its fire, and disintegrated in infinity to perhaps become a part of the whirling rubble in space. Why fear? The stuff of my being is matter, ever changing, ever moving, but never lost; so what need of denominations and creeds to deny myself the comfort of all my fellow men? The wide belt of the universe has no need for finger-rings. I am one with the infinite and need no other assurance.

XVI
Looking Things Over

Well, that is the way things stand up to now. I can look back and see sharp shadows, high lights, and smudgy inbetweens. I have been in Sorrow's kitchen and licked out all the pots. Then I have stood on the peaky mountain wrappen in rainbows, with a harp and a sword in my hands.

What I had to swallow in the kitchen has not made me less glad to have lived, nor made me want to low-rate the human race, nor any whole sections of it. I take no refuge from myself in bitterness. To me, bitterness is the under-arm odor of wishful weakness. It is the graceless acknowledgment of defeat. I have no urge to make any concessions like that to the world as yet. I might be like that some day, but I doubt it. I am in the struggle with the sword in my hands, and I don't intend to run until you run me. So why give off the smell of something dead under the house while I am still in there tussling with my sword in my hand?

If tough breaks have not soured me, neither have my glory-moments caused me to build any altars to myself where I can burn incense before God's best job of work. My sense of humor will always stand in the way of my seeing myself, my family, my race or my nation as the whole intent of the universe. When I see what we really are like, I know that God is too great an artist for we folks on my side of the creek to be all of His best works. Some of His finest touches are among us, without doubt, but some more of His masterpieces are among those folks who live over the creek.

So looking back and forth in history and around the temporary scene, I do not visualize the moon dripping down in blood, nor the sun batting his fiery eyes and laying down in the cradle of eternity to rock himself into sleep and slumber at instances of human self-bias. I know that the sun and the moon must be used to sights like that by now. I too yearn for universal justice, but how to bring it about is another thing. It is such a complicated thing, for justice, like beauty, is in the eye of the beholder. There is universal agreement on the principle, but the application brings on the fight. Oh, for some disinterested party to pass on things! Somebody will hurry to tell me that we voted God to the bench for that. But the lawyers who interpret His opinions, make His decisions sound just like they made them up themselves. Being an idealist, I too wish that the world was better than I am. Like all the rest of my fellow men, I don't want to live around people with no more principles than I have. My inner fineness is continually outraged at finding that the world is a whole family of Hurstons.

Seeing these things, I have come to the point by trying to make the day at hand a positive thing, and realizing the uselessness of gloominess.

Therefore, I see nothing but futility in looking back over my shoulder in rebuke at the grave of some white man who has been dead too long to talk about. That is just what I would be doing in trying to fix the blame for the dark days of slavery and the Reconstruction. From what I can learn, it was sad. Certainly. But my ancestors who lived and died in it are dead. The white men who profited by their labor and lives are dead also. I have no personal memory of those times, and no responsibility for them. Neither has the grandson of the man who held my folks. So I see no need in button-holing that grandson like the Ancient Mariner did the wedding guest and calling for the High Sheriff to put him under arrest.

I am not so stupid as to think that I would be bringing this descendant of a slave-owner any news. He has heard just as much about the thing as I have. I am not so humorless as to visualize this grandson falling out on the sidewalk before me, and throwing an acre of fits in remorse because his old folks held slaves. No, indeed! If it happened to be a fine day and he had had a nice breakfast, he might stop and answer me like this:

"In the first place, I was not able to get any better view of social conditions from my grandmother's womb than you could from your grandmother's. Let us say for the sake of argument that I detest the institution of slavery and all that it implied, just as much as you do. You must admit that I had no more power to do anything about it in my unborn state than you had in yours. Why fix your eyes on me? I respectfully refer you to my ancestors, and bid you a good day."

If I still lingered before him, he might answer me further by asking questions like this:

"Are you so simple as to assume that the Big Surrender (Southerners, both black and white speak of Lee's surrender to Grant as the Big Surrender) banished the concept of human slavery from the earth? What is the principle of slavery? Only the literal buying and selling of human flesh on the block? That was only an outside symbol. Real slavery is couched in the desire and the efforts of any man or community to live and advance their interests at the expense of the lives and interests of others. All of the outward signs come out of that. Do you not realize that the power, prestige and prosperity of the greatest nations on earth rests on colonies and sources of raw materials? Why else are great wars waged? If you have not thought, then why waste up time with your vapid accusations? If you have, then why single *me* out?" And like Pilate, he will light a cigar, and stroll on off without waiting for an answer.

Anticipating such an answer, I have no intention of wasting my time beating on old graves with a club. I know that I cannot pry aloose the clutching hand of Time, so I will turn all my thoughts and energies on the present. I will settle for from now on.

And why not? For me to pretend that I am Old Black Joe and waste my time on his problems, would be just as ridiculous as for the government of Winston Churchill to bill the Duke of Normandy the first of every month, or for the Jews to hang around the pyramids trying to picket Old Pharaoh. While I have a handkerchief over my eyes crying over the landing of the first slaves in 1619, I might miss something swell that is going on in 1942. Furthermore, if somebody were to consider my grandmother's ungranted wishes, and give *me* what *she* wanted, I would be too put out for words.

What do I want, then? I will tell you in a parable. A Negro deacon was down on his knees praying at a wake held for a sister who had died that day. He had his eyes closed and was going great guns, when he noticed that he was not getting any more "amens" from the rest. He opened his eyes and saw that everybody else was gone except himself and the dead woman. Then he saw the reason. The supposedly dead woman was trying to sit up. He bolted for the door himself, but it slammed shut so quickly that it caught his flying coat-tails and held him sort of static. "Oh, no Gabriel!" the deacon shouted, "dat aint no way for you to do. I can do my own running, but you got to 'low me the same chance as the rest."

I don't know any more about the future than you do. I hope that it will be full of work, because I have come to know by experience that work is the nearest thing to happiness that I can find. No matter what else I have among the things that humans want, I go to pieces in a short while if I do not work. What all my work shall be, I don't know that either, every hour being a stranger to you until you live it. I want a busy life, a just mind and a timely death.

But if I should live to be very old, I have laid plans for that so that it will not be too tiresome. So far, I have never used coffee, liquor, nor any form of stimulant. When I get old, and my joints and bones tell me about it, I can sit around and write for myself, if for nobody else, and read slowly and carefully the mysticism of the East, and re-read Spinoza with love and care. All the while my days can be a succession of coffee cups. Then when the sleeplessness of old age attacks me, I can have a likker bottle snug in my pantry and sip away and sleep. Get mellow and think kindly of the world. I think I can be like that because I have known the joy and pain of deep friendship. I have served and been served. I have made some good enemies for which I am not a bit sorry. I have loved unselfishly, and I have fondled hatred with the red-hot tongs of Hell. That's living.

I have no race prejudice of any kind. My kinfolks, and my "skin-folks" are dearly loved. My own circumference of everyday life is there. But I see their same virtues and vices everywhere I look. So I give you all my right hand of fellowship and love, and hope for the same from you. In my eyesight, you lose nothing by not looking just like me. I will remember you all in my good thoughts, and I ask you kindly to do the same for me. Not only just me. You, who play the zig-zag lightning of power over the world, with the grumbling thunder in your wake, think kindly of those who walk in the dust. And you who walk in humble places, think kindly too, of others. There has been no proof in the world so far that you would be less arrogant if you held the lever of power in your hands. Let us all be kissing-friends. Consider that with tolerance and patience, we godly demons may breed a noble world in a few hundred generations or so. Maybe all of us who do not have the good fortune to meet, or meet again, in this world, will meet at a barbecue.

APPENDIX

Zora Neale Hurston gave the manuscript of *Dust Tracks on a Road* to the James Weldon Johnson collection at Yale University's Beinecke Library in response to Carl Van Vechten's request. She noted in the January 14, 1942, dedication of the manuscript to the collection: "Parts of the manuscript were not used in the final composition of the book for publisher's reasons."

The manuscript is in Box I of the Hurston Papers, beginning with folder 10 and extending to Folder 15. Folders 12–15 contain a typed manuscript that was clearly the final version, and the published book was typeset from this typescript. Folders 10 and 11 include both typescript and autograph chapters that either were excised from the final version or were substantially altered prior to printing.

I have included three of these later chapters here, because they provide valuable insights into Hurston's process of composition. "My People, My People!" did become Chapter 12 of the published book, but in a much revised form. It is significant because Hurston talks much more frankly about race in this manuscript version than in the autobiography. Written in 1937, while she was in Haiti, the chapter demonstrates once again the difficulty of fixing Hurston's thoughts on the subject.

"The Inside Light—Being a Salute to Friendship," written just before the book was sent to the publisher, reveals Hurston's capacity for friendship, and her willingness to publicize the attachments. It is a useful chapter for those tracking down people who knew Hurston, and particularly valuable for Hurston's characterization of the relationship with Fannie Hurst, which differs somewhat from the published version.

The most important of the three, however, is "Seeing the World as It Is," which contains very controversial statements about both race and politics. Obviously written prior to December 7, 1941, the chapter contains too many anti-American statements to be published after Pearl Harbor. Significantly, this chapter was intended to be the final chapter in the first draft of the book, which makes Hurston's pro-Japanese statements and her criticism of U.S. imperialism even more noteworthy. Apparently she wished initially to end on this radical note.

In all, the three chapters reveal a writer at work, one who benefited from her editor's advice, but one who also had her true feelings considerably distorted by the editorial process. With this appendix we have a better feeling for Hurston the writer, who obviously did not feel that her international opinions were "irrelevant" to her autobiography—as her editor claimed—or that her views of her people needed to be filtered through the editorial apparatus.

The text printed here reproduces Hurston's words faithfully, although a few misspellings and punctuation errors have been corrected to insure that the passages read smoothly.

"My People, My People!"

"My People, My People!" This very minute, nations of people are moaning it and shaking their heads with a sigh. Thousands and millions of people are uttering it in different parts of the globe. Differences of geography and language make differences in sound, that's all. The sentiment is the same. Yet and still it is a private wail, sacred to my people.

Not that the expression is hard to hear. It is being thrown around with freedom. It is the interpretation that is difficult. No doubt hundreds of outsiders standing around have heard it often enough, but only those who have friended with us like Carl Van Vechten know what it means.

Which ever way you go to describe it—the cry, the sigh, the wail, the groaning grin or grinning groan of "My People, My People!" bursts from us when we see sights that bring on despair.

Say that a brown young woman, fresh from the classic halls of Barnard College and escorted by a black boy from Yale, enters the subway at 50th street. They are well-dressed, well-mannered and good to look at. The eyes of the entire coach agree on that. They are returning from a concert by Marian Anderson and are still vibrating from her glowing tones. They are saying happy things about the tribute the huge white audience paid her genius and her arts. Oh yes, they say, "The Race is going to amount to something after all. Definitely! Look at George W. Carver and Ernest Just and Abram Harris, and Barthe is getting on right well with his sculpture and E. Simms Campbell is holding his own on *Esquire* and oh yes, Charles S. Johnson isn't doing so badly either. Paul Robeson, E. Franklin Frazier, Roland Hayes, well you just take them for granted. There is hope indeed for the Race."

By that time the train pulls into 72nd street. Two scabby-looking Negroes come scrambling into the coach. The coach is not full. There are plenty of seats, but no matter how many vacant seats there are, no other place will do, except side by side with the Yale-Barnard couple. No, indeed! Being dirty and smelly, do they keep quiet otherwise? A thousand times, No! They woof, bookoo, broadcast, and otherwise distriminate [*sic*] from one end of the coach to the other. They consider it a golden opportunity to put on a show. Everybody in the coach being new to them, they naturally have not heard about the way one of the pair beat his woman on Lenox Avenue. Therefore they must be told in great detail what led up to the fracas, how many teeth he knocked out during the fight, and what happened after. His partner is right there, isn't he? Well, all right now. He's in the conversation, too, so he must talk out of his mouth and let the coach know just how he fixed *his* woman up when she tried that same on *him*.

Barnard and Yale sit there and dwindle and dwindle. They do not look around the coach to see what is in the faces of the white passengers. They know too well what is there. Some are grinning from the heel up, and some are stonily quiet. But both kinds are thinking "That's just like a Negro." Not just like *some* Negroes, mind you, no, like all. Only difference is some Negroes are better dressed. Feeling all of this like rock-salt under the skin, Yale and Barnard shake their heads and moan, "My People, My People!"

Maybe at the other end of the coach another couple are saying the same thing but with a different emotion. They say it with a chuckle. They have enjoyed the show, and they are saying in the same tone of voice that a proud father uses when he boasts to others about that bad little boy of his at home. "Mischievous, into everything, beats up all the kids in the neighborhood. Don't know what I'm going to do with the little rascal." That's the way some folks say the thing.

Certain of My People have come to dread railway day coaches for this same reason. They dread such scenes more than they do the dirty upholstery and other inconveniences of a Jim Crow coach. They detest the forced grouping. The railroad company feels

"you are all colored aren't you? So why not all together? If you are not all alike, *that's your own fault*.
Once upon a time you were all alike. You had no business to change. If you are not that way, then it's just
too bad. You're supposed to be like that." So when
sensitive souls are forced to travel that way they sit
there numb and when some free soul takes off his
shoes and socks, they mutter, "My race but not My
taste." When somebody else eats fried fish, bananas,
and a mess of peanuts and throws all the leavings on
the floor, they gasp, "My skinfolks but not my kinfolks." And sadly over all, they keep sighing, "My People, My People!"

Who are My People? I would say all those hosts
spoken of as Negroes, Colored folks, Aunt Hagar's
chillum, the brother in black, Race men and women,
and My People. They range in color from Walter
White, white through high yaller, yaller, Punkin color,
high brown, vaseline brown, seal brown, black, smooth
black, dusty black, rusty black, coal black, lam black,
and damn black. My People there in the south of the
world, the east of the world, in the west, and even
some few in the north. Still and all, you can't just
point out my people by skin color.

White people have come running to me with a deep
wrinkle between the eyes asking me things. They have
heard talk going around about this passing, so they
are trying to get some information so they can know.

So, since I have been asked, that gives me leave to talk right out of my mouth.

In the first place, this passing business works both ways. All the passing is not passing for white. We have white folks among us passing for colored. They just happened to be born with a tinge of brown in the skin and took up being colored as a profession. Take James Weldon Johnson, for instance.

There's a man white enough to suit Hitler, and he's been passing for colored for years.

Now, don't get the idea that he is not welcome among us. He certainly is. He has more than paid his way. But he just is not a Negro. You take a look at him and ask why I talk like that. But you know, I told you back there not to depend too much on skin. You'll certainly get mis-put on your road if you put too much weight on that. Look at James Weldon Johnson from head to foot, but don't let that skin color and that oskobolic hair fool you. Watch him! Does he parade when he walks? No, he smiles. He couldn't give a grin if he tried. He can't even Uncle Tom. Not that I complain of "Tomming" if it's done right.

"Tomming" is not an aggressive act, it is true, but it has its uses like feinting in the prize ring. But James Weldon Johnson can't Tom. He has been seen trying it, but it was sad. Let him look around at some of the other large Negroes, and hand over the dice.

No, I never expect to see James Weldon Johnson a

success in the strictly Negro Arts, but I would not be at all surprised to see him crowned. The man is just full of that old monarch material. If some day I looked out of my window on Seventh Avenue and saw him in an ermine robe and a great procession going to the Cathedral of St. John the Divine to be crowned I wouldn't be a bit surprised. Maybe he'd make a mighty fine king at that. He's tried all he knew how to pass for colored, but he just hasn't made it. His own brother is scared in his presence. He bows and scrapes and calls him The Duke.

So now you say "Well, if you can't tell who my people are by skin color, how are you going to know?" There's more ways than one of telling, and I'm going to point them out right now.

A

Wait until you see a congregation of more than two dark-complected people. If they can't agree on a single, solitary thing, then you can go off satisfied. Those are My People. It's just against nature for us to agree with each other. We not only refuse to agree, we'll get mad and fight about it. *But only each other!* Anybody else can cool us off right now. We fly hot quick, but we are easily cooled when we find out the person who made us mad is not another Negro.

There is the folk-tale of the white man who hired five men to take hold of a rope to pull up a cement block. They caught hold and gave a yank and the little stone flew way up to the pulley the first time. The men looked at one 'nother in surprise, and so one of them said to the bossman: "Boss, how come you hire all of us to pull up that óne little piece of rock? One man could do that by hisself." "Yeah, I know it," the bossman told him, "but I just wanted to see five Negroes pulling together once." Then there is the story of the man who was called on to pray. He got down and he said, "Oh Lord, I want to ask something, but I know you can't do it. I just *know* you can't do it." Then he took a long pause.

Somebody got restless and said, "Go ahead and ask Him. That's God you talking to. He can do anything."

The man who was praying said, "I know He is supposed to do all things, but this what I wants to ask."

"Aw go on and ask Him. God A'Mighty can do anything. Go on, brother, and ask Him and finish up your prayer."

"Well, alright, I'll ask Him. O Lord, I'm asking you because they tell me to go ahead. I'm asking you something, but I just know you can't do it. I just *know* you can't do it, but I'll just ask you. Lord, I'm asking you to bring my people together, but I *know* you can't do it, Lord. Amen."

Maybe the Lord *can* do it, but he hasn't done it yet.

It do say in the Bible that the Lord started the disturbance himself. It was the sons of Ham who built the first big city and started the tower of Babel. They were singing and building their way to heaven when the Lord came down and confused their tongues. We haven't built no more towers and things like that, but we still got the confusion. The other part about the building and what not may be just a folk-tale, but we've got proof about the tongue power.

So when you find a set of folks who won't agree on a thing, those are My People.

B

If you have your doubts, go and listen to the man. If he hunts for six big words where one little one would do, that's My People. If he can't find that big word, he's feeling for, he is going to make a new one. But somehow or other that new-made word fits the thing it was made for. Sounds good, too. Take for instance the time when the man needed the word *slander* and he didn't know it. He just made the word distriminate [*sic*] and anybody that heard the word would know what he meant. "Don't distriminate [*sic*] de woman." Somebody didn't know the word total nor entire so they made bodacious. Then there's asterperious, and so on. When you find a man chewing up the dictionary and spitting out language, that's My People.

C

If you still have doubts, study the man and watch his ways. See if all of him fits into today. If he has no memory of yesterday, nor no concept of tomorrow, then he is My People. There is no tomorrow in the man. He mentions the word plentiful and often. But there is no real belief in a day that is not here and present. For him to believe in a tomorrow would mean an obligation to consequences. There is no sense of consequences. Else he is not My People.

D

If you are still not satisfied, put down two piles of money. Do not leave less than a thousand dollars in one pile, and do not leave more than a dollar and a quarter in the other. Expose these two sums where they are equally easy to take. If he takes the thousand dollars, he is not My People. That is settled. My People never steal more than a dollar and a quarter. This test is one of the strongest.

E

But the proof positive is the recognition of the monkey as our brother. No matter where you find the brother in black, he is telling a story about his brother the monkey. Different languages and geography, but that same tenderness. There is recognition everywhere of the monkey as a brother. Whenever we want to poke a little fun at ourselves, we throw the cloak of our shortcomings over the monkey. This is the American classic:

The monkey was playing in the road one day and a

big new Cadillac come down the road full of white people. The driver saw the monkey and drove sort of to one side and went on. Several more cars came by and never troubled the monkey at all. Way after while here come long a Ford car full of colored folks. The driver was showing off, washing his foot in the gas tank. The car could do 60 and he was doing 70 (He had the accelerator down to the floor). Instead of slowing up when he saw the monkey, he got faster and tried to run over him. The monkey just barely escaped by jumping way to one side. The Negro hollered at him and said, "Why de hell don't you git out of de way? You see me washing my feet in the gas tank! I ought to kill you." By that time they went on down the road. The monkey sat there and shook his head and said, "My People, My People!" However, Georgette Harvey, that superb actress, said that she had spoken with our brother the monkey recently and he does not say "My People" any more. She says the last monkey she talked with was saying "Those People, Those People!" Maybe he done quit the Race. Walked out cold on the family.

F

If you look at a man and mistrust your eyes, do something and see if he will imitate you right away. If he does, that's My People. We love to imitate. We would rather do a good imitation than any amount of some-

thing original. Nothing is half so good as something
that is just like something else. And no title is so cov-
eted as the "black this or that." Roland Hayes is right
white folksy that way. He has pointedly refused the
title of "The Black Caruso." It's got to be Roland
Hayes or nothing. But he is exceptional that way. We
have Black Patti, Black Yankees, Black Giants. Rose
McClendon was referred to time and again as the
Black Barrymore. Why we even had a Black Dillinger!
He was the Negro that Dillinger carried out of Crown
Point when he made his famous wooden gun escape.
Of course he didn't last but a day or two after he got
back to Detroit or Buffalo, or where ever he was be-
fore the police gave him a black-out. He could have
kept quiet and lived a long time perhaps, but he
would rather risk dying than to miss wearing his title.
As far as he was able, he was old Dillinger himself.
Julian, the parachute jumper, risked his life by falling
in the East River pretending he knew how to run an
aeroplane like Lindbergh to gain his title of Black
Eagle. Lindbergh landed in Paris and Julian landed in
New York harbor, but, anyhow, he flew some.

What did Haiti ever do to make the world glad it
happened? Well, they held a black revolution right
behind the white one in France. And now their Senators and Deputies go around looking like cartoons of
French Ministers and Senators in spade whiskers and
other goatee forms. They wave their hands and arms

and explain about their Latin temperaments, but it is not impressive. If you didn't hear them talk, in a bunch, they could be Adam Powell's Abbysinia Baptist Church turning out, and nobody would know the difference.

In Jamaica, the various degrees of Negroes put on some outward show to impress you that no matter what your eyes tell you, that they are really white folks—*white* English folks inside. The moment you meet a mulatto there he makes an opportunity to tell you who his father was. You are bound to hear a lot about that Englishman or that Scot. But never a word about the black mama. It is as if she didn't exist. Had never existed at all. You get the impression that Jamaica is the place where roosters lay eggs. That these Englishmen come there and without benefit of females they just scratch out a nest and lay an egg that hatches out a Jamaican.

As badly as the Ethiopians hated to part with Haile Selassie and freedom, it must be some comfort to have Mussolini for a model. By now, all the Rasses and other big shots are tootching out their lips ferociously, gritting their teeth and otherwise making faces like Il Duce. And I'll bet you a fat man against sweet back that all the little boy Ethiopians are doing a mean pouter pigeon strut around Addis Ababa.

And right here in these United States, we don't miss doing a thing that the white folks do, possible or impossible. Education, Sports, keeping up with the Joneses and the whole shebang. The unanswerable retort to criticism is "The white folks do it, don't they?" In Mobile, Alabama, I saw the Millionaires' ball. A man who roomed in the same house with me got me a ticket and carried me to a seat in the balcony. He warned me not to come down on the dance floor until the first dance was over. The Millionaires and their lady friends would want the floor all to themselves for that dance. It was very special. I was duly impressed, I tell you.

The ball opened with music. A fairly good dance orchestra was on the job. That first dance, exclusively for the Millionaires, was announced and each Millionaire and his lady friend were announced by name as they took the floor.

"John D. Rockefeller, dancing with Miss Selma Jones!" I looked down and out walked Mr. Rockefeller in a pair of white wool pants with a black pin stripe, pink silk shirt without a coat because it was summer time. Ordinarily Mr. Rockefeller delivered hats for a millinery shop, but not tonight.

Commodore Vanderbilt was announced and took the floor. The Commodore was so thin in his ice-cream pants that he just had no behind at all. Mr. Ford pranced out with his lady doing a hot cut-out. J. P. Morgan entered doing a mean black-bottom, and so on. Also each Millionaire presented his lady friend with a five-dollar gold piece after the dance. It was reasoned the Millionaires would have done the same for the same pleasure.

G

Last but not least, My People love a show. We love to act more than we love to see acting done. We love to look at them and we love to put them on, and we love audiences when we get to specifying. That's why some of us take advantage of trains and other public places like dance halls and picnics. We just love to dramatize.

Now you've been told, so you ought to know. But maybe, after all the Negro doesn't really exist. What we think is a race is detached moods and phases of other people walking around. What we have been talking about might not exist at all. Could be the shade patterns of something else thrown on the ground—other folks, seen in shadow. And even if we do exist it's all an accident anyway. God made everybody else's color. We took ours by mistake. The way the old folks tell it, it was like this, you see.

God didn't make people all of a sudden. He made folks by degrees. First he stomped out the clay and then he cut out the patterns and propped 'em against the fence to dry. Then after they was dry, He took and blowed the breath of life into 'em and sent 'em on off. Next day He told everybody to come up and get toenails. So everybody come and got their toenails and fingernails and went on off. Another time He said for

everybody to come get their Nose and Mouth because
He was giving 'em out that day. So everybody come
got noses and mouths and went on off. Kept on like
that till folks had everything but their color. So one
day God called everybody up and said, "Now I want
everybody around the throne at seven o'clock sharp
tomorrow morning. I'm going to give out color tomorrow morning and I want everybody here on time.
I got a lot more creating to do and I want to give out
this color and be through with that."

Seven o'clock next morning God was sitting on His
throne with His great crown on His head. He looked
North, He looked East, He looked West, and He
looked Australia and blazing worlds was falling off of
His teeth. After a while He looked down from His
high towers of elevation and considered the Multitudes in front of Him. He looked to His left and said,
"Youse red people!" so they all turned red and said
"Thank you, God," and they went on off. He looked
at the next host and said, "Youse yellow people!" and
they got yellow and said "Thank you, God," and they
went on off. Then He looked at the next multitude
and said, "Youse white people" and they got white
and told Him, "Thank you, God," and they went on
off. God looked on His other hand and said, "Gabriel,
look like I miss some hosts." Gabriel looked all around
and said, "Yes, sir, several multitudes ain't here."
"Well," God told him, "You go hunt 'em up and tell
'em I say they better come quick if they want any

color. Fool with me and I won't give out no more." So Gabriel went round everywhere hunting till way after while he found the lost multitudes down by the Sea of Life asleep under a tree. So he told them they better hurry if they wanted any color. God wasn't going to wait on them much longer. So everybody jumped up and went running up to the throne. When the first ones got there, they couldn't stop because the ones behind kept on pushing and shoving. They kept on until the throne was careening way over to one side. So God hollered at 'em, "Get back! Get back!!" But they thought He said, "Git black!" So they got black and just kept the thing agoing.

So according to that, we are no race. We are just a collection of people who overslept our time and got caught in the draft.

ZORA NEALE HURSTON
July 2, 1937
Port-au-Prince, Haiti

"The Inside Light—Being a Salute to Friendship"

Now take friendship, for instance. It is a wonderful trade, a noble thing for anyone to work at. God made the world out of tough things, so it could last, and then He made some juice out of the most interior and best things that He had and poured it around for flavor.

You see lonesome-looking old red hills who do not even have clothes to cover their backs just lying there looking useless. Looking just like Old Maker had a junk pile like everybody else. But go back and look at them late in the day and see the herd of friendly shadows browsing happily around the feet of those hills. Then gaze up at the top and surprise the departing sun, all colored-up with its feelings, saying a sweet good night to those lonesome hills, and making them a promise that he will never forget them. So much tender beauty in a parting must mean a friendship. "I will visit you with my love," says the sun. That is why the hills endure.

Personally, I know what it means. I have never been

as good a friend as I meant to be. I keep seeing new heights and depths of possibilities which ought to be reached, only to be frustrated by the press of life, which is no friend to grace. I have my loyalties and my unselfish acts to my credit, but I feel the lack of perfection in them, and it leaves a hunger in me.

But I have received unaccountable friendship that is satisfying. Such as I am, I am a precious gift, as the unlettered Negro would say it. Stripped to my skin, that is just what I am. Without the juice of friendship, I would not be even what I seem to be. So many people have stretched out their hands and helped me along my wander[?]. With the eye of faith, some have beheld me at Hell's dark door, with no rudder in my hand and no light in my heart, and steered me to a peace within. Some others have flown into that awful place west and south of old original Hell and, with great compassion, lifted me off of the blistering coals and showed me trees and flowers. All these are the powers and privileges of friendship.

So many evidences of friendship have been revealed to me, that time and paper would not bear the load. Friendships of a moment, an hour, or a day that were nevertheless important, by humble folk whose names have become dusted over while the feeling of the touch remained, friendly expression having ways like musk. It can throw light back on a day that was so dark that even the sun refused to take responsibility for it.

It was decreed in the beginning of things that I should meet Mrs. R. Osgood Mason. She had been in the last of my prophetic visions from the first coming of them. I could not know that until I met her. But the moment I walked into the room, I knew that this was the end. There were the two women, just as I had always seen them, but always in my dream the faces were misty. Miss Cornelia Chapin was arranging a huge bowl of Calla lilies as I entered the room. There were the strange flowers I had always seen. Her posture was as I had seen it hundreds of times. Mrs. Mason was seated in a chair and everything about her was as I knew it. Only now I could see her face. Born so widely apart in every way, the key to certain phases of my life had been placed in her hand. I had been sent to her to get it. I owe her and owe her and owe her! Not only for material help, but for spiritual guidance.

With the exception of Godmother, Carl Van Vechten has bawled me out more times than anyone else I know. He has not been one of those white "friends of the Negro" who seeks to earn it cheaply by being eternally complimentary. If he is your friend, he will point our your failings as well as your good points in the most direct manner. Take it or leave it. If you can't stand him that way, you need not bother. If he is not interested in you one way or another, he will tell you that, too, in the most off-hand manner, but he is as true as the equator if he is for you. I offer him and his wife Fania Marinoff my humble and sincere thanks.

Both as her secretary and as a friend, Fanny Hurst has picked on me to my profit. She is a curious mixture of little girl and very sophisticated woman. You have to stop and look at her closely to tell which she is from moment to moment. Her transitions are quick as lightning and just as mysterious. I have watched her under all kinds of conditions, and she never ceases to amaze me. Behold her phoning to a swanky hotel for reservations for herself and the Princess Zora *and* parading me in there all dressed up as an Asiatic person of royal blood and keeping a straight face while the attendants goggled at me and bowed low! Like a little girl, I have known her in the joy of a compelling new gown to take me to tea in some exclusive spot in New York. I would be the press agent for her dress, for everybody was sure to look if *they* saw somebody like me strolling into the Astor or the Biltmore. She can wear clothes, and who knows it is her? On the spur of the moment she has taken me galloping over thousands of miles of this North American continent in my Chevrolet for a lark, and then just as suddenly decided to return and go to work. In one moment after figuratively playing with her dolls, she is deep in some social problem. She has been my good friend for many years, and I love her.

To the James Huberts, of Urban League fame, I offer something precious from the best of my treasures. If ever I came to feel that they no longer cared, I would be truly miserable. They elected me to be a Hubert and I mean to hold them to it.

To the Beers, Eleanor Beer de Chetelat, and her mother, Mrs. George W. Beer, twenty-one guns!

I am indebted to Amy Spingarn in a most profound manner. She knows what I mean by that.

Harry T. Burleigh, composer of "Deep River" and other great tunes, worked on me while I was a student to give me perspective and poise. He kept on saying that Negroes did not aim high enough as a rule. They mistook talent for art. One must work. Art was more than inspiration. Besides, he used to take me out to eat in good places to get me used to things. He looks like Otto Kahn in brownskin *and* behaves like a maharajah, with which I do not quarrel.

Of the people who have served me, Bob Wunsch is a man who has no superiors and few equals. Where the man gets all of his soul meat from, I really should like to know. All the greed and grime of the world passes him and never touches him, somehow. I wish that I could make him into a powder and season up the human dough so something could be made out of it. He has enough flavoring in him to do it.

The way I can say how I feel about Dr. Henry Allen Moe is to say that he is twin brother to Bob Wunsch. You cannot talk to the man without feeling that you could have done better in the past and rushing out to improve up from where you are. He has something glinty inside of him that he can't hide. If you have seen him, you have been helped.

I have said that I am grateful to the Charles S. Johnsons and I mean it. Not one iota of their kindness to me has been forgotten.

I fell in love with Jane Belo because she is not what she is supposed to be. She has brains and talent and uses them when she was born rich and pretty, and could have gotten along without any sense. She spent years in Bali studying native custom. She returned to America and went down into the deep South to make comparative studies, with me along. Often as we rode down lonesome roads in South Carolina, I wondered about her tremendous mental energy, and my admiration grew and grew. I also wondered at times why she liked me so much. Certainly it was not from want of friends. Being born of a rich Texas family, familiar with the drawing rooms of America and the continent, she certainly is not starved for company. Yet she thinks that I am a desirable friend to have, and acts like it. Now, she is married to Dr. Frank Tannenbaum, Department of History, Columbia University, and they have a farm up the state and actually milk cows. She draws and paints well enough to make a living at it if she had to, has written things in anthropology that Dr. Margaret Mead approves of, milks cows, and sets her little hat over her nose. How can you place a person like that? I give up. She can just keep on being my friend, and I'll let somebody else explain her.

I value Miguel and Rose Covarrubias for old time's sake. Long before they were married, we polished off many a fried chicken together. Along with Harry Block, we fried "hand chicken" (jointed fried chicken to be eaten with the hand) and settled the affairs of the world over the bones. We did many amusing but senseless things, and kept up our brain power by eating more chicken. Maybe that is why Miguel is such a fine artist. He has hewed to the line, and never let his success induce him to take to trashy foods or fancy plates.

James Weldon Johnson and his wife Grace did much to make my early years in New York pleasant and profitable. I have never seen any other two people who could be right so often, and charming about it at the same time.

Walter White and his glamorous Gladys used to have me over and feed me on good fried chicken in my student days for no other reason than that they just wanted to. They have lent me some pleasant hours. I mean to pay them back sometime.

There are so many others, Colonel and Mrs. Bert Lippincott, Frank Frazier, Paul and Eslanda Robeson, Lawrence Brown, Calvin J. Ferguson, Dr. Edwin Osgood Grover, Dr. Hamilton Holt, H. P. Davis, J. P. McEvoy, Edna St. Vincent Millay, Dr. and Mrs. Simeon L. Carson of Washington, D.C., along with Betram Barker. As I said in the beginning of this, that I was a precious gift, what there is of me. I could not find space for all of the donors on paper, though there is plenty of room in my heart. I am just sort of assembled up together out of friendship and put together by time.

Josephine Van Doltzen Pease, that sprout of an old Philadelphia family who writes such charming stories for children, and our mutual friend, Edith Darling Thompson, are right inside the most inside part of my heart. They are both sacred figures on my altar when I deck it to offer something to love.

How could I ever think I could make out without that remarkable couple Whit Burnett and Martha Foley? I just happened to put his name down first. Either way you take that family, it's got a head to it. One head with whiskers to it, and one plain, but both real heads. Even little David, their son, has got his mind made up. Being little, he gets overruled at times. But he knows what he wants to do and puts a lot of vim into the thing. It is not his fault if Whit and Martha have ideas of censorship. I have no idea what he will pick out to do by the time he gets grown, but, whatever it is, you won't find any bewildered David Foley-Burnett wandering around. I'll bet you a fat man on that. Two fat men to your skinny one.

Another California crowd that got me liking them and grateful too is that Herbert Childs, with his cherub-looking wife.

Katharane Edson Mershon has been a good friend to me. She is a person of immense understanding. It makes me sit and ponder. I do not know whether her ready sympathy grows out of her own experiences, or whether it was always there and only expanded by having struggled herself. I suppose it is both.

She was born of Katherine Philips Edson, the woman who put the minimum wage law for women on the statute books of California. It was no fault of hers that dirty politics later rubbed it out. She did many other things for the good of California, like fighting for the preservation of the Redwood forests. She sat, a lone woman, in the Washington Disarmament Conference, and, after forty, sent her two sons through good colleges by the sweat of her brow.

So Katharane Edson Mershon probably inherited some feelings. Anyway, she took life in her hands and hied herself away from home at sixteen and went forth to dance for inside expression. She did important things in the now famous Play House of Pasadena, conducted a school of dance, and was a Director for the famous school of Ruth St. Denis. After she married, she spent nine years in Bali, conducting a clinic at her own expense. More than that, she did not do it by proxy. She was there every day, giving medicine for fever, washing sores, and sitting by the dying. Dancing was her way of doing things, but she was impelled by mercy into this other field. Her husband was with her in this. His main passion is making gardens, but he threw himself into the clinic with enthusiasm.

For me, she gave me back my health and my hope, and I have her to thank for the sparing of my unprofitable life.

Jack Mershon, husband of Katharane's heart, is the son of William B. Mershon of Saginaw, Michigan. This William B. went into the Michigan forests and hacked him out a fortune. Tough as whit leather, with a passion for hunting and fishing, he nevertheless is one of the best informed men in the world on Americana, with especial emphasis on the Northwest. He has endowed parks, settlements, replanted whole forests of millions of trees in Michigan, and done things to make Saginaw a fine city, which the younger generation knows little about, because he himself says nothing.

Jack like his wife ran off from home and supported himself on the stage. He is soft in manner, but now and then you can see some of the gruff old stuff of William B. Mershon oozing through his hide. That same kind of mule-headedness on one side and generosity on the other. He will probably never be a hard-cussing, hard-driving empire builder like his old man, but what he aims to do, he does.

Mrs. Mershon invited me out to California, and a story starts from that. Being trustful and full of faith, I hurried out there. She fed me well, called in the doctors and cleared the malaria out of my marrow, took me to I. Magnin's and dressed me up. I was just burning up with gratitude and still did not suspect a thing.

Then I began to notice a leer in her eye! This woman had designs on me. I could tell that from her look, but I could not tell what it was. I should have known. I should have been suspicious, but I was dumb to the fact and did not suspect a thing until I was ambushed.

One day she said to me off-hand, "You ought to see a bit of California while you are out here."

"Oh, that would be fine!" I crackled and gleamed at the idea. So I saw California! At first, I thought it was just to give *me* some pleasure, but I soon found out it was the gleeful malice of a Californiac taking revenge upon a poor defenseless Florida Fiend.

She fried me in the deserts, looking at poppies, succulents (cactus, to you and everybody else except Californiacs), Joshna trees, kiln dried lizards, and lupin bushes. Just look at those wild lilacs! Observe that chaparrel! Don't miss that juniper. Don't say you haven't seen our cottonwood. Regard those nobles (California oaks).

Next thing I know we would be loping up some rough-back mountain and every hump and hollow would be pointed out to me. No need for me to murmur that I had to watch the road while driving. Just look at that peak! Wow! You can look down over that rim. When I took refuge in watching the road, she switched technique on me. Her husband, Jack Mershon, was pressed into service, so all I had to do was to sit in the back seat of the Buick while Katharane twisted my head from side to side and pointed out the sights.

From San Diego up, we looked at every wave on the Pacific, lizards, bushes, prune and orange groves, date palms, eucalyptus, gullies with and without water that these Californiacs call rivers, asphalt pits where the remains of prehistoric animals had been found, the prehistoric bones in person, saber-tooth tigers, short-faced bears (bears, before bears saw Californiacs and pulled long faces), old-fashioned elephants that ran mostly to teeth, saurians, and what not. Then there were barracuda and shark meat, abalones, beaches full of people in dark sun glasses, Hollywood, and slacks with hips in them all swearing to God and other responsible characters that they sure look pretty, and most of them lying and unrepentant. Man! I saw Southern California, and thought I had done something. Me, being from Florida, I had held my peace, and only murmured now and then a hint or two about our own climate and trees and things like that. Nothing offensive, you understand. I wouldn't really say how good it was, because I wanted to be polite. So I drew a long breath when we had prospected over Southern California, and I had kept from exploding.

"Now, I shall take you to see Northern California—the best part of the state," my fiendish friend gloated. "Ah, the mountains!"

"But, I don't care too much about mountains," I murmured through the alkali in my mouth.

"You are going to see it just the same. You are not going back east and pretend you saw none of the beauty of my state. You are going to see California, and like it—you Florida Fiend. Just because your Florida mud-turtles have been used to bogging down in swamps and those Everglades, whatever they are—and they don't sound like much to me, is no reason for you to ignore the beauties of California mountains. Let's go!"

So we went north. We drove over rocky ridges and stopped on ledges miles up in the air and gazed upon the Pacific. Redwood forests, Golden Gates, cable cars, missions, gaps, gullies, San Simeon—with William Randolph Hearst, Monterey—with history, Carmel—with artists and atmosphere, Big Sur and Santa Barbara, Bay Bridges and giant Sequoia, Alcatraz, wharves, capital buildings, mountains that didn't have sense enough to know it was summer and time to take off their winter clothes, seals, seal-rocks, and then seals on seal-rocks, pelicans and pelican rocks, and then that [?] Pacific!

Finally, back at Carmel, I struck. A person has just so many places to bump falling down rocky cliffs. But did I escape? No, indeed! I was standing on a big pile of bony rocks on Point Lobas, when I announced that I thought I (sort [of]) had the idea of California and knew what it was about.

"Oh, no!" Katharane grated maliciously. "Seen California! Why, this is the second largest state in the union! You haven't half seen it, but you are going to. I've got you out here and I mean to rub your nose in

California. You are going to see it, I'm here to tell you." So on we went. I saw, and I saw and I *saw!* Man! I tell you that I saw California. For instance, I saw the hats in San Francisco! Finally, I came to the conclusion that in Los Angeles the women get hats imposed upon them. In San Francisco, they go out in the woods and shoot 'em.

Then after I had galloped from one end of the state to the other and from edge to ocean and back again, Katharane Mershon up and tells me, "All I wanted you to see was the redwoods!" I mean to write to the Florida Chamber of Commerce and get them to trick a gang of Californiacs to Florida and let me be the guide. It is going to be good, and I wouldn't fool you. From Key West to the Perdido river they are going to see every orange tree, rattlesnake, gopher, coudar, palm tree, sand pile, beach mango tree, sapodilla, kumquat, alligator, tourist trap, celery patch, bean field, strawberry, lake, jook, gulf, ocean, and river in between, and if their constitutions sort of wear away, it will be unfortunate, but one of the hazards of war.

But California is nice. Even nice! Of course they lie about the California climate a little more than we do about ours, but you don't hold that against them. They have to, to rank up with us. But at that this California is a swell state, especially from Santa Barbara on north. Of course, coming from Florida, I feel like the man when he saw a hunch back for the first time—it seems that California does wear its hips a bit high. I mean all those mountains. Too much of the state is standing up on edge. To my notion, land is supposed to lie down and be walked on—not rearing up, staring you in the face. It is to biggity and imposing. But on the whole, California will do for a lovely state until God can make up something better. So I forgive Katharane Mershon for showing me the place. Another score for friendship.

Therefore, I can say that I have had friends. Friendship is a mysterious and ocean-bottom thing. Who can know the outer ranges of it? Perhaps no human being has ever explored its limits. Anyway, God must have thought well of it when He made it. Make the attempt if you want to, but you will find that trying to go through life without friendship is like milking a bear to get cream for your morning coffee. It is a whole lot of trouble, and then not worth much after you get it.

11:00 A.M.   July 20, 1941
1392 Hull Lane
Altadena, California

"Seeing the World as It is"

Thing lies forever in her birthing-bed and glories. But hungry Time squats beside her couch and waits. His frame was made out of emptiness, and his mouth set wide for prey. Mystery is his oldest son, and power is his portion.

That brings me before the unlived hour, that first mystery of the Universe with its unknown face and reflecting back. For it was said on the day of first sayings that Time should speak backward over his shoulder, and none should see his face, so scornful is he of the creatures of Thing.

What the faceless years will do to me, I do not know. I see Time's footprints, and I gaze into his reflections. My knees have dragged the basement of Hell and I have been in Sorrow's Kitchen, and it has seemed to me that I have licked out all the pots. The winters have been, and my soul-stuff has lain mute like a plain while the herds of happenings thundered across my breast. In these times there were deep chasms in me which had forgotten their memory of the sun.

But time has his beneficent moods. He has commanded some servant-moments to transport me to high towers of elevation so that I might look out on the breadth of things. This is a privilege granted to a servant of many hours but a master of few, from the master of a trillion billion hours and the servant of none.

In those moments I have seen that it is futile for me to seek the face of, and fear, an accusing God withdrawn somewhere beyond the stars in space. I myself live upon a star, and I can be satisfied with the millions of assurances of deity about me. If I have not felt the divinity of man in his cults, I have found it in his works. When I lift my eyes to the towering structures of Manhattan, and look upon the mighty tunnels and bridges of the world, I know that my search is over, and that I can depart in peace. For my soul tells me, "Truly this is the son of God. The rocks and the winds, the tides and the hills are his servants. If he talks in finger-rings, he works in horizons which dwarf the equator. His works are as noble as his words are foolish."

I found that I had no need of either class or race prejudice, those scourges of humanity. The solace of easy generalization was taken from me, but I received the richer gift of individualism. When I have been made to suffer or when I have been made happy by others, I have known that individuals were responsible for that, and not races. All clumps of people turn out to be individuals on close inspection.

This has called for a huge cutting of dead wood on

my part. From my earliest remembrance, I heard the phrases, "Race Problem," "Race Pride," "Race Man or Woman," "Race Solidarity," "Race Consciousness," "Race Leader," and the like. It was a point of pride to be pointed out as a "Race Man." And to say to one, "Why, you are not a Race Man," was low rating a person. Of course these phrases were merely sounding syllables to me as a child. Then the time came when I thought they meant something. I cannot say that they ever really came clear in my mind, but they probably were as clear to me as they were to the great multitude who uttered them. Now they mean nothing to me again. At least nothing that I want to feel.

There could be something wrong with me because I see Negroes neither better nor worse than any other race. Race pride is a luxury I cannot afford. There are too many implications behind the term. Now, suppose a Negro does something really magnificent, and I glory, not in the benefit to mankind, but in the fact that the doer is a Negro. Must I not also go hang my head in shame when a member of my race does something execrable? If a Negro does something fine, I gloat because he or she has done a fine thing, but not because he is a Negro. That is incidental and accidental. It is the human achievement which I honor. I execrate a foul act of a Negro but again not on the grounds that the doer was a Negro, but because it was foul. A member of my race just happened to be the fouler of humanity. In other words, I know that I cannot accept responsibility for thirteen million people. Every tub must sit on its own bottom regardless. So "Race Pride" in me had to go. And, anyway, why should I be proud to be a Negro? Why should anybody be proud to be white? Or yellow? Or red? After all, the word "race" is a loose classification of physical characteristics. It tells nothing about the insides of people. Pointing at achievements tells nothing either. Races have never done anything. What seems race achievement is the work of individuals. The white race did not go into a laboratory and invent incandescent light. That was Edison. The Jews did not work out Relativity. That was Einstein. The Negroes did not find out the inner secrets of peanuts and sweet potatoes, nor the secret of the development of the egg. That was Carver and Just. If you are under the impression that every white man is an Edison, just look around a bit. If you have the idea that every Negro is a Carver, you had better take off plenty of time to do your searching.

No, instead of Race Pride being a virtue, it is a sapping vice. It has caused more suffering in the world than religious opinion, and that is saying a lot.

"Race Conscious" is about the same as Race Pride in meaning. But, granting the shade of difference, all you say for it is, "Be continually conscious of what race you belong to so you can be proud." That is the effect of the thing. But what use is that? I don't care which race you belong to. If you are only one quarter honest in your judgment, you can seldom be proud. Why waste time keeping conscious of your physical aspects? What the world is crying and dying for at this moment is less race consciousness. The human race would blot itself out entirely if it had any more. It is a deadly explosive on the tongues of men. I choose to forget it.

I have asked many well-educated people of both races to tell me what this Race Problem is. They look startled at first. Then I can see them scratching around inside themselves hunting for the meaning of the words which they have used with so much glibness and unction. I have never had an answer that was an answer, so I have had to make up my own. Since there is no fundamental conflict, since there is no solid reason why the blacks and the whites cannot live in one nation in perfect harmony, the only thing in the way of it is Race Pride and Race Consciousness on both sides. A bear has been grabbed by the tail. The captor and the captured are walking around a tree snarling at each other. The man is scared to turn the bear loose, and his hand-hold is slipping. The bear wants to go on about his business, but he feels that something must be done about that tail-hold. So they just keep on following each other around the tree.

So Race Pride and Race Consciousness seem to me to be not only fallacious, but a thing to be abhorred. It is the root of misunderstanding and hence misery and injustice. I cannot, with logic, cry against it in others and wallow in it myself. The only satisfaction to be gained from Race Pride anyway is, "I ain't nothing, my folks ain't nothing, but that makes no difference at all. I belong to such-and-such a race." Poor nourishment according to my notion. Mighty little to chew on. You have to season it awfully high with egotism to make it tasty.

Priding yourself on your physical make up, something over which you have no control, is just another sign that the human cuss is determined not to be grateful. He gives himself a big hand on the way he looks and lets on that he arranged it all himself. God got suspicious that he was going to be like that before He made him, and that is why Old Maker caught up on all of His creating before He made Man. He knew that if Man had seen how He did it, just as soon as a woman came along to listen to him, Man would have been saying, "See that old striped tiger over there? *I* made him. Turned him out one morning before breakfast." And so on until there would not have been a thing in Heaven or earth that he didn't take credit for. So God did the only thing he could to narrow down the field for boasting. He made him late and kept him dumb.

And how can Race Solidarity be possible in a nation made up of as many elements as the United States? It could result in nothing short of chaos. The fate of each and every group is bound up with the others. Individual ability in any group must function for all the rest. National disaster touches us all. There is no escape in grouping. And in practice there can be no sharp lines drawn, because the interest of every individual in any racial group is not identical with the others. Section, locality, self-interest, special fitness, and the like set one group of Anglo-Saxons, Jews, and Negroes against another set of Anglo-Saxons, Jews, and Negroes. We are influenced by a pain in the pocket just like everybody else. During the Civil War Negroes fought in the Confederate Army because many Negroes were themselves slaveowners, and were just as mad at Lincoln as anybody else in the South. Anyone who goes before a body and purports to plead for what "The Negro" wants is a liar and knows it. Negroes want a variety of things and many of them diametrically opposed. There is no single Negro nor no single organization which can carry the thirteen million in any direction. Even Joe Louis can't do it, but he comes nearer to it than anyone else at present.

And why should Negroes be united? Nobody else in America is. If it were true, then one of two other things would be true. One, that they were united on what the white people are united on, and it would take a God to tell what that is; and be moving towards complete and immediate assimilation [sic]. Or we would be united on something specially Negroid, and that would lead towards a hard black knot in the body politic which would be impossible of place in the nation. All of the upper class Negroes certainly want political and economic equality. That is the most universal thing I can pin down.

Negroes are just like anybody else. Some soar. Some plod ahead. Some just make a mess and step back in it—like the rest of America and the world. So Racial Solidarity is a fiction and always will be. Therefore, I have lifted the word out of my mouth.

A Race Man is somebody, not necessarily able, who places his race before all else. He says he will buy everything from a Negro merchant as far as possible, support all "race" institutions and movements and so on. The only thing that keeps this from working is that it is impossible to form a nation within a nation. He makes spurts and jerks at it, but every day he is forced away from it by necessity. He finds that he can neither make money nor spend money in a restricted orbit. He is part of the national economy. But he can give the idea plenty of talk. He springs to arms over such things as the title of Carl Van Vechten's book, *Nigger Heaven*, or Will Rogers saying over the radio that most of the cowboy songs were nothing more than adaptations of "nigger tunes." He does this because he feels that he is defending his race. Sometimes the causes are just, and sometimes they are ridiculous. His zeal is honest enough; it is merely a lack of analysis that leads him into error.

As I said before, the Race Leader is a fiction that is good only at the political trough. But it is not nearly as good as it used to be. The white political leaders have found out more or less that they cannot deliver wholesale. Many of them are successful in a way, but not in any great, big, plushy way. The politician may try ever so hard, but, if people won't follow, he just can't lead. Being an American, I am just like the rest of the Yankees, the Westeners, the Southerners, the Negroes, the Irish, the Indians, and the Jews. I don't lead well either. Don't just tell me what to do. Tell me what is being contemplated and let me help figure on the bill. That is my idea, and I am going to stick to it. Negroes are so much like the rest of America that they not only question what is put before them, but they have got so they order something else besides gin at the bars, which is certainly a sign of something. So I have thrown over the idea of Race Leadership, too.

I know that there is race prejudice, not only in America, but also wherever two races meet together in numbers. I have met it in the flesh, and I have found out that it is never all on one side, either. I do not give it heart room because it seems to me to be the last refuge of the weak. From what little I have been able to learn, I know that goodness, ability, vice, and dumbness know nothing about race lives or geography. I do not wish to close the frontiers of life upon my own self. I do not wish to deny myself the expansion of seeking into individual capabilities and depths by living in a space whose boundaries are race and nation. Lord, give my poor stammering tongue at least one taste of the whole round world, if you please, Sir.

And then I know so well that the people who make a boast of racial, class, or national prejudices do so out of a sense of incapability to which they refuse to give a voice. Instead, they try to be ingenious by limiting competition. They are racial cardsharps trying to rig the game so that they cannot lose. Trying to stack the deck. If I choose to call these cardpalmers poor sports, then the burden of proof is on them. I give the matter the corner of my eye and smile at the backhand compliment, for I know that if I had been born where *they* were born, and they had been born where *I* was born, it is hardly likely that we ever would have met. So I smile and not bitterly, either. For I know that Equality is as you do it and not as you talk it. If you are better than I, you can tell me about it if you want to, but then again, show me so I can know. It is always good to be learning something. But if you never make me know it, I'll keep on questioning. I love to be in the presence of my superiors. If I don't catch on right away, crumble it up fine so I can handle it. And then again, if you can't *show* me, don't bother to bring the mess up.

Since I wash myself of race pride and repudiate race solidarity, by the same token I turn my back upon the past. I see no reason to keep my eyes fixed on the dark years of slavery and the Reconstruction. I am three generations removed from it, and therefore have no experience of the thing. From what I can learn, it was sad. No doubt America would have been better off if it never had been. But it was, and there is no use in beating around the bush. Still, there seems to me to be nothing but futility in gazing backward over my shoulder and buking [sic] the grave of some white man who has been dead too long to talk about. Neither do I see any use in buttonholing his grandson about it. The old man probably did cut some capers back there, and I'll bet you anything my old folks didn't like it. But the old man is dead. My old folks are dead. Let them wrestle all over Hell about it if they want to. That is their business. The present is upon me and that white man's grandchildren as well. I have business with the grandson as of today. I want to get on with the business in hand. Since I cannot pry loose the clutching hand of time, I will settle for some influence on the present. It is ridiculous for me to make out that I'm Old Black Joe and waste my time rehashing his problems. That would be just as ridiculous as it would be for the Jews to hang around the pyramids trying to get a word with Old Cheops. Or for the English to be billing the Duke of Normandy the first of every month.

I am all for starting something brand new in cooperation with the present incumbent. If I don't get any cooperation, I am going to start something anyway.

The world is not just going to stand still looking like a fool at a funeral if I can help it. Let's bring up right now and lay a hearing on it.

Standing on the watch-wall and looking, I no longer expect the millennium. It would be wishful thinking to be searching for justice in the absolute. People are not made so it will happen, because, from all I can see, the world is a whole family of Hurstons. It has always been a family of Hurstons, so it is foolish to expect any justice untwisted by the selfish hand. Look into the Book of Books and it is not even there. The Old Testament is devoted to what was right and just from the viewpoint of the Ancient Hebrews. All of their enemies were twenty-two carat evil. They, the Hebrews, were never aggressors. The Lord wanted His children to have a country full of big grapes and tall corn. Incidentally, while they were getting it, they might as well get rid of some trashy tribes that He never did think much of, anyway. With all of its figs and things, Canaan was their destiny. God sent some-body especially to tell them about it. If the conquest looked like bloody rape to the Canaanites, that was because their evil ways would not let them see a point which was right under their nose. So you had to drive it in under the ribs. King David, who invented the "protection" racket in those days before he was saved by being made king, was a great hero. He only killed and pillaged to help out his own folks. He was a man after God's own heart, and was quite servicable in helping God get rid of no-count rascals who were cluttering up the place.

The New Testament is not quite so frank, but it is equally biased. Paul and the disciples set up a New Order in Palestine after the death of Jesus, but the Jews gave it nothing but their shoulder-blades. So now the Orthodox Jew became a manifest enemy of right. To this day, the names of Pharisee and Sadducee are synonymous with hypocrite and crook to ninety-nine and a half percent of the Christian world. While in fact, the Pharisees were an order small in number, highly educated, well born, and clean-living men whose mission was to guard the purity of the creed. The Sadducees were almost as lofty. Naturally, in the turmoil of the times, they got embroiled in politics in the very nature of the form of their government, but so have both branches of Christianity.

Then there is the slaughter of the innocents by Herod. One thing strikes me curious about that slaughter. The unconverted Jews never seemed to have missed their babies. So Herod must have carefully selected babies from families who forty years later were going to turn Christian. He probably did not realize what a bad example he was setting for the new religionists. He could not have known that centuries later Christians would themselves slaughter more innocents in one night than his soldiers ever saw.

Those Jews who would not accept Christianity look

very bad in the New Testament. And two thousand years have gone by and all the Western World uses the sign of the Cross, but it is evident that the Jews are not the only ones who do not accept it. The Occident has never been christianized and never will be. It is an oriental concept which the sons of hammer-throwing Thor have no enzymes to digest. It calls for meekness, and the West is just not made meek. Instead of being proud to turn the other cheek, our boast is beating the other fellow to the punch.

We have even turned the Gospel of peace into a wrestle, we club each other over the head to prove who is the best missionary. Nature asserts itself. We can give up neither our platitudes nor our profits. The platitudes sound beautiful, and the profits feel like silk.

Popes and Prelates, Bishops and Elders have halted sermons on peace at the sound of battle and rushed out of their pulpits brandishing swords and screaming for blood in Jesus' name. The pews followed the pulpit in glee. So it is obvious that the Prince of Peace is nothing more than a symbol. He has been drafted into every army in the Occident. He must have a delegate behind every cannon. We have tangled with the soft and yielding thing for twenty long centuries without any more progress than letting the words take up around the house. We are moral enough, just not Christians. If we love meekness as we say, then Napoleon should be pictured in a nun's robe, Bismarck in a cassock, and George Washington in a Gandhi diaper. The pedestals should read "These stones do honor to our meekest men. Their piety laid millions low. Praise the Lord!" The actual representation would reveal the confusion in our minds. According to our worship, Joe Louis rates a Cardinal's hat.

But back to Mahatma Gandhi. His application of Christian principles is causing us great distress. We want the people to hear about it from Greenland's icy mountains to India's coral strand, but we do wish that they would not lose their heads and carry the thing too far, like Gandhi does for instance. It is a bad thing for business.

No, actual justice is somewhere away off. We only see its flickering image here. Everybody has it on his tongue and nobody has it at heart. Take, for instance, the matter of conquest.

The Kings of Dahomey once marched up and down West Africa, butchering the aged and the helpless of the surrounding tribes and nations and selling the able off into Western slavery. The Dahomans would have been outraged if anybody had said they were unjust. What could be more just? The profits were enormous. But they did feel that there was no more justice in the world when the French came in and conquered them. The French would have shrugged down the Pyramids if they had been told that they were not just. What could be fairer? The Germans have now conquered the French and the French wonder how those Germans can be so lacking in soul. But the Germans open their blue eyes in amazement. Why, nothing could be more reasonable and just. If the world cannot find pure justice among the Germans, they will never find it anywhere. If the French want to be unfair enough to begrudge them their little profit on the deal, it shows how narrow and mean-minded a Frenchman really can be.

There is no diffused light on anything international so that a comparatively whole scene may be observed. Light is sharply directed on one spot, leaving not only the greater part in darkness but also denying by implication that the great unlighted field exists. It is no longer profitable, with few exceptions, to ask people what they think, for you will be told what they wish, instead. Perhaps at no other period in the history of the world have people lived in such a dreamy state. People even waste time denouncing their enemies in open warfare for shooting back too hard, or too accurately. There is no attempt to be accurate as to truth, however. The whole idea is to be complimentary to one's self and keep alive the dream. The other man's side commits gross butcheries. One's own side wins smashing victories.

Being human and a part of humanity, I like to think that my own nation is more just than any other in spite of the facts on hand. It makes me feel prouder and bigger to think that way. But now and then the embroidered hangings blow aside, and I am less exalted. I see that the high principles enunciated so throatedly are like the flowers in spring—they have nothing to do with the case. If my conclusions are in error, then the orators and copybooks were wrong to start off with. I should have been told in the very beginning that those were words to copy, but not to go by. But they didn't tell me that. They swore by jeepers and by joe that there were certain unshakeable truths that no man nor nation could make out without.

There was the dignity of man. His inalienable rights were sacred. Man, noble man, had risen in his might and glory and had stamped out the vile institution of slavery. That is just what they said. But I know that the principle of human bondage has not yet vanished from the earth. I know that great nations are standing on it. I would not go so far as to deny that there has been no progress toward the concept of liberty. Already it has been agreed that the name of slavery is very bad. No civilized nation will use such a term any more. Neither will they keep the business around the home. Life will be on a loftier level by operating at a distance and calling it acquiring sources of raw material, and keeping the market open. It has been decided, also, that it is not cricket to enslave one's own kind. That is unspeakable tyranny.

But must a nation suffer from lack of prosperity and expansion by lofty concepts? Not at all! If a ruler can find a place way off where the people do not look like him, kill enough of them to convince the rest that they ought to support him with their lives and labor, that ruler is hailed as a great conqueror, and people build monuments to him. The very weapons he used are also honored. They picture him in unforgetting stone with the sacred tool of his conquest in his hand. Democracy, like religion, never was designed to make our profits less.

Now, for instance, if the English people were to quarter troops in France, and force the French to work for them for forty-eight cents a week while they took more than a billion dollars a year out of France, the English would be Occidentally execrated. But actually, the British Government does just that in India, to the glory of the democratic way. They are hailed as not only great Empire builders, the English are extolled as leaders of civilization. And the very people who claim that it is a noble thing to die for freedom and democracy cry out in horror when they hear tell of a "revolt" in India. They even wax frothy if anyone points out the inconsistency of their morals. So this life as we know it is a great thing. It would have to be, to justify certain things.

I do not mean to single England out as something strange and different in the world. We, too, have our Marines in China. We, too, consider machine gun bullets good laxatives for heathens who get constipated with toxic ideas about a country of their own. If the patient dies from the treatment, it was not because the medicine was not good. We are positive of that.

We have seen it work on other patients twice before it killed them and three times after. Then, too, no matter what the outcome, you have to give the doctor credit for trying.

The United States being the giant of the Western World, we have our responsibilities. The little Latin brother south of the border has been a trifle trying at times. Nobody doubts that he means to be a good neighbor. We know that his intentions are the best. It is only that he is so gay and fiesta-minded that he is liable to make arrangements that benefit nobody but himself. Not a selfish bone in his body, you know. Just too full of rumba. So it is our big brotherly duty to teach him right from wrong. He must be taught to share with big brother before big brother comes down and kicks his teeth in. A big *good* neighbor is a lovely thing to have. We are far too moral a people to allow poor Latin judgment to hinder good works.

But there is a geographical boundary to our principles. They are not to leave the United States unless we take them ourselves. Japan's application of our principles to Asia is never to be sufficiently deplored. We are like the southern planter's bride when he kissed her the first time.

"Darling," she fretted, "do niggers hug and kiss like this?"

"Why, I reckon they do, honey, Fact is, I'm sure of it. Why do you ask?"

"You go right out and kill the last one of 'em tomorrow morning. Things like this is much too good for niggers."

Our indignation is more than justified. We Westerners composed that piece about trading in China with gunboats and cannons long decades ago. Japan is now plagiarizing in the most flagrant manner. We also wrote that song about keeping a whole hemisphere under your wing. Now the Nipponese are singing our song all over Asia. They are full of stuff and need a good working out. The only hold-back to the thing is that they have copied our medicine chest. They are stocked up with the same steel pills and cannon plasters that Doctor Occident prescribes.

Mexico, the dear little papoose, has been on the sick list, too. Gangrene had set in the upper limbs, so to speak and amputation was the only thing which could save the patient. Even so, the patient malingered for a long time, and internal dosage had to be resorted to on occasion. The doctor is not sure that all of the germs have been eradicated from the system as yet, but, when the patient breaks out of the hospital, what can the doctor do?

In great and far-sighted magnanimity, no cases have been overlooked. The African tribesmen were saved from the stuffiness of overweening pride and property just in the nick of time.

Looking at all these things, I am driven to the conclusion that democracy is a wonderful thing, but too powerful to be trusted in any but purely Occidental hands. Asia and Africa should know about it. They should die for it in defense of its originators, but they must not use it themselves.

All around me, bitter tears are being shed over the fate of Holland, Belgium, France, and England. I must confess to being a little dry around the eyes. I hear people shaking with shudders at the thought of Germany collecting taxes in Holland. I have not heard a word against Holland collecting one twelfth of poor people's wages in Asia. Hitler's crime is that he is actually doing a thing like that to his own kind. That is international cannibalism and should be stopped. He is a bandit. That is true, but that is not what is held against him. He is muscling in on well-established mobs. Give him credit. He cased some joints away off in Africa and Asia, but the big mobs already had them paying protection money and warned him to stay away. The only way he can climb out of the punk class is to high-jack the load and that is just what he is doing. President Roosevelt could extend his four freedoms to some people right here in America before he takes it all aboard, and, no doubt, he would do it too, if it would bring in the same amount of glory. I am not bitter, but I see what I see. He can call names across an ocean, but he evidently has not the courage to speak even softly at home. Take away the ocean and he simmers right down. I wish that I could say differently, but I cannot. I will fight for my country, but I will not lie for her. Our country is so busy playing "fence" to the mobsters that the cost in human suffering cannot be considered yet. We can take that up in the next depression.

As I see it, the doctrines of democracy deal with the aspirations of men's souls, but the application deals with things. One hand in somebody else's pocket and one on your gun, and you are highly civilized. Your heart is where it belongs—in your pocketbook. Put it in your bosom and you are backward. Desire enough for your own use only, and you are a heathen. Civilized people have things to show to the neighbors.

This is not to say, however, that the darker races are visiting angels, just touristing around here below. They have acted the same way when they had a chance and will act that way again, comes the break. I just think it would be a good thing for the Anglo-Saxon to get the idea out of his head that everybody else owes him something just for being blonde. I am forced to the conclusion that two-thirds of them do hold that view. The idea of human slavery is so deeply ground in that the pink-toes can't get it out of their system. It has just been decided to move the slave quarters farther away from the house. It would be a fine thing if on leaving office, the blond brother could point with pride to the fact that his administration had done away with group-profit at the expense of others. I know well that it has never happened before, but it could happen, couldn't it?

To mention the hundred years of the Anglo-Saxon

in China alone is proof enough of the evils of this view point. The millions of Chinese who have died for our prestige and profit! They are still dying for it. Justify it with all the proud and pretty phrases you please, but if we think our policy is right, you just let the Chinese move a gunboat onto the Hudson to drum up trade with us. The scream of outrage would wake up saints in the backrooms of Heaven. And what is worse, we go on as if the so-called inferior people are not thinking; or, if they do, it does not matter. As if no day could ever come when that which went over the Devil's back will buckle under his belly. People may not be well-armed at present, but you can't stop them from thinking.

I do not brood, however, over the wide gaps between ideals and practices. The world is too full of inconsistencies for that. I recognize that men are given to handling words long before those words have any internal meaning for them. It is as if we were children playing in a field and found something round and hard to play with. It may be full of beauty and pleasure, and then again it may be full of death.

And now to another matter. Many people have pointed out to me that I am a Negro, and that I am poor. Why then have I not joined a party of protest? I will tell you why. I see many good points in, let us say, the Communist Party. Any one would be a liar and a fool to claim that there was no good in it. But I am so put together that I do not have much of a herd instinct. Or if I must be connected with the flock, let *me* be the shepherd my ownself. That is just the way I am made.

You cannot arouse any enthusiasm in me to join in a protest for the boss to provide me with a better hoe to chop his cotton with. Why must I chop cotton at all? Why fix a class of cotton-choppers? I will join in no protests for the boss to put a little more stuffing in my bunk. I don't even want the bunk. I want the boss's bed. It seems to me that the people who are enunciating these principles are so saturated with European ideas that they miss the whole point of America. The people who founded this country, and the immigrants who came later, came here to get away from class distinctions and to keep their unborn children from knowing about them. I am all for the idea of free vertical movement, nothing horizontal. Let him who can, go up, and him who cannot, stay there, mount down to the level his capabilities rate. It works out that way anyhow, hence the saying from shirt-sleeves to shirt-sleeves in three generations. The able at the bottom always snatch the ladder from under the weak on the top rung. That is the way it should be. A dead grandfather's back has proven to be a poor prop time and time again. If they have gone up there and stayed, they had something more than a lucky ancestor. So I can get no lift out of nominating myself to be a peasant and celebrating any feasts back stairs. I want the front of the house and I am going to keep on trying even if I never satisfy my plan.

Then, too, it seems to me that if I say a whole system must be upset for me to win, I am saying that I cannot sit in the game, and that safer rules must be made to give me a chance. I repudiate that. If others are in there, deal me a hand and let me see what I can make of it, even though I know some in there are dealing from the bottom and cheating like hell in other ways. If I can win anything in a game like that, I know I'll end up with the pot if the sharks can be eliminated. As the Negroes say down South, "You can't beat me and my prayers," and they are not talking about supplications either when they talk like that. I don't want to bother with any boring from within. If the leaders on the left feel that only violence can right things, I see no need of fingernail warfare. Why not take a stronger position? Shoot in the hearse, don't care how sad the funeral is. Get the feeling of the bantam hen jumping on the mule. Kill dead and go to jail. I am not bloodthirsty and have no yearning for strife, but, if what they say is true, that there must be this upset, why not make it cosmic? A lot of people would join in for the drama of it, who would not be moved by guile.

I do not say that my conclusions about anything are true for the Universe, but I have lived in many ways,

sweet and bitter, and they feel right for me. I have seen and heard. I have sat in judgment upon the ways of others, and in the voiceless quiet of the night I have also called myself to judgment. I cannot have the joy of knowing that I found always a shining reflection of honor and wisdom in the mirror of my soul on those occasions. I have given myself more harrowing pain than anyone else has ever been capable of giving me. No one else can inflict the hurt of faith unkept. I have had the corroding insight at times, of recognizing that I am a bundle of sham and tinsel, honest metal and sincerity that cannot be untangled. My dross has given my other parts great sorrow.

But, on the other hand, I have given myself the pleasure of sunrises blooming out of oceans, and sunsets drenching heaped-up clouds. I have walked in storms with a crown of clouds about my head and the zigzag lightning playing through my fingers. The gods of the upper air have uncovered their faces to my eyes. I have found out that my real home is in the water, that the earth is only my stepmother. My old man, the Sun, sired me out of the sea.

Like all mortals, I have been shaped by the chisel in the hand of Chance, bulged out here by a sense of victory, shrunken there by the press of failure and the knowledge of unworthiness. But it has been given to me to strive with life, and to conquer the fear of death. I have been correlated to the world so that I know the

indifference of the sun to human emotions. I know that destruction and construction are but two faces of Dame Nature, and that it is nothing to her if I choose to make personal tragedy out of her unbreakable laws.

So I ask of her few things. May I never do good consciously nor evil unconsciously [*sic*]. Let my evil be known to me in advance of my acts, and my good when Nature wills. May I be granted a just mind and a timely death.

While I am still far below the allotted span of time, notwithstanding, I feel that I have lived. I have the joy and pain of strong friendships. I have served and been served. I have made enemies of which I am not ashamed. I have been faithless, and then I have been faithful and steadfast until the blood ran down into my shoes. I have loved unselfishly with all the ardor of a strong heart, and I have hated with all the power of my soul. What waits for me in the future? I do not know. I cannot even imagine, and I am glad for that. But already I have touched the four corners of the horizon, for from hard searching it seems to me that tears and laughter, love and hate, make up the sum of life.